THE TROUBLE BUSH

The Trouble Bush

By EARL SCHENCK MIERS

Rand McNally & Company   Chicago   New York   San Francisco

FIRST PRINTING, *October, 1966*

With Love
For Starling
Who Lived This Story With Me

CONTENTS

THE TROUBLE BUSH

CHAPTER ONE

How
the Trouble Bush
Was Planted

In the Year of the Stolen Peach, when I was four and the Kaiser started his war, I held my first conversation with God. My cathedral was the stretch of narrow road that led from my uncle's farm down to the brook with the sassafras trees. The sun that August day filtered through the boughs of the old horse chestnuts and speckled leaf patterns upon the sandy ground. My hand clutched five pebbles and with eyes closed I struck a bargain with the Lord: "You see that old chestnut this side of the brook? If I hit it, just once out of five, I'll get along."

I let go with my first heave before my eyes reopened. Awestruck, I saw the pebble smack the tree trunk and rebound into the water. I had implored heaven for simple reassurance and had been rewarded with a miracle. The odds against any four-year-old cerebral-palsied child making a one-out-of-one strike like that must be incalculable. Wild excitement shook me. Someone up there not only listened but also understood.

There was likewise someone behind that tree who now bounded into the road as though under attack from the pine robbers who once had terrorized this section of New Jersey. At twelve my sister Edith was a scraggly half-woman with burning brown eyes afire with the rebellion of early adolescence.

"You hit me and I'll sting your ass," she said.

I pranced back, shrieking: "Dirty mouth, dirty mouth, Edith is a dirty mouth!"

"Oh shut up!" my sister said. She wadded her mouth with sassafras bark until both cheeks stuck out in piggish lumps. For a moment she glared at me evilly, clearly contemplating whether to spew into my eye the nasty mess she was chewing, then turned away with the cross, unhappy manner of the guilt-stricken. Presently the sassafras cud splashed like a cannonball into the brook and Edith said: "The peach is gone!"

"Gone?" I repeated with a kind of bug-eyed stupidity. "Where could it go?"

"Down into my gut, that's where it could go," my sister said in a fury of defiance.

The Kaiser, plunging Europe into war, was no greater master of human destiny than Edith in that instant; nor was God, delivering the Ten Commandments to Moses on a mountaintop. Almost daily, in the weeks since we had started our vacation on the old farm, we had been indoctrinated with the marvels of that peach. It weighed more than a pound. It was perfect in coloring, skin texture, shape. Uncle John began the day gazing upon it and at night dreamed of the blue ribbon it would win at the county fair in Freehold. The tree that bore it was not to be looked at, walked around, or breathed on.

No more than Eve after handing the apple to Adam could my sister tell her story coherently. With wicked delight she had snatched the peach. With wicked stealthiness she had borne it, under her blouse, to the privy. There, door locked, she had gobbled it down while reading the harness section in last year's Sears, Roebuck catalog. The devil's odors from beneath, a devil's hornet buzzing overhead added to the awesome trauma of her revolt.

"I pinched my bottom on the crack between the holes," she said. "It hurts awful."

"What did you do with the pit?"

"I dropped it down."

"I could'a made a ring out of it."

Edith admitted that she had not kept her wits; that damn crack was to blame.

Somewhat saddened and suddenly silent, we hunched our backs against an old chestnut and gazed like stone images upon that private maritime possession we called Adam's Brook. If water snakes loitered along its sluggish banks, they were not the vicious sea serpents my sister made of them. Green flies and mosquitoes shared our protected solitude; and I perked up my ears attentively, for there was always the risk of being trampled to death by some fool cow seeking a new spot to leave her trademark.

The brook's name honored Adam Satler, who for almost thirty years had served my uncle as a farmhand. Born "somewhere in Germany" in 1871 and emigrating to America in his middle teens, Adam never had held any other job. One day he had come down the road like the Jew peddler with his pack, creating a neighborhood sensation. He had offered to work for food and a night's lodging and was still employed on the same loose contract. He was irascible, energetic, and fiercely loyal, and his profanity possessed a poetic dimension. He was both as strong and as stupid as an ox and as likely in moments of passion to hang himself over a fence so that he could neither kick nor gouge while his bellows shook the countryside. The day the pigs escaped from their sty and Adam chased them for miles along the brook, filling the air with furious epithets, tripping over tree roots, and soaking himself without catching a single porker, had left him immortal in family legend.

Adam occupied the finished bedroom in the attic; beyond, on a cot, I slept surrounded by spare chamber pots, broken-down furniture, unplanted seeds, mouse droppings, and boxes of discarded clothing. On stormy nights the rain fell like bullets on the roof and the gaunt chimney tops were ghosts, reminding me of Mother's story of my maternal grandfather's death. Embalming then was a city art; in the country a corpse was placed on ice and strapped down until burial. Mother remembered opening the door to the parlor at the precise moment when the straps broke and the corpse popped up as though awakening for supper. She fled from the house in hysterics; and many a night, staring at those dim chimney tops, I had the terrified impression that my grandfather was sitting upright on his death-couch of melting ice.

But Adam's presence nearby comforted me. Adam snored ponderously: no one could mistake that he was alive. Nor could any Prussian nobleman have roamed his estate with greater arrogance than Adam ruled in his private roost. The bed with its corn-husk mattress, the wobbly chair, the dresser with the blurry mirror, all gained a personality from Adam's presence in the room. Tucked away in one corner was that magic Pandora's box: the trunk Adam had brought from Germany. Adam's medal from the Knights of Pythias rested here like a princeling in its crib; and a packet of documents in a soiled envelope tied with

14

a red string and bearing the authoritative inscription, "A. Satler's papers"; and God only knows how many dozens of copies of garishly covered periodicals entitled *Fame and Fortune Weekly* and the *Liberty Boys of '76*; and the suit in which he wished to be buried; and a bottle of wine and five or six bottles of beer; and a photograph of his mother.

I thought the woman in that photograph was a fearsome creature with her angular face and ashen cheeks. Her hair was pulled back to the point of parting from its roots and her dark eyes were like oversized dots in a steel engraving. To Adam she was love and when she had died he had come to America. His father might as well have been dead for all that Adam ever mentioned him. Doubtless it was her memory that made him a knight in armor toward all women and especially toward that frightened, birdlike female called my Aunt Laura, who once had nursed him through an attack of appendicitis. His affection for young children was touchingly tender. He could accept a nervous child like myself as though no difference existed between us. Rarely did any woman or child overextend his patience; his wild Prussian outbursts were reserved for pigs, men, and God. After a dry spell had ruined the crops and then rain fell for days on end, only Adam, turning his gaze from uselessly soaked fields to heaven, could implore: "You Dan' Fool, send it when we need it!" But God must have understood. At least no bolt of lightning struck him down—not Adam, the first "unfamily" person who accepted me.

Edith broke into my reverie. "I'll catch hell," she said. Her self-pity approached near-hysteria: "They'll beat me—they'll kill me—they'll roast me like Joan of Arc."

Adam's Brook, perhaps three hundred yards from the house, suddenly echoed with outraged cries that amounted to anguished oaths.

"Dear God!" Edith moaned. "They've found out!"

As always happened in moments of extreme tension, my

15

palsied arms began to jerk. Tears welled into my eyes. My stomach felt nauseous. Edith's head came up with a snap; her chin tilted with a belligerent thrust. "Nothing's going to happen to you," she said. "Come on!"

Like a tigress, she led her cub back to their lair.

The scene at the farm was breathtaking. Adam had donned the suit in which he wished to be buried and now straddled the Trunk from Germany. Aunt Laura sat on the porch steps in a puddle of tears. My father lurked behind the screen door, a pale figure. My mother hastened across the yard, dragging Uncle John by the arm. All the time Adam shook his fist at my father and filled the air with almost incoherent bellows.

What Adam intended to say, in a literal translation, was (*a*) it was no goddan fault of his what the goddan Kaiser did or how all the goddan fools in Europe ruined their goddan lives; and (*b*) if my goddan father thought it was then he, goddan Adam Satler, wasn't going to live with this goddan family for another goddan minute; and (*c*) as soon as he could get a goddan horse and buggy to take him into goddan Freehold they would all see the goddan last of him.

"Adam, *Adam*," my aunt implored.

"You keep the goddan out of this," Adam shouted.

My uncle said nothing while his moustache twitched. Moments later we heard him driving off in a buggy and knew he would be drunk for days. By then neither Adam nor the peach would matter.

Before dusk Adam carried the Trunk from Germany back to his room—he would never leave Aunt Laura in a crisis. The moon came up and somewhere among the trees in the woodlot beyond the meadow an owl hooted. As my mother said, nothing equaled the peace and quiet of life in the country.

Sadness tinged those end-of-summer days whenever I thought of how soon we would be returning to Brooklyn. The old farm was a world set apart with peculiar challenges to a nervous child. What experience could surpass exploring the icehouse where the milk was cooled and Aunt Laura stored her freshly churned butter and where by a single misstep, or so Adam warned constantly, I could drown beneath the melting ice before my whereabouts was discovered? The tool shed held other diabolical instruments of instant execution I was cautioned never to touch: the scythes used in mowing, the axes for woodchopping, all kept razor sharp. I played with them, my skin covered with goose-pimples of sheer delight: a true revolutionist whose defiance overcame all fears. The dim, so private realm of the haylofts was an obsession with Uncle John, who hid his whiskey here and spoke in gruesome images of how a fall could result in at least broken legs and arms and very likely a broken neck.

To a rebel at the age of four there was no better nesting place for revolt than a hayloft. Below the horses stomped in their stalls. Chickens wandered in and out of the bands of sunlight filtering through the barn roof. A lassitude, produced by the hot and stuffy mixture of hayseed with the odor of manure, was dispelled by the prickly hay which got down inside my pants. Here I held frequent conversations with God and, strongly influenced by Adam, I stated my complaint as I knew it:

"Damn it, why do I have to be different? Damn it, why do I have to live with the shakes? Damn it, why can't I do whatever I want? You listen to me, damn it. I won't be kicked around just because I have the jumps."

That summer, climbing down from a hayloft, I slipped and sprained my ankle, doubtless a warning that even God could get a bellyful of a sassy kid who needed his mouth washed out with soap. I hobbled back to the house, my sniffles growing into wails of despair under the heckling of my mother, Uncle John, and Aunt Laura who, since their warnings had been ignored, seemed to find a grim satisfaction in prodding my swollen ankle, scalding it in hot water and jabbering over my howls of how next time I probably would achieve the ultimate inconvenience to them of killing myself.

I hoped that I would. The hubbub ended unexpectedly—as such outbursts so often did—with a quiet pronouncement from my father: "The boy has to live and grow up just like everyone else." So my tears dried and in time my ankle mended and my trust in Father grew stronger. From as far back as I can remember he understood that if a child with a physical handicap were to make his way, impudence toward grownups was a good prop to place beneath his spirit.

Many signs presaged the ending of summer. Increasingly, during late August days, Aunt Laura reminded the family of how she intended to buy a paper of pins or a comb or a new vinegar cruet when "the Jew came." Sooner or later, pack on back, Simon appeared. Fat, jolly and sweaty, he lumbered up to the porch, flung down his load and cried: "Are you home, Laura?" The house erupted with a carnival spirit. The front parlor with its pump organ, reserved usually for weddings and strapped-down corpses, now was flung open. Simon spread his treasures on the floor, a potentate of the road who haggled over prices and stilled my excitement with a stick of peppermint candy. Afterward he stayed for dinner, providing a bottle of wine to go with the roast chicken. He spread the gossip of the countryside which made him instantly welcome, and I fell asleep to his pleasant voice and the laughter he created. He stayed overnight and was gone with his pack by daylight. Whence he came and whither he disappeared I know not. But in 1914, spring brought the robins and the end of summer brought Simon.

Always our summer on the farm approached its close with the same ritual. One morning Mother packed a picnic luncheon and Father borrowed a farm wagon and team of horses from Uncle John. Edith and I rode on the straw in the back of the wagon, dangling our legs over the tailgate. If, as the team of bays plodded down the rutted road to Colt's Neck, we seemed unnaturally subdued, a sense of quiet contentment explained why; ahead on the front seat sat our parents like a pair of young lovers. This annual outing took us through the scenes of their lost youth. Every farm we passed awakened memories for them. Here one winter Father had tipped the sleigh and dumped Mother in the snow; down in the Cedars they had seen the man with his privates exposed and did not wonder that the poor devil had lived out his last years in an insane asylum; not far beyond was the home of "Aunt Till," who had carved up her husband with a butcher's knife (when was never clear; in this country a good tale lived for centuries). No wonder we two children simply listened: we were traveling over soil where for generations our family had been rooted.

My father handled horses with the skill of the country-born. A descendant of good Dutch stock that had farmed this part of New Jersey almost a century before the American Revolution, he was a tall, strong man with an abundance of straight black hair and the brilliant brown eyes that were a family characteristic. Fun spilled out of him and, judged by the stories he told on these annual outings, he must have been something of a hellion as a young man. Usually Mother called him "Bill," but on this one day, with a special warmth, she addressed him as "Will." She was proud of his enormous strength, his infectious good humor, his abiding gentleness. By formal standards he was not a well-educated man and I doubt if he had been schooled beyond the sixth grade. But that fact added to his nobility in Mother's eyes, for she saw the young boy who had helped support his family after his father's death. Mother clung to the tale that Grandfather Miers had died as a result of wounds suffered in the Civil War, whereas Father insisted that the old man had drunk himself to death and there were worse ways to go.

"Will, you should be more respectful toward your own father," Mother chided.

"Respectful? Good God, what greater respect can you show any man than to call him the best damn judge of likker in ten counties?"

"He had his troubles."

"We all do."

Mother, who doted on country sayings, could not dispute the point. Throughout her long lifetime she reminded us at least once a week: "If all of life's troubles were hung on a bush, you'd still pick your own." Simple and farm-bred though this philosophy may be, it made most of life endurable: death and taxes, droughts and bad prices for crops, a dead son and an afflicted child.

Edith and I, eavesdroppers on the tailgate, learned much as the farm wagon bounced us down the road to Colt's Neck. Mother had been born Emma Mildred Swannell, and her father, who was still respected throughout the county as a gifted cabinetmaker and splendid gentleman, had come from England. He was my maternal grandmother's second husband; and by comparison, if Mother's testimony can be trusted, the first husband had been as common as dirt. Everyone in the county who remembered Grandfather Swannell still called him "Captain Thomas," respecting the rank he had earned in the Civil War; and to my mother, he had lived and died a saint. He had made a practice of never charging wages whenever he built a church.

Father, whipping up the horses as we neared our destination, said: "Em, you were a fine looking girl."

"Better than you deserved."

◆§

An invariable stopping point on our end-of-summer pilgrimage was the General Store that still stands in Colt's Neck. All I recall now is its odors: of the open vats of pickles and jelly, of the leaking kerosene, of the brand new dresses and farmers' work clothes hanging on racks in the back. Once Father not only had managed this store but also had served as the local postmaster and, by Mother's account, had been as good-naturedly ineffective at both tasks as Abraham Lincoln. Here my father first saw my mother coming in for the mail. In time there was always a letter for Emma Swannell from Father: this was how they began and carried on their courtship.

After they were married they lived in a small, nondescript house about a mile down the road from the General Store.

"I was born here, I was born here," cried my sister in one of her nastier moods, knowing I had not been. And so, too, in this house, was born my brother LeRoy, four years my senior, whose name in this Dutch-English family can only be explained by the fact that Captain Thomas once had toured France. Suddenly Father flicked the reins, said "Giddap" to the horses in a very gentle voice, and we turned back to the old Dutch church that stood almost midway between the house and the General Store.

The horses lumbered up a hill to the graveyard behind the church, our destination on this late August outing. A placard out front announced that at the Annual Harvest Home for fifty cents you could have all the fried chicken and pumpkin pie you could eat. The burying ground was a wild place: untended, covered with vines and poison ivy, and not then greatly occupied. A few old families had staked out claims. By late August the flags placed there by the Grand Army of the Republic were as faded and as rain-soaked as the corpses of the men who had gone off in the 1860's to save Mr. Lincoln's Union.

The picnic luncheon Mother had packed was eaten here beneath a fringe of melancholy cedars. Horse stalls then stood behind the church, and Father would not eat before he had watered and rubbed down the animals that had pulled the wagon and had placed the straps of the oat bags upon their necks. Father topped off his lunch with a single bottle of beer.

When lunch was finished, we moved to that mound of earth where my brother LeRoy was buried. On hands and knees, using a sickle, Father cut down the high grass. Mother sat by an upended brick marking the head of the grave and watched each patient stroke as Father chopped down the grass. Finally, when this chore was accomplished, Father crept back, still on his hands and knees; he reached out his farmer's hand with its strong veins and thick wrists, and Mother held it gently.

"Will," Mother said, breaking the silence at last, "I hope some day we can afford to put up a tombstone."

"Em, we will, we will."

My father never kept this promise. Over his entire lifetime he could not find the money to spare from his obligations to the living to indulge a sentimental wish. But his tombstone was like the melodies of those who remain silent in church during hymn singing: in heaven, both are beautiful.

I appreciate now, with the wisdom of more than fifty years, the sublime feeling of that moment in August, 1914, when my parents, holding hands, looked down upon the almost anonymous grave of their dead baby, who had lived hardly more than a year. LeRoy had died from pneumonia. It was the custom those days in the country to say, "It is God's will."

Mother could not say this. "Had I known how to care for this baby," she said then and later, "he would still live."

No sniffler, my mother; when she wept, her tears were genuine. She went to the Trouble Bush and plucked off what she found there, accepting even the mystery of a cerebral-palsied child.

❧

Yet the ordeal must have been excruciatingly difficult for this sensitive, blue-eyed woman. Throughout her lifetime LeRoy was an idealized baby, a symbol of imperishable innocence and perfection. And when she learned that another child lived in her womb, she thanked God that she had been compensated for her lost darling. How deeply both my parents had been wounded by LeRoy's death was revealed by the decision that they could no longer endure the tragic memories of Colt's Neck. So Father left the General Store and Mother packed their few belongings and they moved to Brooklyn, New York.

My understanding is that "city relatives," of whom I have no mental image, helped Father find employment as a house painter. The family settled in a small dwelling on Evergreen Avenue, then a predominately German neighborhood; across the street was a saloon with swinging doors and on Saturdays a three-piece brass band stood outside, banging out melodies transported from the Fatherland. In this surrounding on May 27, 1910, I was born.

The doctor's name was Bender and he was a gruff old German with a rough, insensitive manner who chewed apple cores and spit the seeds into his palm. Long before my mother's time came she guessed that this was no dream-baby she carried; I was turned in the womb and so would arrive backward. Hours before the birth-process began the fluid that nature provides to help a baby find its way into the world drained away: it would be a dry delivery.

My mother's half sister, Aunt Lib, who was nearly blind, was her only comforter in the tiny upstairs bedroom where this butchery occurred. My mother's shrieks reverberated into the street and pedestrians stopped short while Edith, swinging on the gate, announced proudly: "Mama's having a baby." The Catholics all crossed themselves.

Within the room itself Dr. Bender worked methodically. The brass headpiece of the bed was bent under the exertion of my mother's struggle to be free of her child. Blood was splattered on bed and walls, doctor and attendant. "What must be will be," the old German muttered; he was accustomed to scenes of horror in dingy Brooklyn bedrooms. Somehow I was yanked out of my mother's body and placed at the foot of the bed while Dr. Bender worked on stemming Mother's hemorrhages. Sometime during this agony my father returned from work. He stood clutching the door frame, no longer a man of ironlike constitution.

In time Dr. Bender turned from the moaning wreck of a woman to the "blue baby" that was apparently dead. All I know is what I have been told: how with German stubbornness the doctor would not accept the defeat of losing the child; how he shouted at Father and Aunt Lib to arrange on the kitchen table a succession of vessels containing hot and cold water and cursed them both for not having wings with which to fly to this task; how all the while, holding my feet, he swung me like a dervish around his head, then paused to blow his own breath into my lungs; how afterward he stomped into the kitchen and holding me in his hands plunged me from hot water to cold, from cold water to hot, again and again and again; and how sweat poured down his face and dripped from his moustache but the glitter grew in his eyes and triumph crept into his gruff old voice: "A strong baby—he fights back!"

At last, an exhausted man, he felt he could do no more. He left medicine that I was to be given every fifteen minutes. Then, coat slung over his shoulder, he looked from mother to child to aunt to husband and said: "That will be ten dollars, when you can pay me."

For the next three days Father went without sleep, and his anchorage was a chair between his wife and second-born son. He watched the clock as though hypnotized by it; every fifteen minutes he gave me my medicine. On the third day Dr. Bender issued an order singularly gentle for him: "Go to bed. Your son lives, but he has the 'shakes.'"

Modern medicine can explain quite simply what happened in Brooklyn on that May afternoon a half century ago. At birth

24

an infant is highly susceptible to low oxygen intake, and this condition, called anoxia and really a form of suffocation, can result in permanent brain damage. Among the many types of cerebral palsy, mine is known as athetosis.

In 1910 a very kind term for this affliction was "the shakes." Medical science then was terribly primitive in understanding all forms of brain damage, and the superstition largely persisted that the afflicted child—the "marked child"—was a punishment for evil bestowed even unto the third and fourth generation. Many babies born like myself were hidden in dark bedrooms and never seen; some were chained to beds.

On that late August day, in the Year of the Stolen Peach, when we started back from the cemetery on our end-of-summer pilgrimage, we sat together on the front seat of Uncle John's wagon. I remember yet the reassurance of Mother's arm around me, the comfort of my cheek against her soft breast.

"Baby," she said. "My baby."

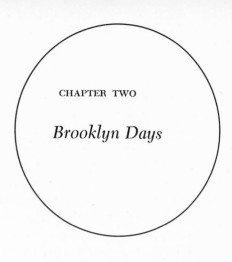

CHAPTER TWO

Brooklyn Days

*I*n *1914,*
Bushwick Avenue was a fashionable Brooklyn thoroughfare
with horse-drawn carriages and an occasional electrically operated automobile. Certainly this street was no place for a four-
year-old cerebral-palsied child, pedalling a tricycle among a
clutter of vehicles, to dash madly ahead with shrieks of "Get out
of the way, get out of the way!" Mother stood by the curb,
shouting in anguish: "Come back! Come back!"

The tricycle tipped crazily as I maneuvered a path through the horse droppings. There was a little bell that I banged imperiously, producing a glorious racket. Startled ladies stared down at the young wildcat whizzing past their carriage wheels. Horses pranced. Drivers pulled hard on their reins and filled the air with epithets that I daresay were suitably profane. A new chant expressed my exhilaration: "Going to Canarsie! Going to Canarsie!" I had not the least idea where Canarsie was, but the name sounded beautiful.

Somehow a giant of a policeman worked his way into the center of Bushwick Avenue. One sweep of his arms lifted tricycle and rider into the air; perhaps he had been to Canarsie, for my continued bellowing of the name awakened no poetic image for him. His face was very red and a glitter lighted his dark eyes. By now quite a crowd had gathered along the curb and my rescuer bore down on it with the majestic stride of an actor determined to ring down a curtain with unforgettable impact.

"Madam," he said, fixing upon my embarrassed mother the indulgent bemusement of an abused public servant, "why don't you tie a rope around this child so that next time you can pull him back to safety?"

A titter ran through the crowd. And an unidentified, mocking voice sing-songed:

> "Brass Buttons, Blue Coat,
> Caught himself a nanny goat."

A frown creased the brow of the policeman who still held me in his arms. "Madam," he asked Mother, "why does this child jerk so?"

"He is a nervous child."

My protector suddenly placed me down on the sidewalk as though at any moment I might go to pieces in his arms. "You— you mean you allowed this child to get out of your sight?"

My mother's face reddened like a fireball. Her head raised stiffly, as though snapped on a wire. With a kind of groping motion, her hand grasped my tricycle.

"Mr. Brass Buttons, Blue Coat," she hissed, "You are a fool!"

Around this infuriated woman the crowd parted respectfully. She was in that moment the personification of her favorite hymn, "Onward, Christian Soldiers."

Head high, a Christian soldier, she marched now with her child, forward to the fray.

≈§

Mother's other half sister, Aunt Louise, lived on Bushwick Avenue and was married to Fred Van Name, a farm boy who now worked in Wall Street and was quite well-to-do. In the coat he hung on the hall rack, Uncle Fred carried peppermint lozenges and new pennies which we children were supposed to steal while he chuckled privately, as though, for a mere pittance, we sold him our birthrights.

The Van Name home on Bushwick Avenue was surrounded by spacious grounds and had a drive leading to a carriage house; there was a downstairs parlor and an upstairs parlor; a basement entrance and a first-floor, walk-up entrance; there was a maid, Lena, whose figure and rapier-like face matched her name; in every room there were cords to pull, causing numbers to appear on a signal-box in the kitchen; and fruit was kept on the dining room table even though no one was sick.

Uncle Fred carried a fine watch on a gold chain. Whenever anyone asked him the time, he snapped the case open and shut, returned the watch to his vest pocket and replied, "I expect it's six o'clock"; but this infuriating habit fitted the character of a man unused to sharing anything graciously: his watch, his home, his money, or his emotions.

On a visit to the old farm, Aunt Louise had invited Adam to

spend a week on Bushwick Avenue. He arrived, resplendent in his burial suit and bearing bags of fresh vegetables, eggs, butter, and chickens. At Uncle Fred's suggestion he was admitted through the rear servant's entrance; at Uncle Fred's suggestion Lena was excused so that Adam could sleep in the attic quarters reserved for the hired help.

Within an hour Adam stormed into Evergreen Avenue, slamming his straw suitcase on the floor. "Goddan," he cried, "goddan. . ." Tears of injured pride glistened in his eyes. Mother and Father, giving up their own bedroom, cajoled Adam into better spirits. He spent a hilarious week with us, as intimately a part of the family in Brooklyn as he was on the old farm, but thereafter he would not even walk on Bushwick Avenue.

Adam brought back an unpleasant memory. Not long before, when Edith had been ill and money was needed for medicine, Mother had told Father: "I'll go see Fred." She had asked for ten dollars.

The loan was given grudgingly: "Please don't make a habit of this, Em." Mother bit her lip and took the money. Father's gentle eyes grew sullen and, henceforth, we had a kind of secret understanding to become sick only when we could afford that extravagance.

I was always uncomfortable in the house on Bushwick Avenue. I was expected to look through only the older issues of magazines for my palsied hands might rip a page of a new issue Uncle Fred had not yet read and he would be annoyed. Quickly Mother hit upon the plan of buying a magazine whenever we visited the Van Names. In happy anticipation she watched me ripping out pictures that caught my fancy, and her reward came in that moment when Aunt Louise erupted in near-hysterics: "Em, Em, my God, look what that child is doing!"

"Louise," Mother said, "since it is *his* magazine I suspect that he can do what he wishes."

I think we were both cruel. Aunt Louise was a handicapped, dependent woman. A pretty, witty girl when she had married Uncle Fred, she had borne three sons and a daughter but during her last confinement had suffered a stroke which left her a semi-invalid with a bladder weakness. Whenever she visited us Father called out gaily, "Get the oil cloth, here comes Louise"; and then, remembering the galling ten-dollar loan, invariably added with a growl: "If it were you, Em, you'd be asked to sit on a kitchen chair."

Mother said, "Blood is thicker than water."

Since Aunt Louise was "blood" (half-measure) she was accepted; since Uncle Fred was not, the wounds he inflicted did not heal so quickly. Poor Uncle Fred—how could he know that history was about to pass him by? How could he know that I, then a cerebral-palsied child, would some day hold more academic degrees than the three sons he sent through the University of Pennsylvania?

Queen Victoria died nine years before I was born, but for Uncle Fred the Age of Victoria was deathless. He loved a country governed by the chosen few; he loved not thinking about the many and why some day they might not be content with a mere subsistence; he loved having his umbrellas repaired by a tinker, who heated his soldering iron in a pot of burning charcoal and charged only pennies for this service; he was satisfied, passing the crippled night watchman at a company gate, and never suspected that one day a cripple might become President of the United States. In this age of caricature Uncle Fred enjoyed and believed jokes about "poor relations" and "niggers" and "Jews"; he chuckled over a comic page about Happy Hooligan, a hobo with a tin can on his head, because in Uncle Fred's mind none of these conditions ever could change.

He was not an evil man: he was simply a prototype being nudged aside by history. So he sent Adam to the servant's entrance. He grudgingly fingered a ten-dollar bill before he loaned it. He asked a cerebral-palsied child not to ruffle the pages of a new magazine. He moved from Bushwick Avenue to Flatbush Avenue and lived in a mansion with a private tennis court. He could not have done better.

My sister idolized Uncle Fred. Since Sally Van Name was close to Edith's age, they were warm companions. Uncle Fred paid the admissions for them both to attend the opera; at his expense they went to the seashore; and to Edith he was the very soul of generosity and the hero of a true-life rags-to-riches drama who, beginning as an office boy, now promised to become a millionaire. That I could feel demeaned in this same household impressed her as silly oversensitivity; but with time I would realize that Uncle Fred was simply like many unperceptive men, handicapped in their inability to recognize the social revolution that was then aborning and someday would alter all our lives.

ᮥᲘ

Three times a year Nana, who was Father's mother, visited us. In her early eighties and after a day-long journey that had begun at dawn, she scattered passersby as she charged down Evergreen Avenue, swinging a leather satchel. There was hardly a streak of gray in the hair on which sat a black straw hat with artificial cherries that bounced like little liberty bells. Exuberantly she bounded into the house, shouting: "Em, Will, Edith, Early, I'm here!" She sat down, breathing a bit heavily; then before she removed her hat, opened the satchel and presented each of us with a gift, warning: "I may not live until Christmas, so take your present now."

Nana's maiden name was Sarah Conover and she was descended from the Couwenhovens, who settled in this part of America in 1635. She remembered a girlhood home in which her grandparents had talked of the events of the American

Revolution; and the greatest moment of her life had been shaking hands with Abraham Lincoln. Years later, visiting Shadow Lawn, the summer White House in Long Branch, New Jersey, she mentioned this fact to Woodrow Wilson. Affectionately, the President grasped my grandmother's hand, gnarled with toil and age, and touched it to his lips.

"Madam," Woodrow Wilson said, "it is my privilege to hold fingers that once clasped those of Abraham Lincoln."

Nana recited the story, once every visit, wiping tears from her eyes; she belonged to an age when patriotism was a proud possession. Out of her worn satchel came the faded weeklies of Civil War days from which she could recount fluently what had occurred at Gettysburg and in the Wilderness and why, since Lincoln was a saint and Jeff Davis was a no-good whipper-snapper, the Union had survived. Divorce was never a word in Nana's vocabulary; if another woman flirted with your husband you took a horsewhip and drove her out of town. And that was how, in Nana's version of the Civil War, Lincoln had handled Robert E. Lee and the rest of those treasonable rascals.

Nana finally killed herself by taking medicines recklessly; when a teaspoon was prescribed she took a "short swig" from a bottle, and when a tablespoon was prescribed she took a "long swig." Advertising then made popular a nutty-flavored laxative that one chewed like candy. Nana chewed it not by the piece but by the package. Her bowels gave out and her intestinal tract collapsed, but for three weeks her great old heart refused to give up.

She was buried on a bleak day beside her husband and I remember the awful sound of the clods of earth falling upon her coffin. I cried convulsively, inconsolably.

When this Civil War widow died, there remained in her pocketbook a single one-dollar bill which was used to buy a collection of Bible stories that I still possess. But I would be eight years old before this evil day arrived and, meanwhile, Nana

32

could make me obey her simplest command with the admonition: "Early, I'll rub switch oil on you unless you behave." I was terrorized by Nana's "switch oil" and would gladly have jumped from the Brooklyn Bridge rather than have one drop rubbed upon me.

On one of Nana's visits the Great School Crisis occurred. It seems incredible that in a metropolis as large as Brooklyn I should never have encountered another cerebral-palsied child. By modern medical statistics, they were there, but where were they kept? They were not on the city's streets or in its parks. They were not in the public schools.

Mother hid nothing; she possessed a nervous child who under the law had rights she intended to obtain. I was to go to school. I cannot recall the name of the principal of P.S. 72 who interviewed us, but I can see her round, florid face covered with perspiration. The principal was an enormous woman with a bosom that spread like lava on the table when she was seated. She spoke like an army sergeant.

"Mrs. Miers, what do you expect me to do with this child?"

"I expect you to teach him."

"A—a—child like this?"

"A child like what?"

"Now, really, you can see for yourself. This child belongs in an institution. Now, tell me—"

My mother also claimed a good-sized bosom and suddenly these two women were standing mountain to mountain with storm clouds gathering over the peaks.

"Tell you what?" Mother repeated. "That you don't understand? That this child is going to receive the education which is his just due?"

It was a breathless moment. The mountains heaved. Across both peaks, lightning flashed.

"Mrs. Miers, I will enroll this child but he won't last a week."

"He'll last or I'll know why."

And so I was entered in P.S. 72 and Mother marched home in triumph. But her confidence had been pricked and she confided her misgivings to Nana: "Maybe I am asking for a miracle."

"Why not?" Nana demanded. "Why do the blowhard Catholics have to claim all the miracles?"

Nana was a hard-shelled Baptist; Father was more reserved about his church affiliation, declaring that he would go to hell before he would be dunked in public with his clothes on.

"You can scarcely expect to be dipped naked," Mother said testily. Clearly, in her mind, there was a severe line between dunking and dipping.

Father's cheerful attitude was that church attendance was a highly commendable habit in other people; both Edith and I were driven like sheep to Sunday School and, of course, Mother, in her pushy way, insisted that her handicapped child must recite a verse at the Rally Day exercises.

Nana made me a white sailor suit with long pants. On the way to Sunday School, chasing Edith across a grassy lot, I managed to streak both legs with green stains. I stood on the platform, seeking to hide this embarrassment by crossing my legs and looking badly in need of a bathroom. My carefully memorized recitation suddenly was blocked as, here and there, a guffaw sounded. I rushed through my piece:

> Jesus loves me,
> This I know,
> For—for—oh, for some damn reason.
> I forgot.

Never again was I prodded into making a public recitation.

❧

From my first day in school until I was graduated from college, I never experienced any exceptional difficulty in obtaining

34

an education. The spirit of the age may have helped me: teachers then were as dedicated as clergymen. Quickly I learned to read and I became almost at once a proficient student of history as though all of Nana's ancestors whispered to me how they had reacted to events gone by. I behaved well in school, being too frightened to act otherwise.

But school was only an incident in those Brooklyn years. Father lost his job and we moved from Evergreen Avenue to a cold-water flat over a store on Ralph Avenue. In the winter of 1917 when a coal shortage closed down even the schools, Mother took in "piece work," sewing up hundreds of cheap neckties on a foot-driven machine that Aunt Louise loaned her. I remember the winter months when, leaving early in the morning for the factory to pick up the day's materials, Mother pulled me on a sleigh; the wind nipped all around me but, coming back, I held the boxes and felt warm. Mother worked all day on the ties and after sunset we returned to the factory. It was dreadfully cold on the sleigh without the boxes.

For Father this period was a miserable time: the violin he kept in the drawer with his box of tools was rarely taken out now. He tramped the streets looking for employment in those years when the suffering of the workingman was considered by the Uncle Freds of America to be as natural as the pains of childbirth: to the few God gave affluence, to the many, the yoke of poverty.

I know how, during this time, Father grew listless and dozed by the coal stove in the parlor. Mother beat her foot on the treadle of Aunt Louise's sewing machine, stitching up neckties. Father hated to start each morning, looking for work, until Mother said, gently, "Will, perhaps I could ask Fred for a loan." At once Father roused like a hibernating bear; and one day he came home proudly, having secured a position that would last for years as janitor for the Bankers Trust Building.

Everything changed. Mother "resigned" her piece work. We

moved from Ralph Avenue to a comfortable third-floor, walk-up apartment on Bainbridge Street, celebrating the event by going to Ebbets Field and watching Uncle Robin's Brooklyn Dodgers lose to the Cincinnati Reds. But by only one run. The Dodgers in those days belonged intrinsically to us, to all working people. When we cried, "Wait until next year," we were describing nothing less than a social revolution.

We were happy as a family on Bainbridge Street. Edith was attending secretarial school and soon hoped to be self-sufficient. Her physical scraggliness was giving way to real prettiness and, as a result, she lost her hostility toward the male animal. Father returned to scratching away on his violin and Mother, who could now afford her own sewing machine, listened with a mouthful of pins as she cut out dress patterns for Edith and herself.

As an athetoid the day still began for me as though I were trying to thread a needle on a moving train. But somehow now it did not matter: we were all getting along. My arms shook, but not badly unless I was made extremely self-conscious of my affliction. I had a speech impediment, but then everyone does: they hesitate, they repeat words, and they learn in time to make these pauses reflect moments of "great introspection." When I drank liquids, the glass had to be held for me; at mealtime, my meat had to be cut; my hair had to be combed for me, and Mother parted it in the middle as though secretly she wanted to split my skull with an ax.

Life on the streets of Brooklyn in those years was exciting. On the curbside we played cards and matched the pictures of famous baseball players that were given away with packs of cigarettes. On the sidewalk we played hopscotch or gambled for pennies, bottlecaps, and the picture-buttons of local politicians, throwing them up against the porch steps. In the street we played "cat" with a sawed-down broom handle; or baseball or football, until we broke a window, when we all disappeared like rats down a sewer. We learned to smoke behind the car

36

barns on Ralph Avenue and, afterward, when the dizziness had worn away, we clung for free rides on the back of trolleys until detected by the motorman, or a policeman, or a drunk from a corner saloon who screamed: "Get the b'jesus off'n there!"

There were "special days": Hallowe'en, a great dress-up, begging day in Brooklyn, when we carried long silk stockings filled with flour and whaled the backsides off each other; and there was always Saturday when, for a nickel, we crowded into the stifling murkiness of a ratty little theater on Fulton Street and sat terrorized through the latest installment of *The Iron Hand*. We punched holes in tin cans, filled them with burning charcoal and raw potatoes, fastening wires to the top and swinging them round and round until the potatoes were baked. Eating these steaming hot on a damp November day, we said: "This is living!" We talked dirty on the streets and clean-mouthed at home; we roller-skated and held contests in vacant lots to see who could pee the farthest; and on warm evenings we sat on the empty vegetable bins in front of the corner grocery store, watching the sun go down, poking and roughhousing and speculating on how badly the Dodgers had been beaten; and singing "It's a Long Way to Tipperary" (which, I thought, must be near Canarsie) and "I'm Forever Blowing Bubbles."

Once a year came Block Night, sponsored by the local Democratic organization. The street was roped off. Japanese lanterns were strung by the hundred from curb to curb. Concessionaires appeared in tents and wagons, selling ices, hot dogs, roast corn, and chances on dolls and stuffed animals. A band banged out music. Watermelons were free, a great vote-catching device. Just how the ward bosses succeeded in selecting the hottest night of the summer for this festival I never discovered. By the hundreds the residents of Bainbridge Street poured out of the rabbit warrens they called home. They ate and laughed and danced and fraternized in the spirit of small towners whose horizons stretched no farther than the length of this city street.

The children raced around in wild delirium and finally, with a wham on the drum to attract attention, the precinct leader mounted the bandstand, wiped away the beer foam from his moustache, and informed his audience:

"By God, you'll never find a streetwalker in this neighborhood."

"Not before she finds you," some wag always shouted back.

ᵉ᷉

Aunt Louise invited Mother and me "out" to lunch, which meant going to Bohack's Market and filling up on free food samples. What Father said of this occasion was colorful but, even within the lenient scope of this chronicle, somewhat unquotable. But Mother's insistence that blood was thicker than water would have worn down the resistance of Old Scratch; she wanted to see Aunt Lib, her dearly beloved, nearly blind half sister who now lived in Red Bank, New Jersey; and when Aunt Louise offered "to treat" to the journey Father agreed and a memorable excursion followed.

Father said afterward: "The rich deserve their money—they bloody well suffer for it!" We traveled to Red Bank the "economical" way. Mother arose at dawn to pack a picnic lunch. Shortly after daybreak Aunt Louise arrived, filled with admonitions about securing the proper transfers so that we would not have to pay extra fare for the two trolleys needed to carry us to Battery Park, where we would catch a steamboat that would transport us across New York Bay and up the Shrewsbury River to Red Bank. If we were lucky, we would arrive at about sunset; by train, for about double the fare, we could have made the trip in three hours.

Of all the scientific achievements of the twentieth century, I admire none more than those that resulted in the death of the trolley. This instrument of human indignity invariably was piloted by a former guillotine head-chopper who now enhanced the execution of his tortures by the constant clanging of a bell. The sadists who constructed trolleys were all his secret allies: if the wheels rolled easily over the tracks the car must be rejected at once. The theory was that trolley passengers must rock to their destinations upon straw-covered, springless seats designed to illustrate every weakness of the human stomach; on sudden stops, these straw-covered seats slipped out of their slots, illustrating as well the imperfections of the human spine.

As we pitched down Fulton Street toward the Brooklyn Bridge and Manhattan Island, the motorman glanced back with a sly leer. He scattered beer wagons out of the way with his clanging bell, happy in the knowledge that if he ever struck one we all would perish like the hapless voyagers aboard the *Titanic*. At the precise moment when, faint with nausea, we were calculating where to deposit our breakfast, the conductor appeared, demanding: "Fare, please." Sickly, we paid him. Afterward, remembering Aunt Louise's admonitions, we each staggered to the rear platform to ask for a transfer.

"You should have asked for it when you paid the fare."

"I didn't think."

Overhead electric sparks spluttered like omens of death. Heat poured in the windows and up through the floor, beneath which the grinding wheels added a new dimension to *Paradise Lost*. "Here," the conductor sneered, tossing transfers which, with luck and prodigious athletic ability, we caught before they flew out the window.

The motorman never loosened his hold on the bellcord as he rocked us across that River Styx then known as the East River. We knew, all at once, why Steve Brodie once had taken a chance diving off the Brooklyn Bridge: he had suffered enough. The trolley stopped with a jolt while the conductor screamed, "Change cars," and promptly disappeared into a saloon before anyone could ask him which car to take. Somehow, ultimately, we reached Battery Park, and an undaunted Aunt Louise said: "Sea air is good for the lungs."

❧

Two steamers, the *Albertina* (on which we sailed) and the *Sea Bird,* then made the run from Battery Park to Red Bank; both were sidewheelers that depended for survival upon the fact that they carried freight cheaper than the railroads. On the upper deck with its pilothouse and smokestacks, a July sun beat down unmercifully; no human being could have endured here. Below were the sheltered lounges, comfortable but overornamented, where Mother, Aunt Louise, and Edith sat around a table littered with their luncheon boxes. For the unwary (or so Aunt Louise claimed) there was a galley where passengers could buy cheese and ham sandwiches encased in moldy bread, coffee brewed in dishwater, fried chicken that could have greased trolley-axles, milk one degree away from curdling, a sickish soft drink called Moxie, and the same Sweet Caporel cigarettes that we smoked behind the car barns on Ralph Avenue.

For a growing boy the lower, or freight, deck was filled with indescribable fascinations. Around the outside ran a small passageway, cluttered with the coiled ropes used in docking. A railing provided a magnificent leaning place for viewing the Statue of Liberty, and the tugs, freighters, and ocean liners making New York the world's busiest seaport. Salt spume lashed over the sides and, beyond, the green water rolled endlessly, casting a hypnotic spell.

Back inside the lower deck life assumed another, but no less exuberant design. Here one could look down into the engine room with its highly polished brass fixtures; heat rolled up from this inner chamber where the heart of the steamer throbbed steadily as an enormous plunger rocked back and forth and turned the side wheels.

The freight was skillfully piled on both sides of the lower deck to provide a broad aisle for the convenience of the vessel's male patrons. Soon little camp stools were opened, board slabs were laid atop, and such games of chance as Black Jack were hawked by gentlemen obviously well-known to the steamer's company, for we journeyed in the last citadel of the old Mississippi River gambler. The bettors drank beer from bottles that they luxuriously threw overboard as they gambled a nickel, a dime, or a quarter. There were a few souls holding the center of attention by risking folding money on the flip of a card.

Since Father could not afford this pastime, which he clearly wished to do, he said contemptuously: "Lawbreakers, every one of them!" The steamer beat a path across the bay, rolling gently, and found its way into the Shrewsbury River. The engines pounded, the side wheels left white avenues of foam, the seagulls screeched overhead looking for scraps from the luncheon boxes, the Moxie drinkers grew sick.

The gamblers never budged from their fixed posts, nor did fascinated onlookers like Father and myself who had selected our own favorites to win and followed each flip of a card as intensely as they. There is a kind of symphonic quality in the remembered conversation of those moments:

"Card?"

"Yes."

"Another?"

"No."

"Nineteen—the dealer has nineteen—pay twenty."

Meanwhile the beer-drinking continued merrily, indulged in by none more vigorously than the captain, who was constantly reappearing on the lower deck. "That fellow," Father said, rather enjoying the unseating of the mighty, "is getting a load on!" The captain guzzled his beer and climbed aloft; moments later he was back. Mesmerized, the Black Jack players fingered their remaining wealth.

41

"Card?"

"Yes, please . . . Christ, no!"

A shock, such as one might expect from an express train hitting a stone wall, rocked the steamer. Campstools, cards, money, Black Jack players sprawled across the deck. Over their heads boxes of freight crashed like angry meteors. A bell clanged, needlessly announcing an emergency. Father held me in his arms, bracing his back against a section of loosened crates. Buried deep within the debris a voice announced:

"That drunken sonofabitch has run us into the river mud!"

Father cried: "Your mother! Edith! Louise!" We staggered up the stairs to the lounge.

⋅⋨

Aside from the fact that Aunt Louise's bladder had let go, no one in the lounge had suffered seriously. Picnic boxes had scattered, however, and hard-boiled egg sandwiches had become yellow streaks upon the carpeting. The attendant was a monstrous old she-adder filled with venom for this crowd of notorious nontippers; she could not conceal her satisfaction at their discomfiture.

"We'll be stuck for hours," she said. "You'll have to row ashore and catch the trolley to Red Bank. That's the cap'n's orders."

Her glance leveled with special malevolence upon Aunt Louise who, having made this excursion many times, was well known for her penny-pinching.

The lifeboats were brought up to the freight entrance, whence a rope ladder, some six or seven feet in length, had to be traversed to reach the tossing boats below. The captain, far less tipsy now, decided that Father should descend and help Aunt Louise into a boat. A crowd gathered, watching in hushed trepidation as Father stood in the bobbing lifeboat and waited, with hands upstretched to receive that mound of flesh known as my aunt. Stomach flat on the deck, this wretched woman dangled her legs over the side.

"Will, do my drawers show?"

"The crabs don't give a damn."

"Will, can I reach the boat?"

"Louise, for God's sake, come on. Your bottom is as big as two elephants and almost as heavy."

"Will, if I fall will I drown?"

"It will take a dredge to dig us both out of the mud." Father now had his hand braced squarely against Aunt Louise.

"Will, maybe I should go back."

"Try it," Father called maliciously. "Just try it!"

Aunt Louise wriggled on the deck; then, emitting a sigh of doom, let go. Somehow—only God knows how—Father guided her into a seat.

When she had caught her breath, she said: "Will, Fred will reward you well for this."

Father refused to meet her glance. "I don't want anything," he said.

An embarrassed silence fell between them. It seemed hours before a trolley had almost bounced us into Red Bank.

"Will," Aunt Louise said contritely, "you're a most dependable man."

Father's tired eyelids fluttered; a smile touched his lips. Mother took his hand and Edith and I nudged closer on the seat.

CHAPTER THREE

A Rum-Scum-
Puppy-Diddle

In the Year

of the Great Syphilis Scare, when I was eight and the First
World War ended, Edith startled the family. A wretched little
blabbermouth, I burst into the apartment with wild excitement:
"Mom, *Mom*, Edith's got a *fella*. I seen 'em on Bainbridge Street
holding hands."

"That's nice," Mother said, not really listening.

"Mom, I seen 'em in the vestibule. They was kissin'."

"In the vestibule?" Understanding and quick vexation heightened the color in Mother's cheeks.

"Mom, how soon will Edith have a baby?"

"Oh, dear God!" Mother said explosively. "What kind of rot
do you hear down on that street? Your father needs to talk to
you."

But Father never did: sex embarrassed him even more than
it did Mother. And by nightfall the family had adjusted to the
discovery that Edith had acquired a steady beau. His name was
Alec Gunther, and he studied accounting in the same business
school where my sister was finishing her secretarial course. He
was a blond-haired, rather mousy boy who lived with his
widowed mother.

"Alec has his cross to bear," Mother said, intending no compliment to Mrs. Gunther. "She's the German type, expecting to
be waited on hand and foot."

Edith, like Father, had learned by now that silence was
golden when Mother fell into a peeve. I did not care about Mrs.
Gunther and my interest in Alec soon centered on a strictly
business-like arrangement: if I were paid enough I kept out of
sight whenever he called on my sister.

At this period a close family friend decided that he could
easily cure my athetosis with a program of rigorous training.
His name was Lamberton and he read the books of Robert
Ingersoll and called himself a freethinker. My trouble in holding
a glass of water, he convinced Mother, arose from a simple lack
of practice. From somewhere he obtained what seemed to me to
be hundreds of glasses, all filled with water, that were waiting
on the kitchen table when we visited him.

"You just pick them up, one after another," he told me gently,
"until you can do so without spilling the water."

"I can't do it."

"You can if you *try*."

Mother turned patient, encouraging eyes upon me; Father

watched with the suggestion of a frown creeping into his taut face; and Mr. Lamberton, a joyous schoolteacher at heart, sat on a stool, swinging his legs. I could feel my tension mounting and my tremors increasing as I viewed those acres of glasses. I considered knocking the whole lot on the floor with one sweep of an arm.

"Start," said Mr. Lamberton, as though he had me in focus under a microscope.

"I've got to go to the toilet. Real bad."

"We can wait."

I had not the least doubt but that the old bastard could and would. I came back from the john with tears in my eyes. Tension now had crept into my legs, a rare occurrence, so that I walked jerkily. I stuttered when I spoke.

"Begin," Mr. Lamberton ordered rather severely while Father's frown deepened.

In misery, I tried. Water splashed crazily around me and glasses shattered on the floor. I soaked myself, my parents and, taking aim at Mr. Lamberton, came close to breaking his nose. My sobs grew convulsive.

"I can't," I screamed, stomping the floor. "I can't, I can't, *I can't!*"

All at once I was in Father's arms. He hugged me in his bearish way and his rough cheek against mine was wonderfully soothing.

"Where is our sense?" Father growled. "Why do we ask this child to do the impossible? If he wants a drink of water, hold the glass for him, or put a sipper in it, and what in Sweet Jesus' name is so important anyhow in holding a water glass?"

"I was only hoping to make him less dependent," Mr. Lamberton said timidly.

"In some things he may just have to depend on other people," Father said. "That won't hurt them or him. Em, mop up this kitchen so that we can take this child home to bed."

The Lamberton incident left wounds that were a long time in healing. The frustration faded but not the conviction that deep within their hearts my parents wished they had not been given an afflicted child. For the first time in many months, I spoke seriously to God. "Why don't You let me hold a water glass? Why do You make everyone so unhappy?"

Since I did not feel any better for this outburst—and since even a youthful mystic acquires cunning instincts—I knew that my message was not getting through.

I tried again: "It isn't right."

I was walking home from school on one of those late afternoons when Brooklyn lapsed into a quiet mood. Only an occasional wagon lumbered over the cobbled streets. The pleasant smell of freshly ground coffee seeped from a corner grocery store. Mothers walked their babies in carriages and little girls on porch steps played with their dolls. An old German woman washed down the sidewalk in front of a brownstone dwelling. I am sure that God had no part in the Big Lie I invented.

"I saw the school doctor," I said at supper that evening.

"About what?" Mother asked.

"About me."

I never have been a good liar; my parents must have known, by my mounting tension, that I was projecting a childhood wish. Gently Mother prodded: "What did he say?"

"That—that I'm going to be all right," I said. "That I won't always have these shakes. Honest, some day I'll get over them."

A long pause followed. Mother held my glass of milk; it felt cool and comforting in my warm throat.

Father said: "Earl, that's fine—that's just fine."

ঙৡ

A sailor a-straddle the hood of a Model T Ford rode down Ralph Avenue, waving a chamber pot on which was printed:

"Kaiser Wilhelm's throne." The end of the First World War left Brooklyn in a delirium. Meeting Mother on the sidewalk, Father grabbed her around the waist and shouted gaily: "Come on, Emmy. Let's dance a Hop Waltz."

The end of the war brought changes quite apart from Aunt Louise's sadness for the fact that the meatless days and scantily filled sugar bowls of "Hooverizing" were now over. Nana, that grand old woman of eternal Christmas, had died, an irreparable loss; and in memory of Nana my parents were determined that Christmas this year should be special.

Most mornings Father cooked his own breakfast and left for work before any of us awakened. Often I had gone to bed before he returned and Mother explained mysteriously: "Your father is doing his bit as Santa's helper." Occasionally, however, he came home early and the evenings turned festive.

The upright piano in the parlor was loved by Edith, who had learned to play by ear. She accompanied Father on the violin as he scratched out the melodies we all sang: World War I favorites like "Roses of Picardy" and "Keep the Home Fires Burning"; and Nana's beloved Civil War songs like "Rally 'Round the Flag" and "When Johnny Comes Marching Home"; and such perennial standbys as "Listen to the Mocking Bird" and "Home, Sweet Home."

Above the artificial logs in the fireplace fluttered a blue gas flame which, had it ever been extinguished undetected, would have asphyxiated us all. Beyond the windows glowed an orange-and-reddish sunset, so brilliant that Van Gogh might have painted it in the winter sky. We could see the lighted cars of the Fulton Street Elevated, flashing by on their way to the Brooklyn Bridge. We were snug and warm, contented and protected.

In the fortnight before Christmas my mother spent every afternoon window shopping on Brooklyn's Broadway. She was a prodigious, inexhaustible seeker of bargains; every window exploded upon her vision as an arena of combat where prices were her personal enemy. And so, as the afternoons sped by, she stored up notes of what she intended to buy, come Christmas Eve, when father brought home his "tip money" from the offices he served in the Bankers Trust Building.

December twenty-fourth was a restless day of pacing and clock-watching and calculating and revising gift lists for Mother; the soup boiled over on the stove; and then toward six o'clock Father came home with more than a hundred dollars, a fantastic sum for that time.

Mother, jamming on her hat, snatched the money and fled. She returned around midnight, after the stores had closed, loaded down like a pack horse. There were games and a toy gun and school clothes for me; there were yards of material for new dresses for Edith; there were socks and ties and long underwear and new violin strings for Father. She sat in a chair, soaking her tired feet in a bucket of hot water, as she wrapped presents until three in the morning.

But it was not Mother's midnight shopping nor the memory of Nana that made this Christmas live forever for me: it was Father. Now I knew why he had been coming home late. He had stayed after hours at the Bankers Trust Building, working on his own ideas. He had made me a truck with headlights powered by a dry cell battery long before such toys appeared in neighborhood stores.

But his masterpiece was the pool table, constructed to lie upon our dining room table. Except for the rubber cushions, the felt covering, and the set of ivory balls, which he somehow managed to find in a pawnshop on the Bowery, he had built this table from scrap materials. Mother crocheted the six pockets from stout green twine. All of the cues were handmade, including two small ones specially weighted to offset my tremors.

Father possessed many characteristics in common with Nana's everlasting hero: like Abe Lincoln, he claimed little formal education and was not much of a book reader; and like Old Abe, when he was not thinking, his nose was stuck in newspapers. The Lamberton incident had aroused his creative instincts; if new habits of muscular coordination were good for a nervous child, they should follow logical patterns. They should be associated with fun rather than with latent fears and they should make allowances for the degree of difficulty involved. The pool table with its weighted cues was his solution; if his notions proved incorrect, then the table could be sold to compensate for the time and money that had gone into constructing it.

The pool table never was sold—we wore it out, playing on it, loving it. Everyone enjoyed the game: Mother, Father, Edith, Alec, all my friends from Bainbridge Street. Afternoon and evening the balls clicked, laughter rang out, and for long periods the upright piano in the parlor stood silent.

By luck or genius, Father had weighted those cues perfectly, and in time I could hold my own against most grownups and beat any kid on the block, for somewhere in his youth Father had become a shark at the game. He knew angles, cushions, when to play safe, how to figure combinations. He delighted in dazzling us with his own repertory of trick shots.

I became his prize pupil, his pet; in team play he would accept no other partner. With a straw in a drinking glass and a weighted cue in my hand, I was now enrolled in Bill Miers' School of Rehabilitation for the Handicapped.

One other memory of that unforgettable Christmas lingers. Tucked in the toe of my stocking was a new five-dollar bill, more money than I had ever owned. I fondled it; I loved it; but all at once I was swept by the realization that Mother had not received many presents. I found this poor, tired woman resting on the couch.

"Mama," I said, holding out my precious bill, "you take it—you buy what you want."

She startled me, smiling and crying together. Her arms embraced me tightly.

"You know what your Nana is telling the Lord right now? I can hear her bragging: 'How do you like them pickin's?' "

<hr/>

The pool table and the upright piano created unexpected emergencies within the next year. Edith finished her secretarial course and quickly found a job. She gave Mother five dollars a week for board and banked another five dollars—Edith was rich.

Since every boy on Bainbridge Street wanted to spend his after-school hours playing pool, I also was rich. My closest friend became Bill Judd, who was almost a brother.

The Judds were a peculiar clan: English in background and as poor as churchmice. Old Man Judd spent his off-work hours in an undershirt sitting by the front windows and keeping watch on the trains of the Fulton Street Elevated. He knew to a second when one was late; and between-times he cursed the day he had left the London waterfront. Old Lady Judd was a sleazy, somewhat vulgar character out of a novel by Fielding or Defoe; she shuffled around the apartment in bare feet and an unconcealing kimono. But on Bainbridge Street Mrs. Judd appeared buttoned up to the throat and corseted to the verge of breathlessness.

Mrs. Judd's opinions of the handicapped were typical of her time and background: the afflicted, to Mrs. Judd, were placed on earth to prove that even unto the third and fourth generation the sins of the fathers endured.

"That poor boy," Mrs. Judd said. "You can't blame the poor, sweet dear. But somewhere, you know—"

Somewhere, she meant, was hereditary syphilis.

I am not sure that my mother could have spelled this word. To her it meant only one thing: you had been wicked; you had

51

lain with a man promiscuously; you would die in a sanitarium, raving mad. Like the memory of my grandfather, breaking through his straps and popping up on his deathbed of ice, the word struck horror in her soul.

I don't think she suspected Father of any great misdoing either, although that may have been a possibility. And who could tell about one's ancestors long gone? Who *knew*?

Mother and Father took blood tests. They awaited the results in agony. To complicate their suffering, a distant relative died of venereal disease contracted from sleeping with a whore in Red Bank: no family can be perfect. There was not, however, a trace of syphilis in the Miers family. But never again was I allowed to play with Bill Judd.

~~~

Meanwhile Edith loved that old upright piano in the parlor. After work, leaving the Ralph Avenue station on the Fulton Elevated, Edith and Alec walked to Bainbridge Street, holding hands. They kissed briefly in the vestibule, then Edith dashed up the three flights of stairs and broke into the apartment, crying: "Mom, I'm home." Soon we would hear her at the piano, singing:

> I left my love in Avalon,
> Beside the sea . . . .

Where Avalon was I could only guess—probably opposite Tipperary, on the other side of Canarsie. But after a time we would hear Edith playing melodies that we did not recognize. Mother would walk down the long hall from the kitchen, holding a stew pot in her hand. "Edith," she asked as she leaned against the door frame, listening, "what tune is that?"

"I made it up."

"It's very pretty."

Mother, retreating to the kitchen stove, could not conceal her pride. "Your sister is a music writer," she said. Her sigh was deeply satisfying.

But not even Mother was prepared for Edith's subsequent announcement. We were finishing supper one evening when Edith said, using that form of address we both reserved for wheedling moments, "*Mama*, I've written the words to a song."

"Good for you," Mother said, mouthing in quiet contentment a spoonful of tapioca pudding.

"But *Mama*," Edith cried, "my lyrics have been accepted!" She dashed to her bedroom and returned bearing a letter that she read breathlessly:

Dear Miss Miers: Your lyrics are excellent and we shall be happy to set them to music and publish same. A fee of fifty dollars will be required to pay the composer, but for this sum you will receive one hundred copies of the completed composition which you may keep or sell to your friends or dispose of in any way you like. Naturally you will receive a royalty of 5 percent—the same royalty that we must pay the composer—on all copies of this composition that we sell.

Miss Miers, we congratulate you upon the talent that your lyrics reveal. You are a fine, sensitive young artist. . . .

There was much more to the letter and Edith read on rapturously to the end. Mother's spoon dropped, untouched, into the tapioca pudding. How did Edith happen to submit her lyrics to this music publisher?

"Mama," Edith confessed, "I read an ad in a magazine. It said: 'Song Writers Wanted—You Write the Words and We'll Write the Music.' I didn't think it would hurt to try."

Mother toyed with the spoon in the pudding. Fifty dollars— Good God, as much as Edith could save in ten weeks or Father could earn in two at the Bankers Trust Building! I do not think my parents then knew anything about "vanity publishing"; like

53

me, underneath, they may have felt electrified by what Edith had achieved. Van Gogh may still have been painting sunsets in the winter sky, the lighted trains of the Fulton Street Elevated may still have been dashing on their way to the Brooklyn Bridge, but Edith had broken the monotony: Edith had become vital. Father said: "Let's play a game of pool." And Edith, easily the worst pool player in the family, outshone us all that evening.

Within a night or so came the miserable experience of our monthly visit with Alec and his mother, who lived in an apartment, similar to ours, some blocks away on Chauncey Street. We sat around the frigid circumference of a dining room table. Lights encased in a green stained-glass shade shown down, as though we were all criminals assembled for questioning.

Mrs. Gunther was about Mother's age, but perhaps stouter; she wore her hair in a net, suggesting that she had just been fished out of the sea. She resented the fact that her husband had left her ten years ago, but in private Father insisted that Mr. Gunther was not dead—he was simply in hiding. Mother steered the conversation away from Mrs. Gunther's physical complaints, never an easy maneuver, to the acceptance of Edith's lyrics.

"Isn't that fine?" Mother asked.

Mrs. Gunther's laugh was fluttery. "Emma," she said, "you know I'm old-fashioned. You and I serve our men. We should. Now arty women. . ."

"Edith has talent," Mother said with the decisiveness of a woman who had just been seized by lockjaw and would die on these words. By now she had memorized the letter from the vanity publisher, quoting glibly: "Edith is 'a fine, sensitive young artist.' "

"Men," Mrs. Gunther responded with equal spirit, "run a family. Men, not women, must take responsibility."

"That depends on what a man wants," Mother said, "a wife or a housekeeper."

I am sure that the resulting silence was as ghastly as Father later claimed. Alec sat mute—his umbilical cord would never be severed within our memory. Edith squirmed, but afterward declared that Alec had given her the idea for a "comic song." Father retained his reputation for diplomatic silence. We left shortly and, walking home, Edith poured out her frustration:

"Mama, Alec didn't back me up! Mama, Alec doesn't care about my song!"

"Tomorrow morning," Mother said, "I'll go to the post office and get the money order for the publisher."

Ultimately, one hundred copies of sheet music arrived on Bainbridge Street. The title of the song long has been forgotten; but the lyrics, as I recall, dealt with love unrequited, which was not inappropriate under the circumstances. The melody, I am sure, was like the cover in purple and black: an old standby, used time and again. Yet there was a magic line on that cover: "Words by Edith Miers."

Father, recalling a bit of folklore nonsense Nana had taught him, expressed our admiration:

"I'll be a rum-scum-puppy-diddle!"

⌐§

Mother's window-shopping at Christmas had taught her the location of every music store on Broadway. With the one hundred copies of Edith's song under her arm, she set out to hawk the family's merchandise. At night she returned home, a happy, fatigued commission salesman: here she had placed ten copies, there another twenty. Eventually she recovered 80 percent of Edith's original investment (naturally no royalties were ever paid). Even Mrs. Judd bought a copy, although the Judds did not own a piano.

We rarely saw Alec now, but Edith did not seem to care. Her evenings, her weekends were spent at the piano, "composing."

Mrs. Judd, however, scarred my life forever. After the Great Syphilis Scare, the frustration of the Lamberton incident or even the triumph of Father's pool table had no lasting meaning to Mother. As she trudged Broadway and its music stores, she also noted the whereabouts of hospitals and clinics. Doctors would tell her what to do with her nervous child . . . and thus began the most dismal cycle of my life.

Nothing could be more lacking in imagination than a Brooklyn clinic in 1919. Here no human being was a hero of the spirit; here the patients sat like cattle, for fifty cents a head, to be hurried in and out as quickly as possible. No beauty surrounded their physical misery, their inner torment. They stared at walls painted in colors as drab as their own emotional misgivings and, miserable beggars that they were, they were expected to respect two realities: they needed help and they could not pay a decent price for needing it.

Meanwhile, a lackluster old trollop, wheezing with dried-up youth, accepted the fifty-cent fee, issued a card that must be surrendered when anyone saw a doctor, and said with an executioner's malice: "Take a seat." She turned away—not hating me personally as a child; she hated everyone.

Ultimately I found a seat, surrounded by bilious walls of yellow. I squirmed. Old men, old women, hacking and coughing, smiled feebly. In summer, somehow, the heat was always breathless, the horseflies numerous.

And so I waited—a number on a card, an ailment. White-frocked doctors and interns flicked in and out, joked with the nurses, stared vacantly at the patients, disappeared behind doors sinisterly marked "Private."

Minutes mounted into hours, hours into days, then into weeks and months and years . . . or so it seemed as I anticipated the calling of our number. At last I was ushered into a cubicle separated by a canvas cloth from fellow sufferers. Here I waited uneasily for the passage of the remainder of the twentieth century before, unexpectedly, a doctor popped in so breathlessly that I had the impression he had just dashed down from the North Pole and must return at once to save the life of a dying Eskimo.

"What's wrong?" the examiner asked.

"The child is nervous."

"For how long?"

"Since birth. He was born backwards."

"Hmmm. Where was he born?"

"At home."

"Hmmm. How are his teeth?"

"Fine."

"Hmmm. And his tonsils?"

"They're out."

"Hmmm. . . ." Clearly this human hummingbird did not believe my mother; he flashed a light down my throat, ran a finger over my teeth, looked suspiciously into my ears, and then inquired explosively:

"Does he wet the bed?"

"Sometimes."

"How much?"

"I never measured it in quarts and gallons."

Obviously the doctor was puzzled; no one in 1919 had taught him how to recognize cerebral palsy or had led him to a small book written a century before by W. J. Little, an English surgeon, that described its symptoms. Looking at me scowlishly, the examiner said at last: "This boy jerks."

"I know that," Mother said. "You tell me why."

But the doctors did not know why; they had been taught nothing about athetosis. Yet for her fifty-cent fee Mother was entitled to advice, and as the visits led us from clinic to clinic, there was at least variety in the suggestions offered.

"Keep the bowels open and make the child take long periods of rest in a room with the shades drawn" was invariable advice,

57

as though there were something especially nerve-wracking in clouds and blue sky and a child's soaring imagination.

One doctor thought electric shock treatments might help; he had just bought a machine that "shot" electric waves through the brain on the theory, apparently, that lights would flash on and bells ring. So I was strapped to a table, wires were placed on both sides of my cranium, and the current turned on. While I lay there, trembling, the doctor suggested that I think positive thoughts and I did—I hoped he would break a leg, be run over by a trolley, and have a dirty pigeon light upon his corpse.

The chiropractors twisted my back, pummeled my arms, swiveled my neck, pumped and punched my legs and took a very dim view of a damaged brain that would not respond to such manly treatment. Another doctor suggested hypnosis, but there Mother balked: what she could not see nor hear she could never believe.

In this period of my life, beginning when I was eight and continuing until sometime after I was ten, I acquired a distrust for the medical profession which, to some degree, would never fade. Lack of knowledge was the invisible handicap these doctors had to bear as athetosis was my outward sign of man's imperfection—but I sensed then, and resent still, their inability to treat the whole person. I was never their equal, their friend, who could have told them Zack Wheat's batting average or how Burleigh Grimes' "spitter" really dropped just before reaching the plate or how to roast a potato in a tincan. They did not seem to care about the person behind a number on a card as they made me dress and undress or snarled at me to relax when I would not have been there if I could relax, or shaved my head for their electric wires or X-rayed me front and back and top and bottom, after flushing me out with oils that could have removed the hair from horses.

And then, marvelously, came a change. Everything was the same—the wait, the impersonal treatment, the miserable cubicle with its canvas partition—but not the old German doctor who strolled in. He was in no hurry. He picked me up, sat me on his lap and said: "You don't belong here."

You never knew the names of the doctors who interviewed you in a Brooklyn clinic, and that was a pity. This old fellow, who chucked me under the chin and rubbed the back of my neck and quieted me within moments, belonged among the giants of his age.

"Madam," he said to Mother, "this boy will always be nervous."

"But—but—" Mother began.

Smiling, the doctor interrupted, placing his hand on the back of my head: "Madam, sometimes God takes away from here." His hand moved to my forehead: "But He gives a little more here, where we learn to think." And then his hand touched my heart: "Here, too, where we learn to understand. If you would help this boy, madam, think, save, scrimp, wash floors if necessary . . . but give him education. Give him all the education he can take. It is the only way."

All the argument went out of Mother. We went home happy, for we both knew that the clinic days had ended. Father listened and nodded: he had won back the only pupil ever enrolled in Bill Miers' School of Rehabilitation for the Handicapped.

And, in a way, the door was now opened for a remarkable personality to walk into our lives. His name was Sam Danks.

CHAPTER FOUR

Above

the Chop Suey

Quite forgotten

today is Ella Wheeler Wilcox, the daughter of a poor Wisconsin farmer who became the philosophical spokesman for the anonymous America to which my parents belonged. Ella was a woman of strong convictions, so devoted to cats that she had no intention of going to heaven if felines were excluded; and such was the affluence she attained through Hearst syndication that she made this pronouncement while reclining on an Oriental couch. Ella preached a sturdy respect for country, home, and materialism. She was living proof that the poor working girl might well dazzle her neighbors without selling her soul to the fleshpots, and her influence upon the age deserves serious consideration from the social historian.

Mother adored Ella, whom she read slavishly. I daresay that Mother might have been taken aback, had she seen her pet languishing on a couch as though waiting for Omar Khayyám with his loaf of bread and jug of wine; but even affectation could not pump Ella dry of the go-ahead, frontier tradition that had produced her. Hers was the spark of those millions like my father and mother who without consciousness were forging a social revolution. Was it Ella or Mother who spoke when we were told: "If fate hands you a lemon, use it to open a fruit stand"? Or: "Aim at the highest and the lowest is always obtainable." Was it Ella's constant harping upon chastity that led Mother and Edith to dress and undress in a closet as though lechers were insects that could fly through any open window?

Like Emerson, the great philosophical spokesman of Nana's generation, Ella told her faithful that they could hitch their wagons to a star; but Ella, always aware of a Wisconsin farm girlhood, knew that one had better exercise hard common sense in the process. Mother believed so, too. She had tramped Broadway for the last time, peddling Edith's songs. Now if my sister really wanted a musical career, she could make the rounds of the regular publishers until she found one with cash of his own to invest.

Edith was delighted. She came to know the toilers in Tin Pan Alley and poor young Alec depressed her even more with his lectures on accounting and why woman's place was in the home. She learned also why her songs were not salable and, to her credit, she studied style and phrasing and impressed us all with her industry and improvement. Then, one evening, she exploded the bombshell.

"Mama, I'm in love. His name is Sam Danks. Mama, he's an

awfully important person—he's the head arranger for Leo Feist, the music publisher above that Chinese restaurant on Seventh Avenue. He makes a lot of money, Mama, and owns an automobile."

Mechanically, Mother began placing dinner on the table. "How long have you known this young man?"

Edith dashed off to comb her hair, calling down the hall: "He's stopping in tonight."

Mother would not budge: "How old did you say he was?"

"Sam's awfully nice, Mama. You'll like him. His first marriage turned out badly, but both his son and daughter are doing well."

"My God!" Mother fairly shouted. "You tell me, Edith—how old is this Sam Danks?"

"Only two years older than Father."

"Only—*what?*"

"Two years," Edith repeated. "He's really mature."

"Does he use a wheelchair?"

"Oh, Mama!" Edith laughed, a bit shrilly. "Wait till you meet him—you'll love him. He said he would be here tonight—right after the rally for Eugene Debs."

"For *whom?*"

"You know, Mama. Debs, the great Socialist leader. Sam's a hard worker for the rights of man. He fights for people like Father, even though he makes as much money as Uncle Fred. What's for dinner?"

"Fried liver."

"Beef or calf?"

"My own," Mother flung back. Her trauma was almost pathetic. Perhaps she was remembering those shocking, unexpected lines by Ella Wheeler Wilcox:

> Whoever was begotten of pure love
> And came desired and welcome into life,
> Is of immaculate conception.

62

When shortly thereafter Father arrived home, Mother led him at once into the bedroom and slammed the door. Very likely to drown out their wild voices, Edith retreated to the upright piano and sang new words to "Avalon":

> I lost my heart at Leo Feist,
> Above the Chop Suey. . . .

~§

I was allowed to stay up until Sam called, perhaps as a reminder to Father that his obligations were numerous and although a chisel would make an effective murder weapon, there must be a better solution. Mother burped unashamedly, for to have digested dinner under the circumstances would have been unthinkable. Hostility wavered on the air like the odor of fried onions. Watching the clock, Father muttered: "Those Socialists are all long-winded." And then the bell rang. Edith ran to the door and shouted down the stairwell: "Sam, Sam, up here!" We heard his footfalls on the carpet.

He was utterly charming. He said to Mother: "You're young enough to pass for Edith's sister." He said to Father: "God, I'm tired—men our age can't act like boys." He patted my head and said warmly: "So this is Early-Morning-in-May . . . your sister talks more about you than she ever will about me." And sinking into a chair with a sigh, he said: "That damn fool Debs, he's been educated above his intelligence." In two minutes, he was one of us. I have never witnessed such salesmanship.

Father said: "I suppose you promised to make a great music-writer out of Edith?"

Sam shook his head. "Her talent," he said, "would not fill an eye-dropper. Commercially, she has nowhere to go."

Father must have blinked a little; he looked at a train on the Fulton Elevated, flashing by on its way to the Brooklyn Bridge. Mother controlled her indigestion, and we agreed that, come Saturday, we would cross the Hudson and go for a drive in New Jersey "on the other side of the United States."

We learned a great deal about Sam in ensuing weeks. He had been born in Nottingham, on the edge of the forest made famous by Robin Hood. His father was rather a substantial man, whose family still ran the hardware business in Notts, and his mother was of somewhat lower class—a serving maid in the idiom of that international authority, Ella Wheeler Wilcox; but Sam, who adored the works of Charles Dickens, put the matter more bluntly—she had been a chambermaid. Sam had traveled Europe before becoming an itinerant musician and actor in America and, playing to a new audience, he could not resist old stories.

Once he told us: "I was crossing the Missouri River on a barge when a friend called: 'Clem, what have ye there?' Clem hacked a little and replied: 'Horse manure and actors,' and we all asked: 'Why can't you put the actors first?'" We laughed, not realizing that Sam was telling a story as old as the traveling vaudevillian in America.

He told me how an Englishman spelled the word saloon: "With a hess, a hay, a hell, two hoes and a hen," and I thought the story extremely funny.

He taught me a song, attributed to his own English childhood, that became the rage of Bainbridge Street:

> I saw Esau kissing Kate,
> She saw I saw 'e saw,
> 'E saw I saw she saw 'e saw
> —We all saw I saw Esau.

Sam drove a Haynes, a well-respected car in that period. It had open sides and a canvas top and isinglass windows to put up when it rained, but not before everyone was soaked to the skin. It had a horn with a rubber bulb that could be honked imperiously, a marvel for any child lording it over those lesser mortals called his playmates. Father ducked his head under the hood, fascinated by this mechanical masterpiece, and within a week understood perfectly how to repair any part.

Mother made a linen duster and bought a veil that went over her hat and face and tied under her chin. She was like a Gibson Girl, slightly outdated, sweeping from porch entrance to car. Doors slammed. The ignition groaned, sputtered, caught fire and we drove off. Almost always we stopped on Flatbush Avenue and Uncle Fred lumbered down from the front porch.

"Nice car, Sam."

"Runs well, Fred."

"Where to this week?"

"I thought we'd spin up to Bear Mountain."

"Well, good luck, Sam. Scratch Anthony's Nose for me." And we all laughed, knowing that Anthony's Nose was the name of the mountain across the river.

On these drives our knowledge of Sam's background increased. His son, Walter, was married, had children, and lived in Ridgewood, New Jersey. His daughter, Charlotte, was an actress in silent movies under the professional name of Charlotte Desmond; there were rumors of a rather hush-hush love affair with a well-known poet.

So not only as a father, but also as a grandfather and as the producer of an enchantress (who, I am sure, was as sinuously distracting to Edith as the screen image of Theda Bara), Sam grew in our minds. His receding, graying hair made him look older than Father; perhaps he should have been sent packing on first acquaintance. But Sam was full of fun and energy and high adventure. We became fond of him and lived for weekends when we could all be together.

◆§

Making up stories became my favorite pastime when I could not sleep. One that I recall was set in Bohack's, the market on

Broadway where the aisles seemed to stretch for miles and Aunt Louise lunched on free samples. In my tale it was not bits of cheese on crackers that were passed out at these booths. With the power of a god I cast a spell over the store; I walked up to the girl in a booth and said, "I wish," and she, nodding knowingly, granted my wish.

For Mother I wished that she could go to the places she talked about when reading the Sunday papers—to Washington, D.C. to see the cherry blossoms, and to Niagara Falls to see where the fool had dropped to his death in a barrel, and to Asbury Park to see the ocean (although why she wanted to go there I never understood, for she hated the water, complained constantly of the sand washing up under her bathing dress, and was terrorized by a sinister force called the undertow that waited to snatch her in its clasp, twirl her around like an eggbeater, and within moments toss her lifeless carcass somewhere along the coast of Spain).

For Edith I wished that she would meet all her "music people" and that Alec would jump off the Brooklyn Bridge and kill himself and stop her from sighing with occasional melancholy: "Oh, Mama, I can't help feeling that I was mean to Alec."

For Father I wished that some day he could fulfill his yearning to move back to the country, nap in a hammock under a tree, putter around his own vegetable garden, and enjoy corn "just pulled and dropped in the pot." And for myself I wished for a two-wheel bicycle and a dog, objects rarely encountered among third-floor apartment dwellers in Brooklyn.

That these fantasies were soon to become realities were all part of Sam's artful courtship. Within a few months Mother was telling Aunt Louise that Edith and Sam had reached an "understanding"; she said it pugnaciously and what she implied was: "It's no damn business of yours how old he is—at least he can support Edith."

66

Another spring found us "house hunting" in New Jersey, where we were to live together as one big happy family. Everyone was excited. "It will be so good for Earl to get away from the city," Edith said. Mother said it too, and Father and Sam. I was the clincher to the deal.

Secretly, I was overwhelmed at the thought of moving away from Brooklyn. I loved the old place with its connected roofs running a block long upon which we raced and screamed and tossed pebbles down on the heads of passersby; and its catacombs of cellars, dark and musty and interconnected where a game of hide-and-seek could last a week, had anyone been able to endure it. I loved its street games: follow-the-leader and duck-on-the-rock, and most of all that glorious neighborhood pastime of catching the corner barber napping so that we could startle him out of his wits by bursting like marauding Indians into his shop. To this delicious divertissement we gave the appropriate name of "Scaring Hoffmyer Pissless."

Poor old Hoffmyer, how he endured I will never know, for age had palsied his hands, not the best asset for a barber; a razor in his grasp sometimes shook like a bowl of jelly; and why Mother insisted on taking me there for a haircut I am not certain unless she figured that if I jerked one way and Hoffmyer another we would come out all right!

But as my favorite author of these years, Horatio Alger, Jr., whose books I read by the ton, would have said, the day of doom approached inexorably. Alger never wasted time on fancy talk and his fans became experts on mortgages. They knew to a penny what interest rates were. The bankers, who were so discredited as a breed in the Depression-Soon-to-Come, may have owed a bust in the nose to Alger for the seeds of distrust he already had sown in our youthful minds. When at last Sam settled on buying a house in Hackensack, New Jersey, I quizzed him about the mortgage until he was almost out of his mind. He was lucky. I could have questioned him with equal expertness

67

about his capital investments, and advised him on when to buy stock on margin, and explained why it was wiser to trust a boot-black than some Wall Street investor like Uncle Fred—we Alger boys were ready for the Revolution.

And then the day of doom arrived. Edith and Sam were to be married. We were packed. The moving van was there and Sam in his Haynes. I stood on the porch steps, choked with emotion. Henceforth others would have to scare Hoffmyer. As deeply and as clearly as a small boy could, I thought:

"Farewell, my love, farewell."

CHAPTER FIVE

The Young
Entrepreneur

The house

in Hackensack, built near the turn of the century, was located
on the corner of First Street and Beech at the foot of that rather
snooty neighborhood known as The Hill. Horse-drawn ice
wagons still lumbered down the street, driven by a sometimes be-
sotted behemoth who, staggering up to the kitchen door with an
ice cake in a canvas sack slung over his back, hissed through the
screen door: "How much, lady—ten cents or fifteen?" On warm

nights old oaken iceboxes dripped gallons of water, but small wonder: nearby stood the coal range, still used for cooking.

A rambling porch, front and side, was an inevitable architectural device in this age before air-conditioning. A large hallway joined the front parlor and dining room, but the family lived in a back parlor or "private room." A kitchen and butler's pantry, a front stairs and back stairs completed the first floor. There were five bedrooms upstairs.

A finished attic became a child's paradise on rainy days. Here was set up what remained of Father's pool table until it was knocked to pieces as a stage for plays put on by children costumed in old suits and dresses pulled from trunks. Here I kept my museum of rocks and leaves, a sign of a city boy's delight in discovering the country. Here I decorated the walls with covers from the *Saturday Evening Post* that gave a wonderful perspective to an American's character whether he was caught with a fan swinging in a hammock, or napping by the side of a stream with a fishing line tied around his big toe, or having a lemon phosphate with his best girl at a marble-topped table with curved iron legs at the corner drug store, or listening to a band concert in the town square.

The cellar, dark and musty, held other charms. One room was converted into that somewhat sacred chamber where, each fall, Father and Sam pressed out two barrels of red wine. The grapes arrived in a truck, box piled on box, and the unloading was a scene no other child witnessed unless he lived near a freight yard.

What weekends these were: Mother always "stole" a box of grapes to make jelly, causing a minor altercation. The sight never to be forgotten was of Father and Sam stripped down to their undershirts and sweating joyously as they turned the press. The juice flowed into buckets which were dumped into the barrels, sacks of sugar were emptied in, and like schoolboys they chortled: "Come Christmas, this will wet our whistles!"

For weeks thereafter they performed a nightly ritual. No sooner were these two men home from work than they rushed to their wine barrels, stirring the mixture with long wooden poles and chuckling over how well their concoction was fermenting. They lived now for that magical Saturday and Sunday when the wine would be ready for bottling. Father built rows of shelves around the room on which each bottle was to be laid with the affectionate pride usually reserved for newborn babies. They would walk to the one little window that permitted the sun to filter into this subterranean paradise, holding up a bottle so that the daylight could shine through.

"Sam, look at that color," Father said, marveling at what they had accomplished. Using a tin dipper, they sampled their wares.

"Bill," Sam asked, "what's wrong with that flavor?"

What was wrong, Mother could have answered, was the fact that both were likely to grow as tipsy as hoot owls and unable to eat dinner by the time the bottling was completed. But she laughed. Such secret vices weld a family together.

Being a good "Alger boy," I knew about what those two barrels of wine cost—very little, really, since the grape pulp was sold to a merchant who stewed it into a brand of cheap bootleg whiskey that may have blinded half the residents of Bergen County. As a Socialist, Sam did not much care what happened to this solidly Republican county.

And as an enlightened "Alger boy," I knew to the penny what Sam had paid for this property: $10,000. He had made a bargain. An acre of ground gave him and Father space for the garden they coveted; here they grew Sam's beloved English squash, vegetable marrow, which was cooked in a cream sauce and when served seven nights a week became thoroughly detestable, although it was never as revolting as Sam's steamed suet puddings, which should have precipitated a second American Revolution. There were two quince trees with low branches that an infant could have climbed, but here a childhood idyll ended: anyone who tasted the fuzzy, yellow-skinned fruit of a quince tree experienced the sensation of biting into a hardened caterpillar.

Edith became pregnant. In the bedroom where Edith now slept alone I discovered hidden in the closet a baby carriage and a bassinet. Mother was aghast to find me sitting on the back porch with the girl next door saying blithely, "Edith and Sam are going to have a kid." The revelation was neighborhood news.

Ben Hecht told the story of how in 1912 a Chicago high school principal had a woman arrested and fined for showing too much of her "leg" when she stepped from a North Avenue trolley. My mother belonged to this generation, and as long as she lived, there would always be something dirty about sex to her. As a subject, sex was not to be thought of, except in the sense that the stork brought babies as the bunny rabbit brought baskets of candy at Easter and Santa Claus came down the chimney shouting "Ho-Ho-Ho" at Christmastime.

Unhappily her son had learned otherwise among his guttersnipe playmates. But what *had* he learned? Mother was no coward; she intended to know. Red-faced and hearts pounding, we faced one another across the dining room table. The result was miserable for both, since my stammering knowledge of how the creative process worked was nearer the truth than she ever could have imagined. I cried with a sense of shame I still believe undeserved. And my mother walked away, too baffled to answer, for in almost gaining a grandchild she had lost part of a son. But Edith's tummy had begun to bulge. Mother could not deny that fact.

Meanwhile Father and Sam, quite unaware of this climacteric in the family, built a greenhouse, for these two enthusiastic gardeners believed that with a little help from God and the sun they could raise flowers for Christmas and grow ripe tomatoes by the Fourth of July. They hammered up the sides to their greenhouse and constructed what to me seemed to be acres of glass roof.

Watching them work, everyone must have envied their incredible energy. They climbed ladders. They nailed down frames and puttied windows. From Friday night, when they returned from New York City, until Monday morning, when they set off again to their paid-for labors, they did not shave although possibly they bathed. Once the glass enclosure was erected, they built a flue that wound beneath the benches and drew its heat from a stove in the "potting room." Neighbors gawked at this marvel, wondering how in hell anyone who supported Eugene Debs could afford such a luxury.

But something went wrong with the flue and, overheating one day, it set the plant benches on fire. From north and south, east and west, volunteer fire companies descended on the greenhouse. Almost giddily, men toppled off the trucks and ran out hose. Not one of them gave a damn about the flue and benches—these were going up in smoke and they knew it.

So they simply enjoyed this fire where a jet of water, under high pressure and aimed at a glass roof, produced sensational results. Satanic delight illuminated their faces as they turned their hoses skyward. Glass popped as the water struck it, and it was a miracle that people for blocks around were not cut to ribbons by flying glass. Putting out that fire became a game, an enchantment: firemen contested for sections of the greenhouse roof to attack. They did not miss a pane.

Sam blamed the needless destruction of his greenhouse not on man's requirement for harmless violence but simply on the Republicans who then controlled Hackensack, and so he threw himself wildly into the hopeless campaign to elect "Fighting" Bob La Follette of Wisconsin, the Progressive candidate, to the Presidency. Meanwhile Father and Sam rebuilt the greenhouse. This time they prudently protected the flue with a sprinkler system.

⊷⧸

A little fox terrier named Teddy became my devoted shadow and his short legs soon wore out chasing after my two-wheeler. So Teddy learned to brace his hind feet over the frame above the pedals and hang his front paws over the handlebars. Thus we rode for hours and I daresay that more than one startled motorist, turning to stare, blamed his dented fenders on "that boy and dog" on their bike.

The change from city to country life was made easily. So far as I know I was accepted into school without even a raised eyebrow, although I must have been the only cerebral-palsied child in the town's entire educational system. But teachers in those years stood apart; they were a community force, devoted professionals, lovers of a craft-art. Some rode to school on bicycles, carefully fastening their skirts with clips so that their bloomers would not show. They spun along with their books in the front basket, their eyes straight ahead, their pompadoured heads proudly raised; they were a vigorous breed of spinsters who seemed to draw power for their pedaling from their tight corsetting; and it was a callow young policeman who did not stop traffic and nod respectfully as they swept around a corner with an arm outstretched.

Mother and Edith, succumbing to the fashion of the early 1920's, might bob their hair, but not these ladies from Elmira and Holyoke, Barnard and Vassar, who clung to their traditions of propriety. Sarah Tyndall, principal of the grammar school, combined the humanity of Nana with the dignity of the pedagogue, and she adored every charge, black and white, as though torn from her own womb. When naughty youngsters were sent to her office, there was no scolding. Above her desk hung a lithograph of Abraham Lincoln. Always she excused herself, saying as she departed: "Until I return I want you to look at this great man

74

and decide if he would have behaved as you did." Lincoln's sad, melancholy eyes held me under a spell; even the wart beside his nose appeared to add to my mesmerization. Presently I was abject with a sense of unworthiness: by dipping some little snot's long braids into an inkwell, I had betrayed Lincoln, home, God, and country.

Ruth Shaw was another of this matchless breed. With such masses of red hair piled upon her head that she should have suffered constantly with migraine, she taught eighth grade English with a passion for language until writing a composition under her became a high adventure in self-expression. And there was that snip of a woman, Agnes Bennett, scarcely four feet tall with her topknot, who taught the bedevilments of mathematics, not from a textbook but from a loving heart. Not only the banker's son from The Hill, but also the colored shoemaker's son from Railroad Avenue and the Jewish boy who worked every afternoon and evening in the newspaper store on Main Street managed to shine as students under "Aggie."

Charlie Piper was one such student; he was a pale, thin boy with a timid smile who never took part in the recess roughhousing. A week went by and we did not see him or really miss his quiet presence; then we learned that he was dead of what I now suspect was rheumatic fever. A pall fell over the school yard; we were unaccountably shocked and seemed almost to walk on tiptoe. The fact that the life of one so near our own age could be snuffed out without warning was one cause of our sobering mood, but Charlie awakened us to a far deeper discovery than that. The truth would grow on us slowly: that we were each perishable, that the span of existence could be extremely brief and, unless we were careful, what was called mortality could be as empty for us as it had been for Charlie.

We played frantically: to release animal spirits, our parents believed, but it was the revolt of youth that was yeasting within us. Under the influence of home, school and church, most of us would piddle away that revolt. We would be shamed into conformity and mediocrity; but the struggle, while it lasted, would be headily intoxicating.

In winter, we skiied and skated, but most of all we enjoyed those tingling evenings sleigh-riding down the hills. Some bolder boy would throw himself astride a girl just as her sleigh was taking off and we would watch him with envy, wondering what it was like.

In spring we tramped the woods, looking for snakes until we reached the abandoned railroad tracks. Here we puffed on Cubebs that we could buy at any corner drugstore and talked about girls. We compiled long lists of synonyms for the various sex regions, male and female. Many of us, who had been told by our parents that self-play led directly to the insane asylum, were sickened by inner guilt, but happily none of us cut off our hands before we discovered that this warning, like so many other adult prejudices which we were expected to respect, was largely a hoax. Away from home, school, and church, we could share the dignity of our own degeneration and had we acted otherwise our glands would have been woefully out of wack. It is no wonder to me that many has been the college freshman who could not wait to get home and tell his parents that their heads were filled with hogwash on this subject.

⋅⋅§

That untutored man, my father, must have remembered some of his own struggle: at least he tried to help me to escape from the tensions of my burgeoning adolescence. One day he came home lugging a discarded Remington Standard which he had bought for a dollar or two from one of the offices in the Bankers Trust Building. He had watched my cerebral-palsied hands trying to write with a pencil; he had seen the calluses on my knuckles, where I pressed down to control my tremors; to him the performance was both ridiculous and unnecessary.

At first I was more frustrated with the typewriter than with a pencil. Watching me, Father said:

"A machine works on principles. The key you strike is governed by a little wire in back that controls the speed with which it strikes the paper. If you hold down the space bar, that wire waits until it is released and so the key will strike evenly, one letter at a time."

Thus I was taught to type, holding down the space bar with a finger of my left hand while striking the keys with a finger on my right: the system works beautifully for an athetoid.

Father decided that I should carry the typewriter to school and from class to class, so Mother put on her best dress and she and Father went to see Sarah Tyndall. The lithograph of Lincoln gazed down on the four of us. Father explained his plan.

"Wonderful!" Miss Tyndall exclaimed. "Why not?"

And so, each Monday, I lugged this monstrously heavy typewriter to school. I walked two miles. I was allowed to use the machine in every class and I do not recall that any schoolmate ever claimed that the clicking of the keys had so distracted him he failed a course. Arithmetic became my best subject. Only a cerebral-palsied child who has learned how to add and subtract, to multiply and divide on an old Remington Standard can explain why, for the manual effort to shift the carriage backward and forward in order to correct a single decimal point becomes too exhausting to justify a mistake.

Every Friday afternoon, despite the two-mile walk, I lugged the typewriter home. Father and I needed it.

❧

How this man divined the agonizing uncertainty boiling up within me I shall never understand. Somehow he must have known that sitting on those abandoned railroad tracks in the springtime, we boys could not discuss girls and sex forever. So we talked of future dreams: of how Bill Conger expected to follow his father into the banking business; of how Jack Mercer wanted to be a successful politician like his old man and live in the biggest house on The Hill; of how Allie Conrad one day would run the hospital as his dad did (poor Allie died of a weak heart before any of us finished college); of how Berry, older than the rest of us and already a freshman at Franklin and Marshall College, planned on running the Lethbridge Construction Company; of how Frenchy Chanut intended to own a chain of restaurants.

Chilled to the bone with fear—and, dear God, I was, no matter how bravely I smiled—I knew there was no future for me as a handicapped son of the maintenance man for the Bankers Trust Company. What *would* I do? How explicit and how urgent were my conversations with God at this period I do not care to recall, but I must confess that His answers were neither explicit nor urgent. You could say that God and I reached a standoff.

Father acted where Providence appeared to hesitate. The tip money that had given us the wonderful Christmas after Nana died now was used to instill within me a sense of economic self-reliance. We were going into business together; we would sell stamps to collectors by mail.

The back bedroom was converted into an office. After his day's labors at the Bankers Trust Building, Father roamed Nassau Street, where New York's stamp dealers then clustered in a ghetto of dingy, bare offices. He bought bundles of stamps. There were as well piles of sheets of bond paper marked off in twenty spaces and called "approvals"; in each space we mounted a stamp, noting the price below. Our enterprise was to be known as the Mohawk Stamp Company—very likely because we were a pair of scalpers at heart. Long evenings we toiled in that back bedroom, arranging and pricing our stamps.

"Who's going to buy them?" Mother asked with a shake of her head. Men, young or old, were incurable romanticists.

Father grumbled at the question, for he had no notion of how to answer. His tip money was now almost exhausted. But we scraped together enough for an advertisement in the classified section of the local newspaper. Mother contributed a dollar, saying gaily: "Easy come, easy go—and don't ask for jelly doughnuts tomorrow!"

We secured one good customer, a retired mailman dying of a heart condition who asked that a representative of the Mohawk Stamp Company call upon him. When I was ushered into the room, he said with a chuckle: "I knew those child labor laws would never work!" Great veins stood out in his temples. He breathed heavily and rubbed his chest as though it hurt. His wife, hovering in the background, annoyed him enormously. "Fan, for God's sake!" he snapped. "Go see your mother and have a good cry!"

"Boy," he said, coming at once to terms, "I can spend two dollars a week."

"For our stamps, sir?"

"No, for a cheerful face around this house."

He was a grand old man, and we had virtually nothing to sell that he needed. He hated the room in which he lived day and night because he could no longer climb stairs. Sometimes I had to fetch the chamber pot from under the couch and stand with my back turned while he "operated." For this service I received an extra quarter.

Nothing peeved him so much as the glass bead portieres that separated his room from the hall; they tinkled in the breeze and he called them his funeral shrouds. Old friends brought him risqué magazines with pictures of naked women and he kept them on the table, confessing with a cackle: "I do it to devil Fan—she's sure I'll have a stroke looking at those French cuties!" His delight was his collection of United States stamps, including many local issues that even then were great rarities. He would turn a page gently, rubbing its edge as though offering a caress; he could tell a story about every stamp.

"No one in this family knows what they're worth," he would break out, and his veins suddenly looked ready to burst. Then he turned good-humored. "They'd sell 'em for scrap paper when I die, but they ain't getting 'em, boy. It's all in my will. An old friend of mine up in Utica, who lives all alone and knows their value—he's the one, boy. He'll know where to sell 'em and"—he gave me a wicked wink—"he'll know how to use the money, too!"

Clearly he hoped that his old chum in Utica would squander every penny on some French cutie. One day my friend was found dead on the porch, having dared for once to break through those tinkling funeral shrouds. Perhaps he had set off to find his own French cutie, whose name would not have been Fan.

The two dollars that I thus earned, added to other tip money that Father had now received, allowed us at last to advertise in a magazine of national circulation. We selected *Popular Science Monthly*—Father enjoyed its articles—offering twenty-five "free" stamps to "any approval applicant" who would send us a dime for "postage and handling." The mail poured in.

Our postman certainly was not joyous at this development. For months he had complained to Mother that I was the worst kid on his route for loading him down with samples and catalogs and prospectuses of the newest business opportunities—anything I could get by sending a penny postcard. He would storm up onto the porch, waving a catalog and shouting at Mother: "My God, Mrs. Miers, look at this—traps for hunting bear and antelope. Where in hell is he going to find bear and antelope around Hackensack?"

For once Mother was stymied. She slapped at a mosquito; those we could find in New Jersey.

Of course, the more the postman complained over the activities of the Mohawk Stamp Company, the happier Father and I were in our back bedroom office. We managed to squeeze out a small profit. In a rudimentary way, I learned accounting and how to answer complaining letters with tact and to mark outrageous prices on shoddy merchandise. The postmarks on the letters we received acquired a special romance: Laramie, Wyoming; Enid, Oklahoma; Wichita Falls, Texas. Chin in hand, I would try to imagine what manner of people these were who bought our stamps. Were they cowboys, oil drillers, trappers of bear and antelope, old men musing over French cuties as they awaited the end of life, housewives, bank clerks—who knew, mayhap even a bank robber? What would they have said if they knew the author of the letters they received was a growing boy with cerebral palsy?

&

First Street provided an interesting boundary in Hackensack. To the west rose The Hill with its homes that often approached the dignity of estates. Names on the gateposts like Zabriskie and Van Pelt were echoes of names heard since the Dutch first settled this region and bought land from the Lenni Lenapes. First Street also contained fine old homes, for it was a remnant of the pre-Revolutionary post road to Newark, and travelers had found it a comfortable spot to rest. The High School was situated here, evidence of its central location; and that commercial tradition which in olden times had placed only an occasional tavern along this route now had sprinkled among the aging houses automobile agencies, a skating rink, a bowling alley, and similar enterprises. East of First Street stretched a low plain that once may have been a swamp leading to the river and was now all filled-in land where wild blackberry bushes abounded.

A long block eastward from First Street, down Beech, ran Railroad Avenue, so named because the tracks of the Erie rattled to the weary rumble of freights and commuter trains bound for Jersey City.

Where First Street ended and Railroad Avenue began was a succession of miserable houses largely inhabited by the Negroes who worked for families like the Zabriskies and the Van Pelts. The porches sagged; rats gnawed at the chicken coops in the back yards; mud holes rather than grass divided houses and streetwalks. Yet the residents were a remarkably pleasant and obliging group. A colored teacher then taught in one Hackensack school; colored boys played on the high school teams; and these Negroes even managed to get along tolerably well with the "pig-Irish," who resided east of Railroad Avenue.

Mother's attitude toward colored people was a strange mixture of old farm prejudice and sentimentality. Negro babies she liked, though she insisted on calling them pickaninnies; she snatched them out of baby carriages, jiggled them in her arms, cooed at them. Toward Negro adults she was stand-offish, recalling her Monmouth County girlhood: Negroes there were hired in harvest season and gotten rid of as quickly as possible for, she had been taught, they stole, possessed loose morals and rarely bathed. It hurt her to have Negroes living so close to her own home and she took out this umbrage on Matty, the colored girl Sam hired to clean the house once a week. "She does the light work and I do the heavy," Mother complained bitterly, and Sam did not help the situation by saying: "Sounds like a damn smart girl." Matty was constantly pregnant, or so Mother declared, adding darkly: "Anybody can be that careless if you fall off stepladders and make having miscarriages an art the way Matty does!" Mother was an artist at exaggeration. But one point was clear: Mother, if she could have her way, did not want *her* son to have "any truck" with this crowd.

The mail of the Mohawk Stamp Company brought us all sorts of "new opportunities," including the chance to become the exclusive representative in Hackensack for the weekly periodicals of a publisher on the south side of Chicago. We sent for sample copies. They were garish, to say the least—and sensational; but they were hair-raising if you enjoyed tales about the snake-worshipers in the back Kentucky hills or how some crazy old coot in Nebraska had carved up eight wives and was butchering his ninth when the police intervened. The profit per copy was four cents on a dime and for the first month the publisher assumed all risk. How could we lose? We ordered a hundred copies and eventually the postman slammed them against the door with the snort:

"Here's your nigger papers!"

With trepidation I set off to sell these wretched publications. In those days the Negro business section clustered around the drab Erie station at the corner of Railroad Avenue and Central. Worried little establishments lined these thoroughfares: a pool room, a barber shop crowded with horse players, a beauty parlor, a luncheonette. A book of horoscopes was the neighborhood Bible, studied avidly each morning by 99 percent of the residents before they invested their pennies, nickels, and dimes with the local policy runner, a gangling youth named Emory, who pimped in off hours. If I came to detest that pink-covered "luck book," moral scruples played no part in my judgment: this gambling on numbers drained off the purchasing power I sought to tap.

But luck favored me early in my excursions into this colored ghetto; I encountered Matty, our house girl, who chatted with Emory in front of the beauty parlor.

"Mawnin', Early," cried Matty. "How come you's here?"

"I could ask the same."

"Lawdy, boy, you can see where I is—like I tells your Ma, here's where I gets straight." Matty meant that within the dim recesses of the beauty parlor, by a mysterious process kept as secret as a voodoo ritual, she intended to have the kinks taken out of her hair.

"That ain't all she here for," added Emory with a giggle.

"Shush your dirty mouth, nigger," Matty scolded, but without rancor. She looked at the bundle under my arm and asked: "Early, what you do with all them papes?"

I explained my mission. Matty bought a copy. She made Emory buy three and he drew a dollar from his cream-colored pants and waited impatiently while I fumbled for the change.

"Wicked money," shouted Matty and they both snickered.

Not all sales came that easily for, as I said, the policy business was rugged competition. But identified as Matty's friend, and as Emory's supplier of trashy reading material, I had gained status. I quickly learned the art of neighborhood bargaining:

"Boy, I tell you what—you take two cents today an' two tomorrow an' by the end of the week we make up the dime."

I pointed to the sign over the poolroom door: "In God we trust—all others cash."

Petulantly: "Don' you trust me, boy?"

"Does Emory?"

"Emory? That nigger won't give you the sweat off his ass to make ice water!" Usually I got the full dime then, and I could sense a growing respect because I was not easily hoodwinked.

There were numerous questions about my physical condition. "Boy, how come you shake like a man who's been ginnin' too much?"

"I was born that way."

"Is that a fact now? They drop you on your head?"

"I don't think so."

"Your mama fall off a stepladder?"

"No."

"She get the frights one night?"

"She never said so."

"Well, it make no dif. You's a good boy an' I buy a pape. Tell me, boy, where you live at on First Street?"

"At 113."

"That's a good number. When you see Emory tell him I wants to see him. I play that number!"

I ate in the luncheonette and the big old woman who ran the place spooned the soup for me.

"That tastes good," I said gratefully.

"Sure it do, baby—that's food to strengthen your gizzard."

She bought a paper and held it upside down. Perhaps she could not read, but this point was not significant. "Needs it to bang down the flies—t'other pape I had wore out."

In the two months that I sold papers in this ghetto, I came to love these people. I lived with what I found. Beneath their raucous, bawdy bumptiousness was a gentleness, a warmth that I treasured. In a sense, we shared the bond of a handicap—they because they were colored in a white man's world, I because I was cerebral palsied in the same world. But we refused to be ruled by self-pity: the young entrepreneur and the policy players believed implicitly that brighter days were ahead if we kept trying.

Of course Matty could not keep her mouth shut and Mother recoiled from having her son grow up under the influence of touts and trollops, as she put the matter to Father. So another idyll ended. Mother's annoyance, I think, was heightened by the fact that Matty spilled out this tale while munching on a bun, for, along with her other accomplishments, Matty was also the inventor of the coffee-break.

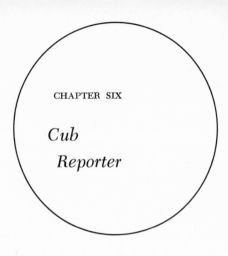

CHAPTER SIX

Cub

Reporter

At the age
of sixteen, I knew—or at least I had seen in the flesh—a *real*
author. He had walked down Main Street in Hackensack with
head bowed moodily as he bumped his way between other
pedestrians. Thus, as he had strolled, he had kept up a medita-
tive conversation:

"And Tom shouted, 'Peewee, you come when I call' . . . But
Peewee, hiding in a treetop, hooted like an owl and dropped a
bag of water on Tom's head. . . ."

86

At this moment my mumbling author had stepped in front of a truck and been brought up short by screeching brakes and the enraged imprecations of the driver:

"Wake up, you dumb bastard!"

An apologetic smile had touched the lips of Percy Keese Fitzhugh; and yet, within a dozen paces, his head once more had been bowed as he plunged into that better world inhabited by Tom Slade, Peewee Harris, and Roy Blakely, whose deeds of valor and nonsense already filled a shelf of books boys adored.

My own head had swirled with wild dreams: how wonderful it would be to become an author like Percy Keese Fitzhugh! Or like Owen Johnson and share the glories of Lawrenceville with Dink Stover, the Tennessee Shad, and the Prodigious Hickey! Or like Ralph Henry Barbour—or James Oliver Curwood —or all those enchanters of my sleepless nights who filled the pages of *Boys Life* and *American Boy, St. Nicholas* and *Youth's Companion.* Collectors today pay handsome prices for first editions of the historical tales of A. C. Henty, a genius who breathed life and truth into history long a-gone. I read such Henty books by the dozen and tossed them aside—foolish, stupid boy!

In this age, books meant much to a family. The new fad of the radio and the old fad of the phonograph really did not alter one's choice of leisure: to read and to listen frequently were pleasant simultaneous occupations.

Sam was a great reader aloud, devoted to Charles Dickens, who in Sam's mind was a far greater apostle than Debs in espousing the cause of the downtrodden. Though we may have seemed like a family depicted in *Harper's Illustrated Weekly* generations before, we often gathered in the back parlor after the evening meal. Sam's glasses slid down on his nose as he opened a book and read to the family.

In those months while Edith awaited the arrival of her baby (he would be named LeRoy Miers Danks in memory of that still unmarked grave in the Colt's Neck Cemetery), magic hours were

spun out. Sam read with an old actor's skill; he possessed an un-
erring inner ear for language so that he could portray characters
as though they were alive. I listened enthralled, sitting in a big
chair with my feet tucked under me. That late summer and fall
we went through *David Copperfield;* in the winter months, while
Edith nursed her baby, we lived with *Bleak House, Sketches by
Boz,* and *Pickwick Papers.*

How well I remember that back parlor and the grief and
triumph that Dickens left there! Who more than I ever loved
Peggoty so completely or hated Mr. Murdock so ferociously?
Who more than I ever was more willin' that Barkis should be
willin'? Who more than I ever responded to the impudent spirit
of Sam Weller who, when prodded to polish the boots for the
gentleman in Room Twenty-two, shot back that electrifying
question in behalf of the bedamned: "Ask number twenty-two
whether he'll have 'em now, or wait till he gets 'em."

Sam did not read Dickens—he lived Dickens. Indeed, he became Dickens: a middle class Englishman in rebellion. There
were interruptions in Sam's reading—for the wine pressing, the
building of the greenhouse, the planting of the garden—but
always we came back to Dickens: to *Dombey and Son* and *Little
Dorrit* and *A Tale of Two Cities.*

Sam read other books—the complete works of James Feni-
more Cooper simply, I suspect, because he had bought them, for
never did any author require quite so many lines for a character
to lift an arm or wipe a nose. He read Anthony Trollope and
Jane Austen and Nathaniel Hawthorne and the Brontë sisters.
Under Sam's prodding I brought dozens of books home from the
town library. At fifteen I had gone through *Paradise Lost* and
Paradise Regained, had fumbled over Shakespeare, but won my
way back to English literature through the plays of James M.
Barrie.

Sometimes I read three or four books in a day, mixing the
pulp paper tales of Dick Merriwell with *Paradise Lost,* the stories

of Percy Keese Fitzhugh with *Old Curiosity Shop*. I hid in the back seat of the car with my books, refusing to hear the call to chores. I read and read and knew that I had to write.

At what age, and under what circumstances, any child will mature no one can predict. Suddenly I had grown up. I knew where I was going, not *how*, but *where*. I deserted the Mohawk Stamp Company and alone Father carried on the business. He never complained. Meanwhile I sat at the old Remington, writing highly imitative stories. I filled reams of paper. Mother said, "Don't disturb him." Sometimes, late at night, I fell asleep, just not able to say what I wanted. I was put to bed—I am sure, gently.

The Lone Scouts of America then was an organization, founded in Chicago, that existed on a very sound notion: across the country, east and west, north and south, were lonely boys seeking to express themselves. To meet this need the Lone Scouts created a series of "tribe" papers published by members and usually paid for by their parents. But the boys published and edited these little papers; they wrote all the copy, arranged all the illustrations, designed all the layouts. Not since the days of Horatio Alger, Jr., had any group of boys been more ruggedly individual.

I was a Lone Scout. I published, sporadically, a tribe paper called *The National Boy*. The stories I wrote were also published in many other tribe papers: in Georgia, in Indiana, in Wisconsin. I worked constantly at the old Remington. I mailed out "contributions" unceasingly. Sometime before the age of fifteen I sold short pieces to *The Country Gentleman* and *Wallace's Farm Weekly*. I also sold a number of made-over jokes to other magazines, averaging about two dollars apiece.

But checks were arriving. Mother cashed them.

"This boy," she said, "has talent."

ᵉᵍ

In 1926 Jim Smith, the city editor of the county newspaper, *The Bergen Evening Record,* was a round-faced, somewhat pot-bellied man with a disposition as gentle as a blanket rubbed against an infant's face. Sitting in his office, however, I was tense, frightened and overwhelmed by my impudence in being here to seek a job. But Mother had heard that the position of writing local high school notes remained open and, never one to throw away an opportunity, had arranged this interview. My ears still tingled from the scrubbing she had given them. I arrived at the Record Building so well groomed that I could have been presented at the Court of St. James. Over the head of this quaking supplicant, a voice asked:

"You wanted to see me, Jim?"

I looked around and there stood Matt Ely, the editor-in-chief of the paper; he was gray-haired and tired, and sloppily sagging at the midriff. Again he asked: "You wish to tell me something?"

"Yes, Matt," Jim Smith said. "Yes, I do. You forgot to button your fly."

"Oh, hell!" Matt Ely walked off, fumbling with his pants, and thus I was taught the first rule of journalism: a reporter is observant.

When Jim Smith said, "Now, Mr. Miers," I gave a jump, for although I was sixteen years of age and about to begin junior year in high school, no one ever had called me mister. "These articles you wrote and brought in," Jim continued, "are pretty well written. We'll give you a try—on space rates at ten cents a column inch—and good luck."

I walked home on a cloud, having secured a job. Tears stung my eyes. Despite my "shakes," a responsible city editor had decided I was worth a chance. He would pay company money for what I produced. Irreverently, I burst into song:

I am Jesus' little lamb,
Yes, by Jesus Christ, I am;
He will wash me clean as snow—
Dirty little job for Je-sus!

Mother also dissolved into joyous tears and together we swung around the back parlor in a kind of pagan victory dance as she cooed: "I knew you could, I knew you could!"

For two days—and one long evening until well after midnight—I toiled over my first story about the opening of school a fortnight hence. I roamed the empty high school building, counting new desks, checking on supplies, noting undusted corners, and the janitor was unaccountably annoyed when he found me inspecting the coal bins.

"Coal's black," he said testily. "That's how the Lord made it."

I wrote and rewrote my story until my arms ached from pounding the old Remington. Convinced at last that I could do no better, I carried my masterpiece to Jim Smith's office.

"Leave it," he said, never raising his eyes from the desk. "I'll read it when I can."

I could not bear to be dismissed this briefly. I hung back in a corner of the editorial room. Before me stretched rows of desks where men with hats on, and women who smoked cigarettes and left lipstick smudges on paper coffee cups, pounded typewriters with an out-of-this-world abstractedness. There was a gloomy air vent overhead. A fly crawled across a wall calendar.

I could see the corner room where Matt Ely toiled and wondered if his fly was buttoned. Next to Mr. Ely's office was a door that bore the legend: "Ross H. Wynkoop, Managing Editor." Suddenly that door was flung open. The wiry man who emerged possessed rumpled hair, piercing eyes, and the smile of a weary cynic.

"Who the hell are you?" he demanded.

I fumbled for words before I answered: "I'm waiting for Mr. Smith to read my story."

"Don't waste your time," I was advised. "Jim can't read. So scoot-ass out of here."

From the far end of the room, where the sports desk was located, I heard a hollow laugh. Embarrassment burned like a celluloid collar around my neck. I fled from the building and that night I could not sleep, thinking of how badly I had failed. So much work and nobody cared a damn!

But next day when the *Record* appeared, there was my story exactly as I had written it, and in bold type at the top of the column was "By Earl S. Miers." I sat in the porch hammock, unable to believe this miracle. Mother rushed off to buy extra copies for all her relatives. I showed my triumph to Matty, who, humming a little tune, said: "I tells Emory."

The phone rang and a voice inquired: "Miers? This is Holran on the sports desk. Come on down: I've got an assignment for you."

I ran all the way, about two miles.

That night I measured up the column inches my first story had occupied. In two days I had earned eighty cents!

ᥱᢌ

Oritani Field with its old wooden bleachers had grown drowsy under the late afternoon sunshine and so, too, had the two semipro teams playing that kind of baseball which now has been converted into an art form by the New York Mets. At the weather-beaten table reserved for the press, sat a boy and his father; the man marked symbols in a scorebook that bore the impressive legend: "Property of the *Bergen Evening Record*," while the boy followed the game in rapt silence, fixing in his mind every deathless detail in this comedy of errors.

I retain no recollection of youth happier than these weekend outings; when rain canceled a game I pouted through the afternoon. Apparently Holran was satisfied with the copy I produced, for a wide variety of other assignments followed in the next few months. I covered auto-racing in Ho-Ho-Kus and polo matches in Oradell, prize fights in Paterson and Union City, and that fiasco of competitive enterprise called wrestling in Newark. I covered canoe races on the Hackensack River and football and basketball games almost everywhere in North Jersey.

My signature above the stories I wrote gave me a community status that was highly satisfying, and since I could not rely on my note-taking I developed a prodigious memory. For a young man too physically handicapped to participate in organized sports, I enjoyed a vicarious experience beyond a psychiatrist's wildest dreams, but the greater profit was in making of human nature a textbook and a guide.

To the sports fan, Paul Cavanagh was almost a great heavyweight who had sparred with Jack Dempsey. To me in a dressing room, while a trainer taped up his cuts, he became a man who faced bitter reality. Paul knew that he lacked the flair of a champion and must stumble through life from one small arena to the next. "I made the wrong choice," he muttered, and the pain in his eyes was more than physical.

I watched a polo player whip his pony after missing a shot and, filled with disgust for what ambition can do to a man, I was seized with uncontrollable nausea.

I stood, numb, quiet, when a corpse was pulled from beneath a burning racing car, and as the other racers whizzed round and round the oval and the crowd cheered and the promoter clutched the fifty dollars and silver-plated loving cup that would go to the winner. I saw only the stunned wife holding a baby as she sobbed: "What do we do without him?"

That extraordinary cynic and managing editor, Ross Wynkoop, summoned me into the hogpen of papers and books he called his office. "We'll see what manner of reporter you are," he said, and a wicked glitter shone in his eyes. "Do me a feature story on the slaughterhouse in East Paterson."

"Why, in God's name?"

"So you'll know what it's like to see blood smeared on floors and walls and ceilings," Wynkoop said as the glitter deepened. "And guts spilled where you can step on them. And legs tossed in piles with gnats buzzing around. And hearts oozing red in a vat. And you forget that these are animal parts. Think of them as human—the kind of mess an ax-killer leaves or what you'll find when some nut tosses a homemade bomb into a crowded theater—and then come back and tell me if you're a reporter!"

It was not difficult locating the slaughterhouse in East Paterson; the stench led me there. Apparently Wynkoop had telephoned ahead that I was coming for no one seemed surprised to see me. My stomach churned at the frightful odor, and my illness grew as a bearded giant, carrying a wire basket filled with dripping intestines, called out cheerily: "Step back, young fella, I don't want to splash you!"

The managing editor's description of what the place would be like had been a masterful understatement. The floor was slimy to the touch of my feet; large green flies buzzed all around and I expected momentarily a flock of vultures to soar through the windows. Hides sweating with fat hung on racks. And a man called a chopper kept swinging his arm up and down, cutting up internal organs and sliding them down a long table, where they splashed into a bucket.

As I stood there, dizzy and faint, Wynkoop's voice pursued me: "Think of them as human." But I remained determined to inspect the entire establishment. I came out looking like a ghost and an hour later I still gulped in fresh air as though I never had tasted the stuff. I wrote my story and Wynkoop said unfeelingly:

"Now go down and look at the stiffs in the county morgue."

"At least they'll be whole."

But Wynkoop chuckled maliciously.

"Not the one they found in Little Ferry last night. Someone

94

bashed in his brains with a hammer. And bit off an ear—for dessert, no doubt."

◆§

Incredibly, I came to love this tyrant. His attitude was that if my handicap made any appreciable difference in the efficiency of my work, I should be sent packing. He saw life as tough and cruel and a devil's paradise and to him crybabies were the moochers and wife-quitters and swindlers and petty hoodlums whose deeds filled the columns of his front page. Years later I would meet his prototype among workers with the handicapped who could watch a crippled child fall and offer no helping hand as he struggled to rise; they would sit, puffing on cigarettes, seemingly indifferent to the child's titanic effort, but ultimately the youngster would stand and on all their faces would be smiles of understanding. There was no easy road to rehabilitation. All men were bedeviled—Wynkoop knew. His own beautiful daughter became a victim of poliomyelitis and would spend her adult life in a wheelchair.

By the hour I followed this man through the composing room, watching him make up the paper. "What's this?" he would ask. "Some slop Miers wrote? Dump it in the hell box!" But he never did. He was a master at his craft, a patient teacher. If I missed getting out of school in time to catch him working on the final edition, he invariably growled at our next encounter, "You decide you've learned it all?" I said honestly, "I'll never know as much as you"; and he muttered, "That's for damn sure, Buster."

Behind the scenes he manipulated assignments to my advantage, and so I was sent to write the stories when Bergen County suddenly acquired a world celebrity. Big Bill Tilden then was in his declining years, grinding out pulp paper fiction and managing a local theatrical company. On our first meeting, I think that he interviewed me rather than I him. He asked intelligent, sympathetic questions about my disability, and seemed awfully anxious that I should never be disturbed by careless remarks others might make. I felt awed by this man whom kings and queens had applauded; with Bobby Jones, Babe Ruth and Jack Dempsey he stood apart as an immortal American sports image. Yet even in Bergen County the rumors persisted that he possessed an Oscar Wilde taint. No one I knew ever had reason to repeat this gossip. Fame, I came to believe, was in itself an affliction.

Even then Tilden was a magnificent athlete. He was a tall man of overpowering coordination, a giant who walked on little cat feet and who, in an exhibition game, could still serve a ball like a pistol shot and cover the back court with the grace of a ballet dancer. He made tennis an aesthetic experience, a form of poetry in motion. He played with any youngster who wished to improve his game and once I was his doubles partner. We won easily, for who could lose playing with Tilden? I had just one shot, a high lob close to the net, and Tilden shouted: "Smack it!" I smacked it all right; at last report that ball is still in orbit around the sun.

"You have quick reflexes," Tilden said with a grin.

Tilden was not alone in discovering this fact. Father saw that I needed a car to cover the range of my assignments and located an old Lexington, a touring model, that was already a museum piece. But Father tinkered with the automobile till he had it running; the brakes he lined with extra care, for he was playing a hunch. No local inspector would give a driving license to any one with "my condition." We were sent to Newark for special tests.

I remember the June day well. It was scorching hot. I had met all the routine requirements, but there was still a doubt. Three inspectors climbed into the back seat; Father and I rode in front.

"We must be sure about his legs," they said. "Have him get the car up to thirty miles an hour and when we cry 'Stop!' have him do so as quickly as he can." We were on a deserted cobbled street close to the Pennsylvania Railroad tracks. I gassed the car up to the desired speed and heard the command:

"Stop!"

My foot slammed down with the force of a piledriver. I looked back. There were no inspectors on the seat. From the tangle of bodies on the floor rose a single voice:

"Give this damn kid a license before he breaks all our necks!"

My success with the Tilden stories, added to the fact that I now had a car to drive, won me another assignment when a second world celebrity came to Bergen County. The home of Ambassador Dwight Morrow in Englewood was within our territory, and when that idol of the first nonstop plane flight between New York and Paris, Charles A. Lindbergh, began courting Anne Morrow, the Associated Press requested that a special man cover the story.

"Go make yourself some real dough," Wynkoop said.

The Morrows lived at the end of a road whence a private drive led through trees to a virtually unseen estate. Here from almost sunup to sunset, twenty or thirty reporters gathered around a closed gate, waiting patiently for Lindbergh to arrive or Anne Morrow to leave. Neither ever appeared. Meanwhile, America waited anxiously for hourly bulletins on this romance of the century. What the nation read was pure fiction. True, one reporter did sneak up to the Morrow home. He pried open a cellar window and fell into a coal bin; he came back, rubbing a sore tail. So we sat around through the boresome hours, waiting, playing blackjack, drinking coffee, eating sandwiches brought in relays from an Englewood drugstore.

One afternoon, for want of something better to do, I went to see the Morrow's clergyman. He was a sweet old man, sorry for all the fuss, sorrier still that no one had been to see him, and so he was in a rather talkative mood. He hinted that the wedding might well occur toward the end of May and I telephoned this story to the Associated Press.

I returned to the *Record* office to find Wynkoop in a rage. The AP teletype of a possible late May wedding had preceded me. He banged the story down on Matt Ely's desk. "That whelp of a cub has beaten us to our own story!" He saw me then and yanked me into his office. "Why? Goddamit, tell me why?"

"I was paid to represent the AP," I said stoutly.

He fixed upon me a withering, vindictive scowl. "If you want to continue working for this newspaper," he advised, "stop being so x-y-z honorable!"

≈§

Clearly, my education was such as only one in many thousands of boys ever receives. Conventional courses in high school were pleasant with a single exception. In junior English—taught by a thin, crotchety woman with mouselike hair, who never married—we discussed one day a story about a wife who left her husband because he drooled while eating.

"I can understand why," the old maid said. "Any woman would have found him disgusting."

I daresay. Sometimes while eating, I drooled.

All at once—and perhaps permanently—I was scarred. Within me had been planted a sense of fright toward approaching the girls I so desperately wanted as friends. My confidence in myself as a whole physical image had been destroyed—in one hour, in one class, by one frustrated spinster.

I walked the streets at night—lonely, so very lonely. In my mind was a caged tiger called sex-awareness trying to break loose, and I could not help it as I strolled in the darkness past the homes of girls I wished to know. Self-pity consumed me, for who can confess this ache to a mother, a father? I wanted a girl —dear God, *how* I wanted a girl—but I was simply too afraid to seek one. In this respect alone, by a single silly old woman, my handicap was thrown out of focus.

Then, unexpectedly, I had a date! The girl next door, who had an Irish prettiness and a bit of a tubby figure, agreed to go with me to an out-of-town football game. I was elated. Mother heard of the plan with a frown, but my days were spent in happy dreams of how I would feel at that game, sporting a girl on my arm just like other fellows in my class. The blow came just before lunch on Saturday.

"You can't have the car," Mother said.

"But, Mom, good God, you know—"

"You're not wasting your money on that girl!"

I shouted; I cussed; I cried. Mother turned away, inflexible. I refused to eat, to talk to anyone.

"You'll get over it," Mother said stubbornly.

But I didn't. What in the name of hell's bells did she think would happen? Mother had her own notions about boys and the "dangerous age" and why they must be protected.

Boys palling around with boys and girls with girls gave Mother a sense of serenity with God. She did not know the half of it. The high school correspondents who worked for the *Record* became a kind of fraternity. We were always together. Late at night, sitting in the editorial room, we told extravagant lies about our virility.

I drove the old Lexington and we often set off for Paterson to see a burlesque show. The theater that housed this entertainment was not too far from the sometimes musky odors of the Passaic River, only a degree removed from the stench of the slaughterhouse in East Paterson.

The stage performance was quite subdued. Slapstick comedians dominated the show. Chorines sang shrilly, danced suggestively, but never removed their clothes. During intermission, brassy-voiced barkers roamed the aisles, offering boxes of candy "with pictures inside of girls in poses, the way you like to see them"; but no one ever secured such a photograph.

Just once, during these Paterson days, did a stripteaser pull down her bra. There, all at once, hung her breasts, fully exposed. We all jumped as though jabbed by an electric cattle prod.

&

In blue coat and white pants, I was graduated from Hackensack High School in June of 1928. Through my work on the *Record,* I had saved a considerable amount of money for an eighteen-year-old boy; and if I worked another year, while taking a postgraduate course in high school, I might well come close to paying the basic costs of four years of college. Mother never had forgotten the advice of the old German doctor in the Brooklyn clinic: if education alone would help me, then I was to go to college even if cashing in Father's insurance policy could provide the only way. But luck had played into Mother's hands, thanks to Jim Smith and Ross Wynkoop; and now politics also helped.

The Presidential campaign of 1928 was remarkable in many respects. There existed in North Jersey a vigorous Roman Catholic segment, grimly resolved that Al Smith's religion must not handicap him in the canvass against Herbert Hoover. Long before my graduation from high school, journalistic scuttlebut had informed me that a weekly newspaper, *The Bergen Democrat,* was to be launched in behalf of Smith's candidacy. I sought a place on its staff and was hired.

The editorial offices were situated in the front of an otherwise unoccupied third floor of a building on Main Street. Behind, over an airshaft, were the private quarters of the editor and publisher, a bug-eyed old lecher with salt-and-pepper hair who spent the day reading books that must be delivered by Railway Express (since they were barred from the U.S. mails) and hiring secretaries he hoped to seduce. His partner appeared toward noon, grinning vacuously and telling everyone his secret ambition was to write a gossip column under the pseudonym of "C. Wanda Knockonit." He laughed more hollowly than anyone I ever have known. Other oddballs, male and female, secured employment. Merit had really very little to do with serving on the staff of this publication which did not depend on the number of copies it sold but on the amount of advertising it secured through political pressure.

I wrote practically all the copy that went into the *Democrat,* including columns of biographical material about Al Smith, which I am sure no one ever read. The editor, his partner, and the advertising manager knew that Smith could not win; miracles were for religion, not politics. I remember one issue when all the advertising rates were tripled, for we were printing 25,000 copies to be delivered to the big Smith rally in Sea Girt. The incredible fact is that we did print that many copies. I rode on the truck that delivered them to Sea Girt.

We arrived on a field so cluttered with tents and politicians that we could not even find the Bergen County delegation. We wandered up one row of headquarters tents and down the next. No one listened or cared that we had a newspaper in hot support of Al Smith, but by luck we bumped into our advertising manager who, at the moment, was propositioning a female delegate from Essex County. What now?

"Dump 'em," he said. "We've got the dough."

So we dumped them, all 25,000 copies, on that field of political honor.

＊

By the time Hoover had won the election I had shifted jobs, becoming sports editor of a new semiweekly tabloid, in that last year before the Great Depression when everyone was making money and new enterprises were easy to finance. I was admitted to Rutgers University and had the money to pay the bills before the summer ended. I went down to see my old friend and tutor on the *Record.*

THE TROUBLE BUSH

"Scoop," I said, addressing Wynkoop with rare familiarity, "can I have a job when I graduate?"

"No."

The answer was an unexpected blow. "Why not?" I asked. I had counted on Wynkoop.

He pushed back his papers, his books. The eyes that looked at me were suddenly gentle.

"You'll do better," he said.

CHAPTER SEVEN

The Breakaway

*I*n *New Jersey,*
toward September, highs and lows play hopscotch on the
weather map and a Bermuda High creeps up the watershed of
the Alleghenies and pants its muggy breath upon the state from
seacoast to mountainside. Invariably, on the hottest day of young
September, New Jersey's colleges and universities begin new
academic years. With the backs of automobiles piled full of the
trash teenagers believe essential to sustaining them for any pro-

longed absence from home, puffing parents and their progeny set off like nomads for the halls of ivy.

On a scorching day in 1929, Mother and I started for New Brunswick where, with luck, I hoped to survive as a student at Rutgers University. We departed with a skid of tires, neither of us quite sure that we were ready for this final severing of the umbilical cord. I was now past nineteen, or two years older than Mother had been on her wedding day, yet I still remained her troubled baby. A force beyond ourselves drove us onward. This hour of destiny had been decided long years before in a Brooklyn clinic.

About ten miles from home, in the town of Rutherford, our adventure almost fell apart.

"Mom," I said, stricken with a wave of despair, "we forgot the straws."

Mother stopped the car with a jerk that nearly snapped our necks. As other automobiles flashed by, we littered the roadside with mountains of junk. The bookcase Father had made looked ridiculous leaning against the fence of a garbage dump. Beside this scarlet-bright skeleton rested the new portable typewriter Edith and Sam had given me. Piles of clothes with their hangers were spread upon the fence. Lamps and lampshades tipped drunkenly beside a ditch. An old morris chair and footstool finally slid down the bank into the stagnant breeding pool of mosquitoes. Sort frantically though we did, we found no straws. We had left them, piled box upon box, on the kitchen table in Hackensack.

Those straws were props beneath my sense of dignity, my independence. Did we turn back? My mother, once she had set her heart on an objective, never turned back. Somewhere in Rutherford we would find straws. For an hour we visited all manner of local emporiums without success. Apparently no one in Rutherford would be caught owning such contraptions.

Mother swept from store to store and I can see her yet: a

woman going through menopause and suffering with hot flashes which, God knows, the sun of that steaming September day did not help. She strode along the streets of Rutherford in a dress with artificial red flowers pinned on her bosom and, like swinging danger signals, they warned other pedestrians to step aside. Her son was going to college. With drinking straws.

Her victory came unexpectedly in a run-down candy store with a soda fountain where the cracked marble top had been clumsily patched. But there all at once stood the prize—"sippers," wrapped two together, and stuck in a glass container brownish with fly specks. A rancid smell filled the place, matching the trays of melted chocolates in the showcase and the rows of glasses that were dusty from disuse. Presently a little unwashed woman in a faded kimona sidled through the curtain that divided the store from her private pigsty.

"I'd like to buy these straws," Mother said.

"They ain't for sale."

"I need them badly."

"So do I."

"Well, at least you'll sell my son a pack of cigarettes."

"Down here," the slattern said, shuffling toward the front of the store in her bedroom slippers. Mother hesitated just long enough to transfer the straws from the holder to her pocketbook. We left hurriedly and were driving off as the old hoyden appeared in the doorway, screaming:

"Bring back my straws, you lousy thief!"

Mother chuckled. She was a most determined woman.

Soon Mother lapsed into brooding silence, for other problems possessed her. Resolutely she drove on toward New Brunswick, cussing the drivers who got in the way while the hot flashes washed in waves across her face.

"Your father has always shaved you," she said. "What will you do?"

"There are barbers in New Brunswick."

"Who will cut your meat for you?"

"I'll find someone."

I had to believe that people were decent and would give me the help I needed if I were utterly honest and told them why I required assistance, for even at this tender age I had acquired the essential wisdom of how to live graciously with an affliction: I must put those around me at ease so that they could offer help without embarrassment.

For Mother, each town that spun by seemed to stir up another concern. At Rahway my mother insisted: "You change your underwear every day"; and I answered: "My God, I've been doing that every day since I outgrew diapers." At Colonia my mother warned: "Have the barber cut your hair short since it's easier to comb that way"; and with growing annoyance, I answered: "I don't care if he shaves my head like a cue ball." At Metuchen my mother said: "If your father could have gone to college he would have made more money and everything would have been simpler for you"; and I answered: "Pa did the best he could."

Tears touched the edges of Mother's eyes as though, silently, she confessed: "Yes, yes—Will is a brave man, a hard worker, a doer and not a whiner." And even had he been a millionaire that fact could not have altered the nature of my brain damage. All my problems would have been the same—the few *special* problems created by a visible disability and all the *general* problems that went with growing up. Only the physical environment of my body could be called abnormal. The man within, who had yet to emerge, would have existed under any circumstances.

We were a pair of innocents, mother and son, when presently we crossed the Raritan River. There, all at once, was the college, standing on a hill. "We've made it," Mother said. There was awe in her voice. Together, we had traveled a long distance from a fifty-cent clinic in Brooklyn.

≈§

Freshman Week preceded the opening of regular classes. We were taught how to use the University Library, and how to follow our noses from one building to the next, and then we were herded together in a huge auditorium for an English placement examination.

Another, more personal kind of terrorism hung over the campus for these days also constituted "Pledge Week" when the fraternities selected new members. A few freshmen—the promising athletes—were pledged almost upon arrival, and there were a dozen or so who were accepted as "legacies" by fraternities to which their fathers or near relatives had belonged. The others merely waited in hope and anguish. Rutgers, then, was not the institution described in the college catalog but two universities divided between the "ins" and the "outs"; fraternity house parties not only dominated the social life of the campus, but fraternity politics also decided who should be elected class officers, who should join the honorary societies, who should edit the school's publications. At night, lying on their beds, hands under their heads, freshmen waited for the tap on the door that meant they had been chosen. Eventually, fretfully, they slumbered. If the knock never came, they believed that, somehow, they had been judged inferior.

No one ever knocked at my door. In that age, no fraternity would have considered pledging an athetoid, unless by a stroke of ill-fortune he chanced to be an important legacy, any more than a fraternity would have selected a Negro. I keenly felt this rejection that said so clearly a lad with "the shakes" would be an embarrassment, most of all during house parties. At night I turned my head against the pillow and thought, dry-eyed,

"Damn them!" Friends of the morning would return at noon wearing pledge pins. They were no longer the same friends.

Rebellion—that streak of impudence without which, no handicapped person can rise above the ignorance and superstition surrounding him—stirred deeply. A variety of four-letter words expressed neatly what I thought of the entire fraternity system. Nor would I accept the belief that fraternities had to run the whole campus. There were on the campus more neutrals than fraternity men, who needed only organization to become the dominant political force in the college. Sam's years of raving about the coming Socialist revolution had not been wasted. I intended, by God, to break the system.

The first weekend my parents visited the campus they found a sign on the dormitory bulletin board: "NEUTRALS SUPPORT MIERS FOR CLASS PRESIDENT." Mother was so pleased she had another hot flash, although I assured her that I had absolutely no chance of winning. But four years of college lay ahead; we neutrals were forming a nucleus of an organization that would grow with time. From those members of the administration who, as old fraternity boys, now revered the system as though it were as sacred and as indispensable to a stable society as membership in a church and a good country club (to say nothing of a discreet association with a reliable bootlegger), my defiance elicited two responses: it was one of those silly attempts at secession that would wither with the sunlight; or it was the unholy experiment of dangerous radicals who should be flunked out of college at the first opportunity.

Meanwhile, during Freshman Week, we were assembled in the Chapel to learn the college songs and cheers. We laughed uproariously at the hoary quip: "Any of you fellows who feel real horny are welcome to try out for the college band." We heard impassioned lectures about the history and traditions of Old Rutgers, which was chartered in 1766 by George III as Queen's College. Portraits of former Rutgers graduates cluttered the walls of the Chapel. They were a dingy crowd, more or less, solemn and humorless, and most of them were Dutchmen who had wanted a school of their own to escape the heresies that the Episcopalians were teaching at Columbia and the Presbyterians at Princeton.

The great historian of the college then was a one-time president, William Henry Steele Demarest, Class of 1883, who, since he could not control his false teeth, was known to the students as "Whistling Willie"; yet there was a breathless majesty when he described how S-S-Simeon DeWitt, Class-*s-s* of 1776, had been the geographer who had charted the route by which Wash-*sh-sh*-ington had cornered Cornwallis-*s-s* at Yorktown. Dr. Demarest's hand swept from portrait to portrait as the stories spilled out in an endless flow and the wooden pews blistered our wriggling behinds. Still, the warmth and dignity of this old man made us love the college for his sake; we stopped calling him "Whistling Willie" and told ourselves it was a most unusual man who could pronounce benediction and whistle taps at the same time.

The week ended with the hazing of the freshmen by a group of idiots called sophomores. We were required to crawl along College Avenue with one knee on the curb and the other on the pavement while a fire hose, spraying the road, added to our misery. The inane theory behind this common torment was that we were being welded together as a class. The fags among the sophomores cheered on the masochists who held the fire hose for, as we quickly divined, only perverts had been admitted to the Class of 1932. I had crawled about half the length of a block when a hand touched my shoulder and a gentle voice commanded:

"Get up, son—this isn't for you."

I flushed with resentment. Damn it, here I was once more being set apart—the unwanted fraternity pledge who could not even be soaked to the skin with dignity.

Smiling down at me was a short man with graying hair. His name was Earl Reed Silvers and he wore a hearing aid which, I later learned, he switched off so that he could sleep through faculty meetings. Dozens of books for boys had streamed from his old Oliver typewriter. They were stories about boys who played fairly, shed shameless tears when the old school lost a football game, acted like sexless nitwits in the presence of girls, joined the right fraternities, and thereby became a credit to God and country. I had read many of his books, and captured by the dream of going to school like one of his heroes had saved $1,800 from my newspaper work to realize this ambition, but the little man who now clutched my arm and pulled me back from the shouting and knee-bruising and hose-spraying along College Avenue so heightened my tension that I trembled all over.

"You let me go," I blubbered. Hot tears of anger rolled down my cheeks.

"No," he said stubbornly. "You come with me."

Stormily I obeyed, walking into one of the finest friendships of my lifetime.

◄§

October 24, 1929, was that history-shattering "Black Thursday" on Wall Street when more than 16,400,000 shares of stock were traded at an average loss of forty points. That the college, the country, and the world stood on the threshold of the Great Depression would not be recognized for months. Yet before the members of the Class of 1933 received their sheepskins, journalism majors like myself would write practice stories about a clownish little Austrian named Adolf Hitler, Franklin D. Roosevelt would launch his first hundred days of social revolution, and the patterns of our lives would change forever.

This change ate gradually into everyone's experience. Boys who had gone to college filled with the joy of the breakaway from home ties became, as the years passed, secretly guilt-stricken over what their escape suddenly entailed. Many dropped out, including a number of fraternity legacies, simply because all at once their families were struggling to keep a roof over their heads and food in their bellies. Those who remained became far less prone to sneak down to the speakeasy on Easton Avenue and douse their insides with that nauseous prohibition concoction called needle beer while gazing at photographs of females in various poses of pornographic disarray. Although even whoring came down in price in New Brunswick, fewer classmates suffered the affliction immortalized in the limerick about that poor devil from Dundee.

When I think of myself in those late autumn months of 1929 wearing a derby hat and gray spats, I shudder at the silly ass I must have seemed. Happily the derby hat was stepped on in the excitement of the ride to an out-of-town football game in Easton, Pennsylvania, where we had heard there were whole blocks lined with cat houses, and the spats were sensibly tossed into the closet and forgotten. I owned a tuxedo, which I wore half a dozen times a year, whereas my father, whose employment now became touch-and-go, did not own a new suit during the remaining ten years of his life.

Sam lost his job and a good part of his investments. Like so many in those months of deepening depression he became impoverished almost overnight. For a time Sam tried raising flowers commercially but he possessed no flair for this kind of enterprise. The only real money he earned thereafter was with a pickup band he organized, playing weekends at weddings and dances.

Down on the farm Uncle John took to the jug and let the place go to hell, and Adam Satler, finding a job in the Freehold rug mill, supported Aunt Laura until that sad day in 1940 when angels fluttered over his bed and his burial suit was removed from the Trunk from Germany.

In this upside-down world Father, Mother, Sam, and Edith would not think of my leaving college.

"Times will get better," Sam said; he had not devoted a lifetime to loving Micawber for nothing. And when in my junior year my own financial resources became shaky, he loaned me his last $300 to help out. "Every investment I ever made," he said, "turned out lousy. Maybe you'll be the exception."

❦

Under the pressure of the sacrifices our families were making to keep us in college, I suppose that we should have all excelled as students. We did not. The opinion was prevalent, perhaps unjustly, that the college needed money and as long as we could pay term bills we would have to approach complete idiocy to be flunked out. Nor was getting through college in that time any great mental achievement. Some thirty years later college, as I knew it, becomes a series of vignettes set in the shabby classrooms of old and moldering buildings.

In one two-hour session each week Houston Peterson taught logic and philosophy. This was all the time he could spare for Rutgers since he also taught at Cooper Union and gave the distinct impression that between times he ascended unto heaven and aided God in running the universe. Pete wrote books about Darwin and Huxley and Conrad Aiken, claiming that he corrected the proofs while attending the Six-Day Bicycle Races, for such excitement quickened his mental processes. He was Billy Sunday on a lecture platform—with a dash of W. C. Fields—as he strutted around the room, flicking cigar ashes on floor and clothing and not infrequently, when the session ended, he could have passed for a chimney sweep. He never forgot any book he ever had read and, each week, he was an intellectual Niagara Falls over which we plunged in a barrel. We adored him—the old pro, the best ham on the faculty.

William B. Twiss was nicknamed "Cap," in tribute to his army service, and taught American Literature and Advanced Composition as though waging a war of attrition with words and once, during an especially long pause between sentences, someone said aloud: "My God, he's dead." But Cap was too mild-mannered to take offense. He recognized that other classes were napping in the same building and he was too much of a gentleman to disturb these siestas with an outburst of umbrage. Surprisingly what he taught *stuck*, and in later years his gentleness endured in mind and heart as a warm image.

Occasionally, when a professor was ill, a graduate student from Princeton was drafted for temporary duty. My most vivid recollection is of a faultlessly attired young man who clearly looked down at our campus set in its factory-town surroundings. The class was psychology and we were experimenting with ink blots, which were supposed to create pictures in our minds. When my turn came, the instructor flashed a card before my eyes and demanded, in a sort of how-in-hell-did-you-ever-get-in-college tone:

"What do you see?"

"An ink blot on a white square," I said.

His lips stiffened. "Try this."

Another person's anger, superimposing tension upon tension, brings out the worst in an athetoid. I snapped:

"Another ink blot."

"And this."

"Ditto."

Like Mother, he seemed to be having hot flashes. The words fairly rasped from his throat: "One more, please."

My own face had grown warmish. "There, sir," I said, "are two girls chasing a frightened senior across the campus and his pants are falling down. On the steps of Kirkpatrick Chapel a drunken night watchman is laying the housemother of one of the dorms. The dean, hiding in the bushes, is splitting his sides with laughter."

And so were the members of the class. The instructor slammed down the card on his desk. I suppose, had the college not needed the tuition so badly, I might have been tossed out on my fanny.

No nickname ever marred the dignity of Allen Sinclair Will, the Father of the School of Journalism, who was, in addition, a bona fide member of the editorial staff of *The New York Times*. White-haired and standoffish, as prim as though he arrived each Tuesday and Thursday wrapped in waxed paper, he claimed a Southern background that left him plainly unhappy over the one Negro boy in the class. From the heights of his professional achievement, Dr. Will taught us like a bird pecking at a room full of silly worms. The trouble, as I saw it, was the fact that teaching journalism amounted to spreading over two years what any intelligent person with a modicum of literary ability should be able to learn in two weeks. Insofar as Dr. Will became Public Enemy Number One to me, and nearly ruined my life, I confess to a deep-rooted prejudice toward him.

There were dozens of other professors—some stimulating, some dull, some gifted, some academic hucksters—and what we sang about them in that lusty ballad, "The Faculty of Rutgers," reduced novels like *Fanny Hill* to appropriate reading in vacation Bible schools. By and large these professors—most of whom we secretly admired—were no wackier than the students they taught. A remarkable amount of knowledge was crammed into our bony heads; more, very likely, than we deserved. But then, the age helped us for in those years history ended with the League of Nations, nuclear physics was an unexplored field, and computers did not measure man's ability to comprehend man's inhumanity to man. Gaining a college degree then may not have been as difficult as earning a creditable high school diploma today and if you majored in journalism, it may have been easier.

عگ

Vignettes of classmates—some dead, some living—flash across my mind. There was one boy who, as the depression deepened, kept in his dormitory an enormous packing box of canned food which he shared with nobody. How he ever consumed so many tins of sardines without meowing like a cat remains an unfathomable mystery.

Across the hall lived a lad who owned all the hundreds of little five-cent blue books published by Haldemann-Julius in Girard, Kansas; he read them avidly, day and night, never attending classes. Tight money or not, he flunked out at the end of the freshman year.

And there was Bob, who ran away during Christmas vacation rather than return to a home where both parents were blind; ultimately, he was discovered living in a bordello in New Orleans and shortly after he returned to college was found dead under circumstances that were described, officially, as a heart attack. He was a sweet-tempered boy, filled with a love for poetry and philosophy. No one could see his handicap: this locked-up, rending grief for his parents in their shut-up world.

One of my roommates was a thin, wiry fellow completely dominated by a brilliant father who never once came to see him. On weekends, when the campus was overrun by visiting parents, he would disappear until nightfall on long hikes into the country and then throw himself into bed, exhausted, sleeping with his head turned toward the wall. Some nights he awoke, sobbing.

Our housemother in Hegeman, where I lived the first two years, was Eva Lacey Peck, who walked with a limp as the result of a once-broken leg, but who hid her deeper afflictions—an unsuccessful marriage and a dead child—so that all the boys in

Hegeman were her sons who could do no wrong. A hellion was simply a youth displaying healthy animal spirit. In Earl Reed Silvers there was the same secret loneliness—a son who had died in infancy; year in, year out, he gathered about him his own special clique of undergraduates, seeking that son.

Rutgers was much smaller then. Its entire enrollment was less than the present entering class. As student to student, as student to faculty, we dwelt in an atmosphere of intimacy that long since has disappeared.

My freshman year roommate took pleasure in covertly watching me, stop watch in hand, and counting my tremors while awake and asleep. Resting, he said, I was "normal," which was somehow comforting and by the end of the first semester I suspect that he knew more about the essential nature of cerebral palsy than did the college physician.

There were two football players who always left class early and raced across campus to the building where Lozier Englander, his legs withered from poliomyelitis, had to be carried up and down stairs. I can hear little Lozier still—a happy, undaunted rebel, a worthy member of the impudent breed of the unconquered visibly handicapped—sassing his benefactors: "Careful—take it easy, you bastards—that's my backside you're bumping on those steps!"

College was not a place where we went to learn how to live; here we lived. Nor were the lessons of the classroom often as remote as we believed; through the Lozier Englanders, or a blind boy named Carl with his seeing-eye dog, we grew to understand what Houston Peterson meant by the epic vision: man could become a hero of the spirit.

No small part of the "higher" education we absorbed came in that greatest of all collegiate institutions—the bull session. It was a rare day when we were in bed before one or two o'clock in the morning. A dozen of us, crowded in someone's room, talked and talked: about books, music, girls, masturbation, bootleg whiskey, sports, parents, the future, what was wrong with the college, profs, and sex, sex, sex. Each of us memorized at least a hundred bawdy limericks that we recited, over and over, until we knew to a man what had happened to the corsetstrings of the Young Girl from Thrace, and the foul-mouthed essays composed by the Thirty-ninth Duke of Buckingham, and the frightful betrayal of the Old Lady from Pitlocery, and the remarkable agility of the Young Man from Kent, and the equally remarkable conversion of the Gay Young Sultan of Algiers. The dormitory rocked with laughter. Then we wandered off to bed, vicariously purged, the dark tiger in our minds caged. Sleepy-eyed, with the morning's light, we crawled off to classes and invariably were greeted by the same quip from the frowsy-headed waitress who attended the steam tables in the college cafeteria: "What you fellows need for breakfast is a roll in bed with honey." There was a rumor that the cafeteria food was seasoned with saltpeter to cut down our sexual desires; if true, the college should have saved itself the trouble.

The hero of the campus was Paul Robeson, who had graduated from Rutgers in the Class of 1919 as a member of Phi Beta Kappa and an All-American end. His performances in *Emperor Jones* and *Showboat* had made him a national celebrity; and in my generation Rutgers men said proudly: "I go to Paul Robeson's school." Whenever he sang a concert in the gym, unless one bought a ticket well in advance, only standing room in the upper balcony remained when the big night came.

No man, alone in a spotlight on a stage, ever looked taller or more majestic than Paul Robeson. People stood up and cheered, and never have I seen any man, let alone a Negro, so idolized. Then he began to sing, this majestic, natural baritone, and town and gown sat enthralled. His powerful voice reached out to the upper rafters, warm and all-embracing; I could feel my own throat tightening with emotion.

The applause grew deafening; he bowed graciously. He was

gone suddenly, and we talked about his greatness; but not a one of us understood his loneliness, his heartbreak, his growing rebellion. No one could guess then that a day would come when angry alumni would demand that his name be stricken from the rolls of the college.

&

Almost unconsciously, we grew up in college. The hell-raising tapered off. As we matured, in our own slow, giddy, stumbling way, we learned that the essence of wisdom was compassion, a willingness to yield to others a margin for error. Perhaps we learned to laugh at ourselves. I hope so, for acquiring this gift is in itself worth a baccalaureate degree.

No man taught me this truth quite so quickly, or quite so well, as Earl Reed Silvers. Friends who loved him called him Reed, and those who feared his power called him Sil—he knew, I knew, everyone knew that those who said Sil were deeply jealous of the gifts that he possessed. For he inspired love, loyalty, obedience by the simplest of formulas: he gave love, loyalty, and obedience in return.

To those who were "his boys"—all those undergraduates who, in composite, became that son in a lonely grave—his door was always open. They could talk to him about anything: troubles at home, troubles in college, troubles within themselves. Although his title was Director of Alumni and Public Relations, he was really a father-teacher, now a rare character on the American campus.

He could not be sure at what hour of what day a boy was going to awaken intellectually, for boys were not alike, but he had the patience to wait. He gave nicknames to all of his boys and mine was Flash, because of a compulsive temper that took off like a Roman candle and fizzled out almost as quickly. Never once, when high tension overwhelmed me, did he command me to relax, for he understood—as so very few people do—that if I could relax I would not be handicapped.

Our relationship, though beginning awkwardly when Reed jerked me away from the hose-sprayers during Freshman Week, soon settled into a spirit of unusual camaraderie. His office was on the ground floor of Old Queen's, probably the finest example of Georgian architecture in America. This building, in use since 1811, possessed a gentleness, a mellowness that fitted Reed's personality. He was a wonderful listener. Within a term he knew more about me than my parents. He had a laugh—rather, a high-pitched giggle—that was infectious. He giggled at my derby and spats, at my sassiness toward the instructor over the ink blots, at my revolt against fraternities. As the depression deepened and the neutrals grew in power and prestige so that we were a political force to be reckoned with, he giggled most at those colleagues in the administration who, as fraternity boys, had grown older rather than up.

"Hop Brill thinks you'll blow up the D.U. house one night," Reed chuckled. I was not pleased by this comment for Hop, as the university's purchasing agent, had a strong voice in choosing the editor of the campus newspaper, a position no nonfraternity man had held within living memory. "To hell with Hop," Reed said breezily; at heart he was an inveterate manipulator. Again, when I wrote somewhat risqué stories for the college magazine about Mattie and Emory and other Negroes I had known during my newspaper-selling days in Hackensack, Reed laughed at the Dean of Men's concern for my loose morals. "To hell with him, too," Reed said. "You've got talent and style."

In that shaky junior year, when Sam loaned me his last $300, I moved from Hegeman to the attic of a rooming house on Bartlett Street, cramped quarters that I shared with Archie Milligan, a good-humored Irish classmate. To eke out our rent Archie and I made baskets of sandwiches that we sold in the dormitories late at night.

Reed came through handsomely, securing for me the job as campus correspondent for the *Newark Evening News,* the best paying job of its kind. He taught me how to write short stories for the Sunday School weeklies and once or twice a month I would receive a check for twenty-five dollars. The sandwich route was forsaken and I planned in my senior year to move to a two-room suite in Ford Hall, then the Rutgers equivalent of a Gold Coast.

I was determined to become the editor-in-chief of *Targum,* the campus newspaper, without question the most influential undergraduate office in the college. The position not only paid a share of the profits earned by the paper (approximately $400 a year), but also automatically placed the recipient on Student Council and into Cap and Skull, the senior honorary society. My heart was set on becoming editor-in-chief, and Reed encouraged this ambition, but he knew that I was bucking tough opposition: the fraternities, Hop, tradition.

The *Targum* occupied a ramshackle frame building on College Avenue; to me it was a castle. In lieu of any cash remuneration, the managing editor lived in a room on the second floor and apparently never washed for the bathtub was littered with old newspapers and gin bottles (gin sold for two dollars a fifth if you knew on which door to knock on Holy Hill, where the theologians lived). Never had I labored harder than in this old building. Our standards, self-imposed, were far above the quality of anything we were taught in the School of Journalism; and the editor was a czar, a tyrant, who treated freshmen and sophomores like Mexican peons—his was a majestic office, dazzling and lovely for his ego.

Without Reed, I never would have broken the tradition and become editor-in-chief; that pent-up tension that made me a rebel and hell-cat was too often apparent and once sent half the residents of the men's campus marching two miles across town to the College for Women (N.J.C.) on a night's spree that rocked the town. No one had told us that there was an unwritten agreement between the college authorities and local police restricting undergraduate high jinks to our own side of the city. I doubt if that knowledge would have stopped us, anyhow. A pep rally had fired our spirits. No one wanted to go back to his studies.

"Let's wake up the gals across town," I suggested.

Soup Campbell, an apple-cheeked junior, gave a practical reason for this deviltry. We both covered Rutgers news for various papers. The story of the march would line our pockets with more money than we had seen in a long time. "Hell," Soup said, "this is front page copy."

Little Abe Etkin, a classmate rushing by, was stopped short by Soup clutching the seat of his pants. "Go through the fraternities, spreading the word," Soup prodded Abe, who was off in a dash.

College Avenue was soon thronged with students tumbling from their rooms. Some came in coats tossed over their pajamas. They brought horns, clackers, cow bells. The crowd kept growing, its mood almost riotous.

"Jesus," little Abe puffed, "what a story."

Soup, Abe, and I took the lead. In unison we shouted: "Forward, men!"

"Move! Get going! We'll sleep tonight in N.J.C.!" came the raucous retort of our fellow hellions.

What a wonderful night we had, tearing the town apart! Police cars screeched in all directions. Ash cans rolled noisily across sidewalks. Down George Street, New Brunswick's main thoroughfare, we swept like an eruption of lava. We shouted, sang, hip-hip-hurrahed for the old school. At N.J.C. the girls hung out the windows, waving panties and bras at us. Since Soup, Abe, and I were all Reed's "boys," we confessed the truth to him next morning. He giggled, then retired to his office to figure out how he would get us off the hook, should the worst happen. When at last Abe did "leak" the whole story, I was already editor of *Targum*—Hop could not hold this against me.

But poor old Hop had other causes for chewing up cigars and shaking his head. "What this country needs is not so much a good five-cent cigar, as Tom Marshall believed, but more professors who will wave the red banner of intellectual anarchism and toss the bombs of academic revolt," I said in one editorial. To Hop, an upstate New York farm boy who had followed his Republican nose straight into a marriage with one of the most prominent socialites in town, this was heresy. Sam might cheer but Hop only shuddered when *Targum* proclaimed: "Socialism has captured the imagination of the . . . collegiate world." Even that most sacred of institutions, Phi Beta Kappa, was not immune from ridicule.

When letters poured in by the dozens, in protest, in support, Hop shook his head, then broke into a laugh:

"It's a lively paper—that's for damn sure!"

CHAPTER EIGHT

Starling

In the Year
of the Wobbly Stepladder, when I was twenty-two and a senior in college, Father fell into the Christmas tree. The crash resounded throughout the house. Light bulbs shattered and breaking ornaments tinkled in thousands of fragments across the floor. Father lay among the broken branches, holding a bottle of wine above his chest. He had not spilled a drop.

Mother accepted this catastrophe in surprisingly good spirit.

There was still time, she said, to rush out and buy another tree and new lights and ornaments.

Sam swore bitterly. "In a year when we can't afford one tree we have to get two!"

Mother sniffed. What did Sam know about Nana, who would rise from her grave if we failed to have a Christmas tree! Father, a spectacle of sheepishness, crawled from the wreckage.

But Sam was gentle toward Father. "That worn out ladder should have been thrown out years ago," he said consolingly. "But those infernal women—" meaning Mother and Edith— "would rather friz their hair than spend the money to keep us from breaking our necks."

I expected the family fur to fly. I was wrong. No one wanted to involve Father, who in recent months had been suffering with severe internal pains. Sometimes, Sam told me confidentially, Father would be doubled up on the job; sometimes, coming home from New York, he would sit on the sidewalk with his legs tight against his stomach until the cramps passed and people would step around him as though he were some hapless derelict. Somehow he had managed to keep going, refusing medical help as long as he could. Doctors were fakirs and robbers. Who could afford them and still have a pound of coffee in the house?

By now the depression had begun to eat deeply into the family structure; actually, by late 1932, a second depression had been piled upon the first. Shantytowns called Hoovervilles fringed many towns and cities. America recoiled from newsreel films of federal troops armed with tanks, tear gas and bayonets, driving the "Bonus Expeditionary Force" from the nation's capital. A Chicagoan lamented: "We saw a crowd of some fifty men fighting over a barrel of garbage outside the back door of a restaurant. American citizens fighting for scraps like animals!"

Increasingly within a great many homes like ours America drifted toward a matriarchal society. The tomatoes that Sam forced in the greenhouse Mother sold at a handsome price in early July to the one luxury vegetable market in town. Throughout the summer she canned hundreds of jars of vegetables that Sam raised in the garden. She preserved eggs in big earthen crocks and "laid down" what seemed to be tons of sauerkraut. With a farm girl's instinct she was determined that the family would not starve when winter came. Two nurses from the nearby hospital were taken in as boarders and Edith practiced typing and shorthand preparatory to seeking a secretarial position.

Jobless Sam clung to his dignity in the firm belief that the Socialist Revolution would soon overtake us. Father worked at dirt-cheap wages for a private contractor who splashed one coat of paint on low-cost apartments, plugged up the rat holes, soldered over the leaking pipes, and called these places ready for occupancy.

What, psychologically, must have been happening to these men I did not perceive. I should have recognized how age and world-weariness had so quickly deepened the lines in their faces. I should have realized that they talked less and napped more. But I was editor of the *Targum*, a member of Student Council, a big wheel on the campus. I was remote, self-centered, doggedly determined to earn my degree. And if these ambitions were not enough to make me "self-contained, and as solitary as an oyster," to use the phrase of Sam's old friend Dickens, I was also in love.

Mother had no sense about girls. If she liked them they were sexless to me: that was why she liked them. And my sister was not any help: her female friends impressed me as silly frumps. Mother's argument in those years of depression was that money spent on college dances should be "kept in the family" and her choice for my social awakening was a cousin five years my senior. "You should love giving her a good time," Mother insisted. I didn't. Nor did I delude myself: the feeling was mutual. To my cousin I was only a convenience while she danced with my classmates and hoped they would date her.

Midway through my sophomore year I found my own girl and I kept her as far away from Mother's scrutiny as I could.

"What's her name?" Mother prodded.

"Teddy Papa."

"Humph!" Mother said, certain I had taken up with some night-spot floozie. "Where does she live?"

"In one of those old mansions along the Shrewsbury in Red Bank." That information stopped her: the neighborhood was not known as a hangout for burlesque queens.

I loved that old house along the Shrewsbury, for entering it was like stepping into the Age of Victoria. In the evening gaslights cast shadows upon high-backed chairs, horsehair sofas and marble-topped tables. Mellowness and gentility and a kind of haunting mustiness overspread the rooms: time and the river dwelt here along with Teddy and her mother. There was also a sense of sadness such as wealth leaves when it slips away through one misadventure or another. Yet Mrs. Papa was a magnificent symbol of a pride and grace that would not bend before the fickleness of fortune or a husband who had deserted her. Teddy, a former student at Goucher College and now a depression casualty, ran a day nursery to assist in keeping the old place going.

Teddy was a fine girl: loyal, warm-hearted, understanding, self-reliant. She was a slim, unaffected, almost pixieish girl with friendly eyes that danced like the flames of a wood fire on a winter's night. She was a hand-holder, as ready as I for puppy love, and she was a sharer of dreams who with a squeeze of her fingers could say: "You can do it . . . nothing is impossible."

Moonlit evenings we would sit for hours on the old river dock, listening to the water lap against the pilings and hearing a perch or carp flutter in a pool left by the tide. I could tell her anything about myself, my family, my life in college and she would listen, providing the wonderful therapy of a confession between a boy and girl. I heard all her problems and by a nod, a word, a touch of my hand gave her such comfort as I could. Thus we rested beneath what Coleridge would have called our "sheltering tree" in old Sam Johnson's "endearing elegance of female friendship."

Yet one evening we both understood our affair was ending. We stood for a long time, silent and holding hands and looking across the moon-bright Shrewsbury. A soft breeze through the trees echoed our loneliness for we both knew that we had yet to seek and find that deeper emotion which became love and marriage.

"You've been good for me, Teddy," I said.

On tiptoe, she kissed me. "Good night, dear," she whispered.

We were almost saying good-bye.

In that year when Father fell into the Christmas tree and I fell in love, Roosevelt opposed Hoover for the Presidency. The election, I wrote in *Targum*, "will be a vote of passion and emotion" in a setting of "national hysteria," sentiments that even Hop Brill could not dispute; but Hop was far less mollified, I suspect, when *Targum* thumped its editorial drums in behalf of Norman Thomas, the Socialist contender. We whipped up real enthusiasm over a campus straw vote and announced the result in the auditorium of the Physics Building. Quite a crowd assembled, including a fair sprinkling of women students from across town.

When the meeting ended, I met *her*. The night was damp, with a threat of drizzle, and she stood, straight and smiling, in a tan raincoat. Since all memories are mere pictures painted in one's own psychic colors, I cannot say what precisely attracted me so instantly. Upturned nose, eyes alight with good humor, a mouth that held a gentle smile . . . something indefinable within me responded. I could not explain it then; I cannot explain it now.

"I'd like you to meet Starling Wyckoff," said Bill Owen, the classmate who introduced us.

We walked only the short distance to where Starling and a friend must catch a bus to the College for Women. Starling, I thought: the name was beautiful. We said good-bye. In my mind her name thrummed on like a poem: Starling, Starling, Starling.

"What do you think of her?" Bill asked as we wandered back across a campus that all at once seemed dark and lonely.

"That's a girl I'd like to marry," I said.

Bill Owen was far older than most seniors, and sometimes he felt those advanced years oppressively; he was studying for the ministry, and tended upon occasion to take godlike stances. "You can't make snap judgments over anything so serious. You——you——" But I was not listening and he lapsed into melancholic silence.

Quickly Starling and I became inseparable. We went to all the dances, concerts, movies, and when there was nothing better to do we sipped chocolate milkshakes at Louie's Luncheonette and simply talked. Bill Owen grew indignant at our "senseless infatuation."

"You're like two children," he said in a fluster, "two children riding round and round on a carousel until you become dizzy and fall off."

"How do you know?"

"It isn't natural."

"Oh, for God's sake," I said, "go slide down a banister. The sublimation will do you good."

Starling and I never doubted. From week to week our love grew stronger. My handicap was never mentioned unless I raised the subject. Starling's smile said: "What does it matter?"

Reed Silvers fretted over our whirlwind courtship. "Flash," he counseled, "moderation is wise in all things"; but Reed had been to a drinking party the night before and was fuzzy-headed with a hangover. "Oh hell," he moaned finally, "what do I know about moderation?" Our one unfailing ally was Mrs. Peck, my old housemother from Hegeman, who, inviting us to visit her rooms, would say: "I'm sorry, I have to go out unexpectedly, but you two stay here and be comfortable and I'll be back in an hour and a half." She would depart with a sly little chuckle.

That Christmas vacation Starling wore my Cap and Skull pin as a symbol of "our understanding." I tried to conceal a growing dismay at the prospect of meeting her parents. Why should they tolerate seeing so lovely a daughter throw away her love on someone who had to have his meat cut, who drank through a straw and could not sip hot coffee unless someone held his cup? "They'll like you," Starling said, adding practically: "I don't see where they have much choice." I forced a smile, then Starling flung open the door with a gay shout: "Hi. Anybody home?"

Houses tell a lot about people: this one was comfortable and neat, homey and warm-hearted. Two straightforward people without a trace of fussiness greeted me cheerfully. A great weight lifted from my heart and that night I had a dream which had a foundation in actuality.

During the years when I attended Rutgers the university had experienced difficulty in keeping a president. Dr. John H. Thomas, who was president when I entered, ran into jealousies and criticisms that I never understood, but one day he resigned to become, in time, president of Norwich University. While the Rutgers trustees sought a new president, the position was filled temporarily by Philip Milledoler Brett, who had graduated in the

Class of 1892 and was a direct descendant of the Reverend Philip Milledoler, president of the college in the early decades of the nineteenth century. Phil Brett was a sweet-tempered, thoughtful man whom everyone admired, and when I dreamed of him that night I was reliving a chance meeting with him on Old Queen's campus.

"Reed Silvers tells me a lot about you," he said.

"Reed is a generous man, sir."

Dr. Brett smiled. "We all know about the struggle you've had and how well you've done. The years ahead won't be easy, but I want you to make a promise."

"Yes, sir. I'll promise you anything."

His hand rested on my shoulder. "One day," he said, "no matter how hard the struggle becomes, you will turn a corner and there all at once you will see the right road and your heart will sing and your head will lift high. So please don't lose patience: keep seeking and seeking until you find that corner."

"Sir," a misty-eyed boy replied, "you're an awfully nice man."

With warmth and affection he gave my shoulder a quick pat, then lowering his head against a stiffening fall breeze hustled his stubby legs across campus.

I awakened from this memory become dream and folded my hands beneath my head. I had turned the corner and found my girl. Phil Brett was right. "Starling, Starling," I whispered, "I'm going to make it—for you, for him."

❧

Starling visited my family before the Christmas holidays ended.

"They'll think you're wonderful," I predicted and Starling said with a note of edginess, "You're prejudiced."

The occasion passed pleasantly and Sam, in an animated mood, announced: "That girl's a jewel." Father was clearly approving and told a story of seeing a couple walking arm-in-arm a few days ago along a New York side street. "Their faces shone," he said, "and they were so happy I felt ten years younger just being near them."

Mother's face said: "Oh my God, all the men in the world are silly romanticists who would get nowhere without a woman's practical mind to save them." Aloud she added: "Only a fool would rush into marriage in these times." And Edith, who danced to Mother's tune like a puppet on a string, declared: "Earl owes Starling a long courtship so that she can enjoy his beautiful letters." Sam slammed on his cap and stomped out to the greenhouse before spending his irritations:

"By God! That's Edith for you—a postmark for a bedpost!"

Starling and I returned to New Brunswick. Almost six months of campus freedom stretched before us, or so we thought. At least we had crammed our way through midterm exams before someone tried to behead us both.

One Saturday morning, brimming over with an idea for an editorial, I unlocked the *Targum* building and wrote the copy while Starling read a book. About an hour later we emerged and walked back to the College for Women. During this interval an informer called Starling's housemother. Did she know that one of her girls had been seen going into an unoccupied college building with a boy? Did she know that this same couple had been seen entering a dormitory (as, indeed, we had at Mrs. Peck's invitation)?

Charged with accusations, the housemother awaited Starling's return. The fact that Starling was house chairman of her dormitory added to the woman's distress. Starling stood her ground. Who was this gratuitous busybody; the house mother refused to say. Starling threatened to carry the case to the dean of women; the housemother begged her not to. But she could not stop Starling from calling and telling me the story. I took off like Haley's comet.

On Saturdays Reed stayed over for the sporting events. I charged into his office, reciting as coherently as I could what had happened. A cardinal rule of human affairs is never to outrage a gentle man: Reed, like my father, was a classic example of that maxim. For five minutes in an impressive display of unrestrained profanity Reed expounded upon all the evil that had befallen the world through the idle gossip of dried-up old maids, then stomped off to find the dean of men.

Frazer Metzger, the dean, had good reason for knowing me: he was Mrs. Peck's brother-in-law. No one who understood him ever doubted his fighting instincts when aroused; he had run for governor of Vermont on the old Bull Moose ticket and had never lost the Teddy Roosevelt gift for exuberant indignation. He heard Reed through, then reached for the telephone and called the dean of women. "I think we can consider the incident closed," he said when he returned the phone to its cradle. When later I asked Starling how her housemother was behaving she giggled and said: "Walking on eggshells."

&

The philosopher-psychiatrist-proprietress of Louie's Luncheonette was Mama Stollman. During those years many students lived on credit at Stollman's. Her greeting never varied: "Hello, dollink, how's by you?"

From the kitchen doorway fat Louie called: "Where's Stollen?"

"She'll be along," I said.

"Dot Stollen!" Louie sighed. "She's got a cute behind."

"Dirty Mouth, back in the kitchen git!" Mama cried snappishly. "Oi, dot man!" she said, bringing her order pad. "Dollink, you don't look too good to Mama."

"I've had a little trouble."

"Oi, trouble!" Mama exclaimed. "What trouble there's been

by me!" And Mama launched into an excited tale of how the *allrightnick* (American Yiddish for an upstart), who this year had been chairman of refreshments for the Soph Hop, had failed to buy his punch by Mama. A quarter a gallon was all this *all-rightnick* had saved and what had happened by everyone? "Womiting," Mama said. "All over the floor everyone womiting."

Upon this cheery social intelligence Starling entered and Mama held her foot against the kitchen door so that fat Louie could not peek. A wave of happiness overcame me, and despite Mama's insistence that trouble hatches like eggs, I was sure that our worries were over for this final term of college.

During the next few weeks events fell into a tranquil sequence. I helped to write and produce a student show to the music of the *Mikado*. When the first term marks were released, I stood on the honors list. So how by me could life be sweeter?

But one morning the mail brought a summons to see Allen Sinclair Will immediately. I tramped over to Van Nest Hall, where the School of Journalism was located, and since my marks had been in the high 90's for three semesters, I possessed no sense of impending catastrophe. Dr. Will was dressed in a double-breasted suit that fit him like a tiger's skin. A sullen glitter shone in his eyes. Without ceremony he came to the point: "I want you to drop out of the School of Journalism."

I recoiled as though he had plunged a fist into my stomach. A furious excitement swept over me. "Drop out? And not graduate this June? What the hell are you talking about?"

His own face was flushed and angry. He spoke as though he were old Herod ordering a mass slaughter of Israelites. "Look at you! Look how you're shaking! Who's going to give you a job?"

"Why the hell wouldn't I shake when you throw me a low blow like this?"

"We run a professional school," my executioner decreed inflexibly. "Every student we ever have graduated has been placed with some newspaper and I won't have you spoiling our record."

I was so tense I must have been hopping around his office like a jack on a stick. Tears streaked my face and very likely my voice grew hysterical.

"What kind of goddam *blufferké* are you?" I shouted, using Mama Stollman's word for a hypocrite. "You give me honor marks and then all at once I'm no longer a human being but just a lousy statistic!"

"That's how it must be."

"That's just how in hell it's *not* going to be."

"Old Herod" pushed out a stubborn chin. "I've written a letter to the dean of the college . . ."

"Write it on johnny paper if you want it to do you any good," I cried. I stormed from his office in a blind rage.

How far I walked before the tremors in my arms and legs and shoulders and head subsided I cannot be certain. My whole being seemed to be wracked with dry, convulsive sobs. "My God," I implored, "why this, why this?" Why should one man—coldly, cruelly, tyranically—threaten to destroy my future for the sake of his personal pride?

I became conscious of stumbling along the Canal Road while drivers honked angrily and glared at me as though I were drunk or crazy. I slipped beneath the guard railing and leaned against a post, staring vacantly at the brackish water. Years ago a student had drowned in this canal, but I gave no thought to suicide.

After a time my spasms quieted. The image of Dr. Will filled my mind. I saw an aging man, professionally competent but crabbed in spirit. Emotionally he walked on a crutch, for his precious record was like drink to an alcoholic. He was no teacher in the sense of Houston Peterson or Cap Twiss. He possessed no strength to give to others. "A hollow man," I said.

Starling crept into my thoughts. What was one old man's blindness compared to this girl's love? Long years would pass before I could explain the emotions of those next few moments and then I discovered the poetry of Sir Edwin Arnold, whose travels in the Far East so filled his mind with Oriental mysticism:

> Somewhere there waiteth in this world of ours
>   For one lone soul, another lonely soul—
> Each chasing each through all the weary hours,
>   And meeting strangely at one sudden goal;
> Then blend they—like green leaves with golden flowers,
>   Into one beautiful and perfect whole—
> And life's long night is ended, and the way
>   Lies open onward to eternal day.

Starling . . . Starling, I whispered to the breeze. I remembered Peter in the Bible meeting the lame man at the temple gate. And Peter said: "I have no gold and silver, but I give you what I have; in the name of Jesus Christ of Nazareth, walk."

Now I must walk—alone, unafraid.

I went back, not to see Will or the dean but the president. All I knew about Robert Clarkson Clothier, who had come to Rutgers from the University of Pittsburgh the year before, was Reed Silvers' affection for the man. A thoroughbred, Reed called him, a man of heart and spirit.

The president received me graciously, saying: "You missed your old friend by five minutes."

"Reed Silvers, sir?"

"No, Dr. Will." A slight smile touched his lips. "I gather you two are a pair of verbal battlers."

I nodded. "We both must have been reading Mark Twain."

"What did he say?"

"When angry, count to four; when very angry, swear."

Dr. Clothier's smile deepened. "What is a *blufferké?*"

"That, sir, is Mama Stollman's Yiddish word for a hypocrite." I could stand the suspense no longer. "Doctor, what is going to happen?"

"What should happen. In June you're going to receive the degree of Bachelor of Letters in Journalism."

✍§

And so I graduated. In those topsy-turvy years of depression, Rutgers seniors estimated that they must wait from five to ten years to accumulate the financial resources necessary for a successful marriage. Mother approved their good sense; Starling and I said: "Nonsense." In the silly poll seniors hold at commencement I was voted "the man who had done most for Rutgers," "the most literary," "the biggest publicity hound," and tied with Morris L. Forer, a brilliant lawyer in later years, as "the man most likely to succeed."

One incident of commencement day lingers in memory. The moment came when Dr. Will, standing in his gown and hood, called for the graduates in journalism to rise and receive their degrees. Our glances met and I could not resist an impish impulse.

I winked.

CHAPTER NINE

The Myth Makers

T*he telephone call*

from Reed Silvers came on New Year's Day:

"Flash, can you come down to New Brunswick tomorrow? I've got a job for you."

I raced to tell Starling. We danced around the room. Our joy was understandable in this deepest of all depression years when, along with most college graduates, we had learned that, in a jobless America, it can be a long, long time from June to December. Starling's parents were far more perceptive than mine in guessing that we were too mushy to resist any excuse for being married and, quite sensibly, they sent her to Katharine Gibbs School in New York City to learn shorthand and typing so that she would have some means of supporting herself if I turned into one of those arty longhairs who preferred a typewriter on an orange crate in an attic to a desk job and a nice apartment.

Yet during these months when discouraged older men were selling apples on street corners and housing dispirited families in shanties built on city dumps, I was busy. Again I could thank Reed for the contract to write a boy's book for D. Appleton and Company. The result was *The Backfield Feud,* a thoroughly miserable piece of work that should not have been published and never repaid its modest advance against royalties.

Appleton's reception room in those days was booklined, dusty, and threadbare and the elderly woman who looked up when I entered had a way of suggesting she really had been expecting Nathaniel Hawthorne or Ralph Waldo Emerson in this room where time must have stopped a century ago. John L. B. Williams, stout and a bit of a puffer, then controlled Appleton's editorial policies. God knows, poor John Williams labored mightily to make something out of this hackneyed manuscript with which Reed had stuck him, but he never had a chance. Starling could have told him why, for she had been reduced to tears trying to help the dunderhead with whom her heart had stuck her.

But no school of journalism taught a student how to write with flair and style and self-confidence; quite the opposite was true and may still be, for all I know. One day all I was taught would have to be unlearned. Models and imitation and a common mold of mediocrity could produce hacks but not creative people. Lessons about words and sentences and grammar were the piddling part of it—the tools, like a carpenter's hammer and saw, with which the building had to be erected. Underneath

138

there must be the writer himself: hearing with his inner ear, feeling emotion deeply and perhaps disastrously, perceiving with his own God-given intelligence, and somehow finding the strength and patience and wisdom to get all this down on a sheet of blank paper.

Happily, neither Starling nor I realized how dark and difficult and strewn with danger the road ahead could be on that New Year's Day in 1934 as we danced around the room. I had a job . . . we were started! What Reed had failed to tell me was that I was being hired under a federal grant as a statistician, for which I was as little qualified as if I had been named ambassador to the Court of St. James, but Reed, the master manipulator, simply giggled. "Flash, it's the old game of hocus-pocus. You'll be assigned to me as a statistical assistant, which means you'll be a writer since we don't keep statistics, and by June I'll convince the president that you're so indispensable, I'll have you on the college payroll."

Reed loved to talk about himself and rare was the day when, feet crossed on the desk and corncob pipe puffing, he could not find an hour to spare for these reminiscences. His grandfather, a doctor, had been known in Rahway politics as "the bald-headed eagle of Seminary Avenue," which explained one side of Reed's personality. His mother's oldest sister, Aunt Emma Reed, discovered a pile of boyish poems he had written and she persuaded a friendly printer to publish them in a little booklet entitled *The Rill and Other Poems*. Then a nosey newspaperman, doubtless writing on space rates, splashed a story about the "Boy Poet of Rahway" in the columns of the old *New York World*, together with a photograph of "a rather sappy looking boy in white knickers and blue coat," and Reed became a local celebrity. At least Reed's mother and Aunt Emma were happy, which seemed little enough to compensate for the struggle they had known since his father had died when the lad was only seven. The family managed a more or less hand-to-mouth existence, with Reed's mother taking in sewing; and in 1909, or the year before I was born, he could not have attended Rutgers without a scholarship even though the tuition then was only a hundred dollars a year. When with tenderness and nostalgia he recalled these early years he became a writer of compelling sensitivity:

". . . In those days when you were young, Pointer's Beach was a place where the sons of dressmakers and the daughters of clerks congregated for an hour or two of dancing. It was the only place we could go, we children of the poor. Twenty-five cents would give us a pass to the dance hall for the entire evening, the trolley ride cost only a nickel, and there was a long pier on which we could walk in the moonlight."[*]

One of the close bonds between us was the fact that Reed's early years in Rahway reminded me of my own childhood in Brooklyn. When he talked of his mother sewing into the late evening hours, I relived that stormy, hungry winter when Mother pulled me on the sleigh to the necktie factory where she picked up or delivered her piecework. Except for a brief three-month stint on a newspaper, Reed never had worked anywhere but at Rutgers. Time and again he told me: "The college has been good to me, Flash, and it will be good to you." He spoke solemnly, as though under oath.

⁓§

I trusted him implicitly; he was the straw that kept my secret, half-realized dreams afloat. A reading of the letters that Starling has saved from these months reveals a lovesick young ass living lachrymosely from one weekend to the next when he could be with his girl again. Dean Metzger appointed me a preceptor so that I could live free amid the flaking plaster and

---

[*] Earl Reed Silvers, *The Editor Accepts*, 81.

sagging beams of old Winant's Hall. Toward late spring one of those wonderful brain trusters in Washington decided that statisticians should receive eighty rather than sixty cents an hour and all at once I received over $100 in retroactive wages. I was rich in this age when rent was cheap and you could buy a whole chicken for seventy-five cents and, if you were in a celebrating mood, could add a bottle of the best domestic sparkling Moselle for only a dollar. Starling, a prodigious note taker, had everything worked out: two people could eat well, including a daily bottle of milk, for eight dollars a week. And Reed, who never let up on his campaign concerning my "indispensability," kept his promise and a letter from the president announced that I had been hired by the college as an assistant editor of university publications at a salary of $75 a month.

"Now we can start on our next campaign," Reed said exultantly. "You'll need Starling as your secretary!"

Occasionally a worrisome tone crept into my letters to Starling. Mother's moods, I wrote, were not to be taken seriously, and since I now even talked like Reed I intimated that at the proper time I would "handle" her. For the soundest of reasons— it was pay day—we picked August 25, 1934 for our wedding.

Mother emoted, though I do not recall that she actually wrung her hands, and for a spell there was quite a tempestuous little scene. Then, very quietly, my mild-mannered father broke in: "Emma, this argument has gone far enough. The boy has to live his own life and we can thank God that he has won the love of such a grand girl." A silence fell as though the Almighty had spoken, and in astonishment I looked at Father who, without blinking an eye, was master in his own household. Sam chuckled and to bedevil Mother began practicing Mendelsohn's "Wedding March" on the piano. But Mother knew how to pay him back: she and Edith held a shouting contest as they discussed the new dresses they would require for the wedding.

And so, on the twenty-fifth day of August, Starling and I

were married in her parents' home in Little Falls. The walls were banked with summer flowers and Sam slammed out the wedding march with satisfied vengeance and in a sweet and tender ceremony, we exchanged our vows. Afterward we dashed off to catch the train for New Brunswick, fretting the whole way over whether a friend had kept his promise and slipped my pay check under the door.

The rathole apartment that we called our first home was situated above a store on Church Street, one of the older sections in this pre-Revolutionary city. The hallway, dark and musty-smelling, led to stairs that creaked even above the clack and rattle of the street noises. When the door opened, Starling cried: "Joy to the world—the check has come!" I carried her across the doorsill and into the collection of junky furniture we had scrounged from our family attics.

"It's not much," I said, sheepishly.

"It's ours—it's wonderful—we're together!" We were both teary-eyed and so deeply, so ecstatically in love, but the spell was quickly broken by the beating of the dumbwaiter ropes against the walls, followed by the landlord's outraged voice booming up the shaft:

"Goddamit, you pig-people on the third floor, wrap your goddam garbage so it won't all fall apart in my goddam hands!"

So began our wedding night on a Saturday in August. We had not counted on a serenade but presently a Salvation Army band appeared on the corner, thumping out "The Battle Hymn of the Republic" with an enthusiasm that rattled windows for blocks around. Still, I suppose that for a theme song to a life together much can be said for "Glory, Glory Hallelujah!"

❧

I am not a sophisticate about marriage and people who commit adultery bore me. I am quickly wearied by husbands

142

who father their wives and wives who mother their husbands; and spouses who only bed down for specified favors can do their strumpeting in some other household: I do not want them in mine. One divorce I can understand and two I can tolerate, but this Hollywood game of Musical Wives attracts me about as much as a moldy lamb chop. I am saddened by homosexuals and lesbians, but the problem is theirs and not mine; and beyond the tiresome pages of novels like *Tropic of Cancer* I have yet to encounter a nymphomaniac. Whereas I have never resisted looking twice at girls who, like June, are "busting out all over," Starling would be the first to admit that if I married her for this reason I sure was near-sighted.

There was speculation over why Starling had married a visibly handicapped man. Some college gossips whispered that she was pregnant and when we deliberately waited five years before having our first child they whispered that I was impotent. One psychologist warned Starling that overmothering tended to smother such marriages, but this poor man, worn out from worrying over other people's problems, died under circumstances strongly suggesting suicide. Since the nature of human nature is mankind's greatest bedevilment, there were those who repeated the old cliché about the family of a handicapped person becoming a handicapped family.

I know why our marriage worked. Ben Hecht had part of the answer when he declared that a successful marriage requires an element of genius—*that*, at least; and Ambrose Bierce had another part when he defined marriage as "a community consisting of a master, a mistress, and two slaves, making in all, two"; and Henrik Ibsen another part when he said that "marriage is a thing you've got to give your whole mind to." What the gossips and worryworts never could understand about our marriage was the simple fact that Starling, in her own mind, had not married a handicapped man. Instead, she had chosen a husband with special problems as many women do and with certain small adjustments we could live as peacefully and as comfortably as any couple.

For a woman entering matrimony, where all at once she is expected to change her mood from faithful wife to comforting mother to bawdy mistress as though turning on and off a water faucet, the tensions that arise have nothing to do with cerebral palsy. I often think of a friend, a newlywed, who used to count to ten before telling himself: "I must not think of sex"; I never counted to five before surrendering to the happy conviction that a dash of healthy lechery was good for a marriage.

But sex is not all of it, as any grown-up should know. When we were first married, Starling's parents offered us fifty dollars a month to help along. The first month we accepted the money, more out of embarrassment than necessity, but then we said: "Thank you very much, but no—we've got to stand on our own feet."

Starling needed a new winter coat, so I wrote advertising copy for a local business concern, and Starling had a good cloth coat with a raccoon collar, for thirty-five dollars purchased a lot in those days.

This faith in ourselves, this drive to get ahead by working day and night, if that was the way to do so, found us within ten months owning a second-hand Ford coupé which was little more than a tin can on four wheels and renting a small, pretty house with a yard, meandering stream, and outdoor fish pond in Bound Brook.

Once more I was following in Reed's shadow, planning my life as he had lived his. Without his writing he never would have been able to provide for his family as graciously as he had. Walter P. McGuire, editor of *Boys Life,* had turned Reed to writing for boys and girls some two decades before, emphasizing how great was the opportunity for a college-trained man. A cabinet filled with letters from his young readers, including the impression of a girl's mouth in lipstick with "I love you" written beneath, convinced Reed that such an author must rank among the great educators of America.

Feet crossed on the desk, corncob pipe puffing sparks and smoke, he giggled over how slim his earnings often had been. When he reached one thousand short stories, he stopped counting; a few had sold for three dollars and his biggest check, received from *Boys Life* for a two-part serial, had been $300. Among his twenty-seven books, five had been written under the pen name of David Stone for the now defunct publishing house of Barse and Hopkins. "They paid two hundred dollars outright and no royalties," Reed chuckled. He had written all five books in five months, stoically turning out one 3,000-word chapter each night. Even the books he wrote for Appleton rarely earned above $1,000 in royalties. "What the hell, it was all gravy. It bought cars and paid for summers in Maine and sent the kids to camp." He was satisfied, or thought he was. Within him, however, a sense of unfulfillment stirred deeply; it would emerge in time, affecting both his life and mine.

Sometimes Reed talked too much. Shortly after Starling and I moved to Bound Brook he persuaded the university to raise my annual salary to $1,500. "Cy," he said, referring to the comptroller, "gave in, but he made it clear, Flash, that this is all a person in your condition should expect." Then Reed saw my face and could have bitten out his tongue. Mistiness stung the edges of my eyes and my stomach had the same hollow feeling of a low blow struck without warning that I had experienced in my interview with Dr. Will. What, in God's name, was "a person in my condition": some sort of luckless freak predestined in heaven to beg for a livelihood?

Glum, dispirited, I sought out Starling. She was sympathetic, calm, and surprisingly indifferent. "Cy Johnson! That fathead! Who cares what he thinks? You're running our lives—he isn't!"

If when I die my family wishes an epitaph on my tombstone, let it read: "He was the lifemate Starling chose."

◄§

Working at a university—not just Rutgers, but any institution of higher learning—is another kind of marriage. A university is a mixture of myth and reality, one presence known to the public and another known privately, and many of its personalities, as comedian Allen Sherman would say, range from crazy-crazy to nice-crazy. Reed, of course, was nice-crazy, as any director of alumni and public relations must be, and those who worked for him were myth makers. In those days, when Rutgers was part private and part public, this myth-making was played for high stakes: to squeeze every dime we could from alumni to whom the image of a private colonial college appealed and to budge from the New Jersey legislature every dollar we could for functioning as a substitute for a state university.

The rules of the myth makers were rigid. We assumed, for example, that anyone who attended the old school had been deliriously happy through every hour of every day on campus, and if he were the decent sort he would never forget as long as he lived how much he owed to alma mater. We thought nothing of taking some complacent, run-of-the-mill school teacher and transforming him in the *Alumni Monthly* into one of the nation's great educators (the image Reed made of himself, pounding out his potboilers for youngsters); and anyone who shed a tear singing of how old Rutgers had "stood" since the time of the "flood" became a hero for swallowing both this lie and lousy rhyme-scheme.

The football season was a time of unrestrained hysteria when members of the athletic department wallowed as shamelessly as Hollywood starlets in an orgy of undeserved publicity. Straight-faced, we reported their statements of how the proselyting of college football players was a wicked, seamy practice, knowing all the time that they really meant to say: "Look, you

146

carping bastards, if you want us to beat Lehigh lay the dough on the line so we can offer the kind of scholarship aid that will bring us linemen who can block and backs who don't stumble over their own feet." If ever novacaine was shot into a player's lamed ankle so that he could go on dying for "dear old Rutgers" and the coaching staff's domestic tranquility, we turned away from the malicious gossips who would circulate such senseless rumors. No one would confirm the frequently repeated story during the years when money was especially tight that one member of the administration proposed releasing a foreign-born teacher because he spoke "broken English"; in this case, happily, the dean stood firm and so a scientist was permitted to discover an antibiotic and to become the university's first and only Nobel Prize winner.

At times myth-making reached ridiculous extremes. An undergraduate who published in the college magazine a mild, but perfectly objective story about a girl who visited an abortionist paid dearly for his "daring." The Archdiocese of Trenton became outraged that, in a publicly supported institution, a student's mind should dwell upon so earthy a subject. Since the Catholic vote is sizable in New Jersey, the governor did not disguise his umbrage. The trustees' appropriations committee thrummed with vibrations of self-preservation, damning the culprit as disloyal, a pale pink and a Jew; and with no sense of absurdity one trustee told me: "If undergraduates want to think about social problems, let them wait until they get out of college to do it!"

In later years, when I became director of the Rutgers University Press, I was constantly at odds with Cy Johnson, who never could decide whether "a person in my condition" was a genius or a fool. When I persuaded Beryl and Sam Epstein, two very fine authors and Rutgers graduates, to write a book about Selman A. Waksman, the discoverer of streptomycin, Cy summoned me. His mood was explosive when he mentioned an alumnus of considerable wealth and old Dutch family background who, Cy hoped, would remember the university handsomely in his will. "What," he demanded, "will —— say when he sees the names of two Jews on this book jacket?" I replied that he could say what he pleased; I was not going to lose any sleep or change the jacket. Soon Cy was embarked on another fretful storm when the publicity for a book about hybrid corn gave prominence to the significant part of Henry A. Wallace in developing this branch of agricultural science.

"What," Cy raged, "will our Republican friends think?"

"I didn't know they could," I answered sassily. The man baffled me.

∽§

Paul Robeson flabbergasted the Rutgers myth makers. I wrote a book about Paul's undergraduate years that had an excellent reception, but the greater reward was the chance to know Paul personally. Since the early 1920's, when Eugene O'Neill had discovered Robeson acting with the Provincetown Players on Cape Cod, the Negro had dazzled audiences in *All God's Chillun, Emperor Jones,* and *Showboat.* I interviewed Paul in the brief periods he could snatch from a busy schedule—in his lawyer's office, in the wings of a theater where he was performing. He possessed a magnificent stature, standing well over a sturdy six feet. He was splendidly all Negro in appearance, personality, and viewpoint. Never would I meet anyone who surpassed this handsome, proud Negro in quickness of mentality. Soft-spoken in conversation, frequently when he made a point laughter boomed out of him. His smile was quick, disarming, infectious, but that smile was often the device of the professional performer who was himself part myth maker; in other moments, when his private thoughts intruded, his eyes grew shadowy as though trying to hide an inner torment.

Robeson's sensitivity would not permit him to keep his resentments forever dormant. He had been born in a Princeton which in those first years of the twentieth century had not recovered from its divided loyalties during Civil War times. Here the smart Negro was expected to know his place and Paul, by Princeton standards, was potentially a "mean nigger" who sassed back.

In 1915, when Robeson reached Rutgers, the football coach wanted to invite him to the training camp at Eatontown, but half the squad rebelled. If Robeson came they were going home. A 10-to-0 defeat by Princeton somewhat sobered these rebels, and they consented to give the Negro a chance. One day in practice they smashed the fingers of one hand to see how much he could take; he was kneed in the groin—his college years were not an untainted idyll. The myth makers later insisted that Robeson did not make the glee club because he never tried, which was a partial truth. But Paul, as the only Negro in a small college, told a different story: glee club concerts were followed by dances and he understood the unwritten rules. In those days the college president called a cheery hello on meeting students; when Robeson appeared the president turned his head. But Paul had weathered these irritations, winning a Phi Beta Kappa key and becoming valedictorian of his class. Twice Walter Camp named him an All-American end. Afterwards he went to Columbia Law School before his future wife turned him toward a career on the stage and in the concert hall.

"Robie is our best known alumnus," Reed, the myth maker, eulogized in the *Alumni Monthly*. No inkling of any unhappiness in college crept into this interview, filled with raptures for the Robeson who "has sung on two continents and in a dozen countries." And Reed continued: "Robie talked about his son, Paul Jr. He is twelve years old and as big as his father . . . he is coming to Rutgers."

Paul Jr. went to Cornell and the myth makers never understood why. But the day had arrived when one of Robeson's classmates told me: "To hell with that Commie! He doesn't belong to us anymore. When we played football with Robie he was the right kind of nigger who knew his place."

I winced, overwhelmed by a sense of helplessness. And I had experienced the same feeling when one day, before Paul's conversion to Communism was either known or complete, I asked the manager of the University Club in New York if there would be any objection should I bring Robeson to lunch. "My God," that poor man said, "don't do it, sir. For your own sake, don't. Our Southern members will raise hell."

Paul shrugged when I told him. "You are naïve, my friend." Then his bitterness spilled over. He told about a private club in an upstate city in New York where he was made to ride in the freight elevator because the members who had come to hear him sing should not be expected to mix with him socially. He mentioned restaurants where, as a celebrity, he was permitted to dine but where his son, as an unknown Negro, was turned away at the door. I could feel how his spirit had been wounded and my heart reached out to say so but I found no words to use.

His thoughts drifted to a winter's night in Boston. He arrived late with a concert scheduled for the following day. Sleet filled the air and his throat tightened with a threatening cold. One hotel after another refused him a room, not all overpolite in making clear that they did not cater to "niggers." His panic heightened. But at this point he paused, those moments vividly alive; then, unexpectedly, he chuckled. "See what a damn fool I was? I knew better. If I went to the best hotel and walked up to the desk asking for a room I would not be turned away. The best don't need to apologize. They never fail you." As a visibly handicapped person I have upon occasion been forced to follow Paul's rule: he was right.

One by one the scars accumulated as Robeson the artist was divided from Robeson the human being by a white man's line we both knew was there. Slowly but irresistibly he seemed to turn against his government, his university, his tormentors. I could not play the myth maker in this case and wrote an article for *The Nation* detailing the facts. Robeson, I said, was a product of a generation already out of step with America. His classmates at Rutgers might scorn him, but recently at Amherst a Negro had been admitted to membership in a national fraternity and Yale had elected a Negro as captain of its football team. The letters, I explained, demanding that Robeson's name be struck from the rolls of the college "came from the older graduates," while the committee that refused to take this action was composed of younger men. And I added:

> Robeson's tragedy is that he does not see how the age and the atmosphere which produced him have already lost much of their hold upon the future. Jackie Robinson, testifying before a Congressional committee, made the change clear. Any difference of opinion between Robeson and Robinson is basically not one between two prominent members of the Negro race or between men of conflicting ideologies; it is a difference in the philosophical attitudes of two generations. In the long run only Westbrook Pegler and his tribe will be unable to comprehend this distinction, but, then, about all Pegler has ever taught us is that no one perspires so profusely as the man beating a dead horse.*

Marshall Field, Jr., wrote me a warm note, saying *The Nation* piece had helped him to understand Robeson, but I had wasted my effort if I wanted to dent the prejudiced minds of his Rutgers classmates.

On campus there were mutterings that I must be a "pale pink," for who else would defend a Robeson at the expense of

---

* Earl Schenck Miers, "Paul Robeson—Made in America," *The Nation,* May 27, 1950.

his university? I worked earnestly at being an effective myth maker, and if in time the experience soured, it was only because it brought a sense of pimping for an intellectual bawdy house. What manner of person would I become if I did not recognize that Paul's black skin was far more of a physical handicap than my cerebral palsy? Or if I took names off a title page because they were Jewish names? Or confused Henry Wallace, the gifted agricultural scientist, with Henry Wallace, a political zany?

I was no pale pink but simply a kid out of college growing up. The kid clung to the lessons Houston Peterson had taught him—in a world of epic visions man became a hero of the spirit—and the emerging adult, who hitherto had judged his parents and forgiven them, now judged his bosses and ultimately forgave them also. In that world of epic visions, survival called for something better than a myth maker. Perhaps, this was all a gifted psychiatrist, Abraham Myerson, was trying to say when he commented: "If a snake and a man were thrown into a well, it would not be the man who was fitter to survive."

Luckily, in those years, a great intellectual ferment was stirring at Rutgers, fomented by a group who were young, ambitious, imaginative, and aggressive. This group was not interested in old images but in their own image. As a result they changed not only the university but also the physical character of the town and campus.

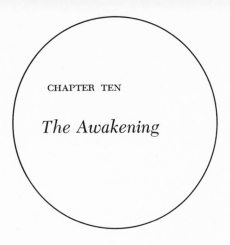

CHAPTER TEN

The Awakening

*T*o *get anything*
done at Rutgers in those topsy-turvy days of the middle 1930's,
whether the problem concerned building a stadium or establish-
ing a university press, everyone started at the same point: somehow by guile or persuasion, trickery or indignation one had to
get around, under, or over Cy Johnson, keeper of the university's
purse strings. In one sense this situation may not have been un-
healthy, for it created a strong camaraderie among the university's "progressive spirits."

To Hop Brill, who as the university's purchasing agent was caught in the center of this internecine warfare, anyone who was not in the room at the moment he was expostulating became "that monkey." Hop tried to evaluate Cy realistically: "That monkey isn't actually mean, there's just a great deal he doesn't know." We protested that Cy had worked four-year stretches at Emory and Wisconsin before coming to Rutgers, so why didn't he know? "That monkey," Hop said, "didn't even know *The Wall Street Journal* existed before I started lending him my copy."

George E. Little, the athletic director, also had come to Rutgers from Wisconsin and knew Cy's ruse, whenever anyone entered his office, of shuffling piles of paper as though he really did not have time to spare. "He signs letters or calls his secretary to fetch this or that report or get some trustee on the telephone, but nuts to that malarky!" George was round-faced, earthy, jolly, and as self-assured as though he had discovered a cure for old age. Aside from Casey Stengel no one talked like George, whose conversations were filled with connotations out of a remote past or out of his dreams as far as anyone could tell. But on one point George was crystal clear: he intended to build a stadium, in large part with federal money and labor, and he did not give two damns if Cy's highly Republican-oriented conscience quaked at these financial shenanigans.

"I'll tell you how I'll do it," George said. "I'll dig a hole. In fact, I'll scoop out the biggest hole those WPA fellas will dig. The public and Cy and the trustees will see that hole. Filling it up again won't satisfy the public for digging it in the first place, so they'll have to build a stadium in it."

George chuckled; he was not bluffing. Today, in the hole he dug, stands one of the handsomest stadiums in America.

Outmaneuvering Cy became a point of pride. He was studied, evaluated, notes on his methods exchanged. And Cy let slip little revelations to his personality: for one, he had a fetish over changing jobs every four years and meant to cling to his present position until death, a kind of security blanket which he grasped to almost ridiculous extremes. If his staff was not terrorized, they were at least stunned by the intensity of his resolution and so they were studied, their weaknesses calculated.

Hop, a firm believer in the new Rutgers that one day must emerge, was, I think, a conscious conspirator on the side of the progressives. President Clothier, an intuitive compromiser like Reed, preferred to come around by small degrees, but he had the cultivated tastes of an old Philadelphia Main Liner along with a Quaker's tendency to embrace Holy Experiments, and among the progressives his instincts were considered to be trustworthy. The most effective approach to Cy was the impersonal; you divorced yourself from a suggestion, only mentioning it because you believed some influential trustee like Phil Brett would think it grand if Rutgers could do thus and so. In this sense, I suppose, we brainwashed Cy.

Yet Cy was no fool, knowing that if he gave a foot it might cost him a yard and if he yielded a yard he might well lose a mile. George Little buzzed around him like a swarm of hornets. It was not enough for George to drive Cy and Hop crazy digging holes and erecting steel framework and pouring concrete and ordering redwood planks from California for his stadium seats; one day a couple of secondhand shells appeared, then a discarded barge was tugged through the Narrows and down the Raritan to serve as a temporary boathouse and Rutgers was launched into the costly sport of rowing. "This will give us class," George said guilelessly of a sneaky business that easily might have driven a comptroller to heavy drink. Hop could not very well deny his complicity in this piece of skullduggery but met his obligations manfully and in time his Class of 1914 built a permanent boathouse.

My duties jelled into what amounted to official responsibility for all university publications and my salary crept toward $3,000. Reed worked according to plan: I was elected an honorary member of Phi Beta Kappa and received an honorary Master of Arts degree and, with the backing of President Clothier and Phil Brett, was admitted to the University Club in New York. "Entrenchments, Flash," Reed said enthusiastically. "These things make you a permanent part of the university. You can be safe here."

I nodded and smiled but there came moments when my spirit felt chilled. Reed would not let up on the theme: "Flash, compared to a university, you can't imagine how tough and nasty the business world can be." In one way, I had a sense of being as caged by my disability as Paul Robeson was by his black skin. And yet I knew that Reed was using me to convince himself. He recalled the day in 1913 when his widowed mother had come down for commencement. She had a new dress for the graduation exercises, a made-over dress for Class Day: Reed saw her, face aglow, a tiny person with a courageous heart. But he did not understand how desperately she wanted to attend the president's reception and meet his professors and classmates. He hustled her onto the 12:27 train, spoiling what should have been the happiest day of her life. "If I had the time and money, I'd go off and write the kind of story she deserves," he said heavily. His pipe went out, his mouth grew pinched. He, too, was trapped.

In time Paul would find one escape, Reed another, and I a third, and each of us, in our way, would reaffirm Robert Browning's observation:

> When the fight begins within himself,
> A man's worth something.

Pure happenstance, the approach of the university's 175th anniversary celebration, helped me. The moving forces behind the planning for this event were Donald F. Cameron, whom

everyone called Scotty, representing the humanities, and William H. Cole, representing the sciences. Wittily cynical, imaginative, determined, full of spunk, Scotty quickly grew into one of my close friends. Scotty had muffed the orals for his doctorate at Princeton and was not anxious to suffer that ordeal again. Yet, knowing the old academic game, Scotty realized that the lack of a Ph.D. well could place a ceiling over his faculty advancement even though he was one of the most effective teachers of undergraduates on campus. In this respect, Scotty faced an insurmountable handicap unless he carved out his own future. The 175th anniversary became that opportunity.

Like George Little's hole that grew into a stadium, Scotty's revolution, as it affected and changed my life, began with an attack on the quality of the university's printing which was tawdry and cheap and as a reflection of the university gave the impression that Rutgers operated in the last log cabins to be found in New Jersey. Reed knew little and cared less about the graphic arts; but Scotty's anniversary committee had the money to spend on a consultant and chose one of the best in Carl Purrington Rollins, who held the proud title of Printer to Yale University.

Blessed Carl! Who, in a few sentences, can revive the wonderful vitality of this gentleman and scholar? Richly endowed with kindness and wisdom, wit and tolerance, he embraced all around him with the warming glow of his personality. His eyesight then was fast failing, yet he could dictate from memory the details of how a title page should be composed and achieve perfection. An elder statesman in the world of book design and typography, he took pleasure in the fact that he had designed a timetable for the New Haven Railroad that was both readable and aesthetically appealing. Cy's defensive antennae vibrated instantly at Carl's presence, and the needling began with the first expense account. A call from Cy's office picked on an item reading "Miscellaneous, 20¢."

Would Mr. Rollins explain that item more fully?

"Certainly," Carl responded. "While riding down from Yale on those two bands of rust called the New Haven I bought a newspaper for five cents, which I finished before reaching New York City. Here, unfortunately, I found it necessary to go to the lavatory, which cost ten cents. To compound matters, I have been troubled with the slows lately so in order to keep my mind undistracted and fresh for my labors when I arrived in New Brunswick, I spent another five cents on a second newspaper to while away the time. I think, sir, it all adds up to the penny— yes, sir, so it does, twenty cents exactly."

There were no further telephone calls from Cy's office.

Carl was an inspiring teacher. Under his tutelage I read Daniel B. Updyke's splendid books on the history and techniques of printing and everything Frederic Goudy had written on type design or Dard Hunter on papermaking. In the evening Starling and I filled the dining-room table with type specimen books. I taught her what was an ascender and a descender and how a serif could give distinction and beauty to the design of type. Caslon, Bodoni, DeVinne, Garamond . . . the names of fifty type faces became household words.

There is only one way a cerebral-palsied person can design printing: someone else copies the models for him. Hour after hour, Starling traced letters, then pasted them where I directed on blank pages. We argued over letter spacing, optical center, the balancing of light and heavy weights of type. We were not ostentatious; we sought no spectacular effects. The task in design was to be appropriate, to mate purpose to beauty of easy visual communication. An old percolator bubbled on the kitchen stove; coffee pried open sleepy eyes and we thought nothing of doing over a layout a dozen times. "I think we're getting somewhere," Starling said, becoming caught up in the spell of the work. We were happy as the result became more satisfying and I would dream over those designs, wanting to make them better.

Impatiently I waited for Carl's next visit to show him what we had accomplished. He would hold the pages flat against his nose, the only way he could see. He could sense my tension, my anxiety to please him. His approval filled the room with sunshine. To his surprise I wrote a little book, *Composing Sticks and Mortar Boards,* which seemed the sensible way for me to learn how effective institutional printing should be designed and produced. Carl reviewed it generously in *The Saturday Review,* telling a friend: "He has a mind like a sponge."

Actually I was having my first intellectual love affair. With Carl as my tutor, doors opened everywhere into this new realm where fine books and good paper and woodcuts and calligraphy were like sunlight and rain replenishing the earth.

Many were the companions of those days of enchantment. Harpers' Arthur Rushmore was one—he and his lovely wife Edna with their Golden Hind Press in Madison, New Jersey where books and laughter and good Scotch whiskey blended into a heady elixir. Another was Richard Ellis, forever lugging his books between shifting establishments in the environs of Philadelphia and New York and never getting them unpacked (together we edited *Bookmaking and Kindred Amenities,* and one bookseller in Miami returned five copies in disgust: we were discussing the wrong kind of bookmaking for his horse-minded clientele). Dear old Fred Melcher, the convivial pilot of *Publishers Weekly,* gave me hours of his time. What I was learning most through such friends was the reward an intellectual passion brings: a man so endowed has no loneliness, no sense of isolation because of an accident of birth; but Reed had no interest in this awakening and, in a subtle way, rather ridiculed it.

Yet Reed was willing to go along with Carl Rollins, for the Printer to Yale University was that sort of charmer, and Carl worked out a two-front campaign for effecting our renaissance in printing at Rutgers. He would educate me and I would educate the local compositors and pressmen. Thatcher-Anderson, the print shop favored by the university, was housed in what once may have been a stable in an alley behind a theater. Hot and mosquito-ridden in summer, cold and drafty in winter, this structure with its sagging floors and beams became my daytime home. In one sense the experience was an echo from my boyhood, reminding me of those days when I had watched Scoop Wynkoop making up the forms of the *Bergen Evening Record*.

The staff grew accustomed to my presence haunting the place. I soon knew where every case of display type was located, and above the clatter of the linotype machines shouted and cajoled, pleaded and probably wept trying to achieve results that would satisfy Carl. Slowly, I won over Bill Gladstone, the head compositor. "Get it right, get it right," he would grumble, mimicking me. "What the hell do I care if it takes all day to letterspace a title page? I get paid the same." But Bill liked doing good work and was a buffer when John Morris, the silent partner, howled that I was bankrupting the firm.

Like so many little men, John possessed the aggressiveness of a bantam rooster. "Presses standing idle by the hour while you fuss over makeready," he expostulated with angry puffs of breath. "A dozen new type faces ordered within a month. Gladstone tied up so that on fifty other jobs we are paying overtime. Good God, you're driving us to the poorhouse."

"You should take pride in your work," Bill teased, again mimicking me.

"Pride he says! Can I eat it? Does it pay the bills? I was happy before that damn Rollins started sticking his nose into my business."

Gladstone looked archly at Little John. "Shall I stop?"

"For God's sake, after all we've invested? You heard him. Get it right."

John Morris went back to the front office, leaving a trail of grumbles. But often his eyes betrayed a sudden gentleness, a flash of enthusiasm. He would hold up a proof sheet from the press after the makeready had been completed and nod. "Show that to your confounded Rollins and tell him to stop clacking over the kind of work we do."

"John," I said, "I'm glad you like me."

"If I didn't love you I'd have driven you away with a shotgun weeks ago!" A sheepish smile crept across his lips. The presses were running now and we could hear the hiss of the dryer as each sheet tumbled into the rack. Bill Gladstone broke up a form so that everything would be in readiness for tomorrow's dogfight. Little John carried the press proofs back to the front office where he could study them in leisure. Maybe pride would not fill his belly, but the spirit also needed nourishment. "Not bad," he muttered, folding up his proofs. "Not half bad." He pushed the time sheet under the blotter. Tomorrow he would tally that up with a breaking heart, but tonight he would sleep with his pride.

The battle was not won quickly or easily, and for long weeks, after standing for hours in that print shop I dragged myself wearily up the hill to my office in Old Queen's. My hands were filthy and ink smudges covered my face. Starling laughed. Soap and water and rest could repair these damages. Meanwhile I was helping to turn journeymen printers into sound craftsmen.

While we were training Thatcher-Anderson to our requirements Carl Rollins decided that for immediate results, such as improving the appearance of the university catalog, we could write specifications that only the better printers in the state could meet. I knew that without Hop's support this scheme was never going to get off the ground and told him so. "Will that monkey back you up?" Hop asked, meaning Carl. I nodded. But how about Cy? "You leave that monkey to me," Hop answered. He picked up the day's *Wall Street Journal* and set off across campus to "soften up" Cy.

And so, like George Little, we dug our hole, and what ultimately we would put into it was a great deal more than Cy or

Hop or Reed or even ourselves suspected. In time a door opened
in Old Queen's and in walked Curlette H. Wilhelm, a man almost
as unbelievable as his name.

❧

Curley's father was a circus man who ran off to South
America. The stars were right in deciding that Curley should
become a self-made man, for no one but Curley could have
produced the intelligent, cunning, incorrigible, clownish, loving, aggressively ambitious, successful, outrageous person that
I came to know and to adore. He was some fifteen years my
senior, this Gulliver among the Lilliputs. A round, jolly face gave
this portly fellow a resemblance to the North Wind in a child's
picture book; his hair was mostly gone, creating an illusion of a
Christmas tree ornament popping through puffs of cotton, and
his rather prominent nose was useful when he fell into a mood
to imitate Jimmy Durante. His energy was inexhaustible, permitting him to work all day and play all night; and if ever there
was a man whose wife did not know that he drank until he made
the mistake of coming home sober, possibly in those years Curley
inspired that joke. His infectious warmth made almost everyone like him: publishers, authors, editors, college presidents, professors, headwaiters, bartenders, race track touts.

Reed was one of the rare exceptions. He was standoffish toward Curley, perhaps because he was a symbol of the Big Business that Reed instinctively distrusted. I was the peacemaker,
smoothing out the ruffles between them that sometimes became
tidal waves. At this time Curley was executive vice-president of
the Haddon Craftsmen, a book manufacturing plant in Camden
that had been entrusted with the university catalog at the dawn
of our new era in printing. Whereas the typography was quite
satisfactory, we judged the presswork to be dreadful. With some
justification Curley blamed this misfortune on the quality of the

paper we had supplied, but Reed, in an obvious mood to cut down Mr. Big Business, demanded a full refund.

Curley slapped a hand against his forehead as though Reed had struck him with a poisoned arrow. "A full refund? My God, what kind of crappus-de-lappus is this?"

Reed glowered, bracing for a fight. Beads of perspiration glistened on Curley's bald top. I suggested a 10 percent penalty as fair and Curley agreed, saying afterward: "Kid, you're all right and I'm on your side from herein." Reed consented grudgingly—"for Flash's sake," he made clear—and he was filled with dark warnings afterward:

"Be careful of that fellow, Flash. You don't know how you can be hurt in the cutthroat world beyond the campus."

I hid a smile. Who but Reed had essayed the role of cutthroat? Increasingly, Reed was living in the past, groping for some unfulfilled part of himself. He never had wanted renown as the boy poet of Rahway but as captain of the Grand Street baseball team. But this honor had gone to Lou Rubin, whose father owned the neighborhood candy store. "If I only had the time and money," he muttered. "There's a real story there."

Meanwhile Scotty and Bill Cole were brimming with new ideas for Rutgers. In order to encourage intellectual growth within the faculty, the establishment of a university press was proposed. Cy, Hop, and Reed were wary, each for his own motive. Hop was the frankest: "What in a nanny's petticoat do you monkeys know about the publishing business?" He expected the answer, growling: "Yeah, yeah, you can say you can learn and once more I get stuck in the middle." With Hop grumpiness amounted to surrender. With Cy the worry was money—not only with us and George Little and every department head in the university with a go-ahead spirit, but also with those trustees who were forever paying architects for drawing up and revising plans for future buildings. "A hobby they play with university money," Hop said.

Reed tried not to admit that he was wearying of his lifetime as the master myth maker. It may be all right for a Bernard Baruch to describe middle age as seventeen years away from the present moment, but Reed could feel the years creeping by. A night out now meant a day in, a telltale sign. Story ideas kept filling his mind: he wanted to break away, to have his chance to grow professionally. He began talking of how the university owed him a sabbatical year and, as this notion grew, anything new within his department, such as a university press, posed a threat. "Some day," he said, "I'd like to be dean of men."

Starling and I had our own motives for wanting to see our opportunities expand, for we were anxious to begin raising a family. We never had accepted Reed's belief that the world beyond the campus was better forgotten since a future of limited horizons placed us in a crippled world, a handicap that could only exist if we surrendered without a struggle.

"You can't hide behind a disability," Starling said. "If you grow in mind and ability—if you can offer services that other people need—what difference does an affliction make?"

⋙

Institutions survive because in situations of tangled emotions a way is found to keep everyone happy. We all agreed that as soon as circumstances permitted, Reed should have his year off, and since he would add to his other titles that of director of the university press while I did all the work, he tended to view the project more cheerfully. The Board of Trustees appropriated $1,200 to start a Press, and the librarian diverted $700 from other funds to aid in its establishment. These sums were the total capitalization of the Rutgers University Press, but in university undertakings, success or failure often depends on whether the bookkeeping is friendly or unfriendly.

To me the Press was a second intellectual awakening, and

in the same warm-hearted way that Carl Rollins led me into the enchantments of the graphic arts my tutor in publishing became Philip Van Doren Stern, who had graduated from Rutgers in 1924 and was now production manager for Simon & Schuster.

Phil was an alumnus who did not fit the image of the myth makers: his years in college had been anything but delirious and if he had not been able to bury himself among the books in the university library he might well have run away from the damn place. Shy by nature, Phil appeared to be reserved and stand-offish, but underneath he was a man of unrestrained intellectual passions. He would talk about Lincoln and the Civil War for hours, for these were his deepest loves. He was happily cynical toward the source of his own basic income, insisting that all publishers dreamed of a day when they could perfect a machine that would take a ream of blank paper at one end and produce a finished book at the other, thus dispensing forever with the nuisance of live authors.

Curley joined Phil in fathering my apprenticeship and I became a starry-eyed youngster sitting at the feet of the masters. My circle of publishing mentors grew: Louis Greene from *Publishers' Weekly*, Harry Dale from the Book-of-the-Month Club, Louis Untermeyer (who eventually edited two books for the Press), and Eddie Patella who sold the South for Groset & Dunlap. From each I learned much: I was a hundred times more mentally alive than I had ever been as a college undergraduate. Knowledge brought confidence; I was ready to go anywhere, including Princeton.

Most Rutgers men in those days nurtured an inferiority complex toward Princeton, which by a crow's flight is about seventeen miles from New Brunswick. For many years this diffidence stemmed from the fact that after beating Princeton 6 to 4 in America's first game of intercollegiate football, the old school had not won another game since that 1869 affair and now had fallen to the low level of not even getting on the Princeton schedule. Another side of this Rutgers sheepishness rose from the physical character of the two communities: New Brunswick is one of those tumbling-down commercial places with which New Jersey is littered, whereas Princeton is one of the world's most beautiful college towns.

Of course to George Little such meekness was the sheerest poppycock. Hell, George said, if he could build a stadium he could schedule Princeton and beat 'em to boot, which is precisely what Rutgers did in the official stadium dedication game. "I'll be down on Lake Carnegie with the Rutgers crew one of these days and they'll know it," George said; he was no shrinking violet. His drive and enthusiasm were contagious as far as I was concerned, and if the Princeton University Press could teach me what I needed to know, that was where I was heading.

Whitney Darrow, Sr., of Scribners, a friend from the University Club, was the fathering spirit behind the Princeton University Press and perhaps he spoke a kindly word in my behalf. Joe Brandt was then the Princeton director and since there is a trace of the Assyrian merchant in most publishers, they envied Joe's string of successful books and complained bitterly over university presses invading the commercial field. But Joe was helped by a staff as good as any in the business: Datus Smith, his editor, was urbane, brilliant, alert; Red Samuels, his sales manager, was cordial, good-humored and knowledgeable concerning the tricks of the trade; and P. J. Conkright, his designer, was of the cut of a Carl Rollins. Joe himself was an imaginative, warm fellow who threw open his door and his heart to a neophyte. I learned all Joe would teach and dreamed of what it meant to build a university press like this.

Hop frowned over these visits. "Don't go getting the idea you'll ever be in a league with those Princeton monkeys," he warned. "Their own presses and building and full-page advertisements in the *New York Times*—ha, there's a laugh for you and most of all for that monkey in the comptroller's office."

"Maybe so," I said reluctantly.

But the day would come when I received an orchid from the Princeton staff. And by special messenger.

CHAPTER ELEVEN

Philadelphia
and
Points West

$O_{n\ a\ bright,}$

sunshiny day in October of 1939, our first child, David, was born. Dr. Emerson Hird, who attended Starling, was a gruff but kindly old fellow with a wisp of chin whiskers that always reminded me of a nanny goat. We should be satisfied with a single child, he advised seriously.

In an oversensitive mood, I suspected that Old Chin Whiskers doubted my ability to feed more than two additional mouths, but after another twenty-five years of association with doctors I changed my mind. Dr. Hird, as the parent of an only child, fell into a pattern among medical people: the chubby ones tend to advise me to put on weight, the skinny ones like to see me slim, and I sometimes imagine that the surgeons lost soap-carving contests in their youths and became anxious to demonstrate to humanity how well they can handle cutting tools.

A box of cigars under my arm, I was dizzily happy over the arrival of what Hop called "Flash's new boy monkey" (a not inept description of an infant at birth). President Clothier beckoned me into the office and I grew conscious of the great warmth between us. "There is only one better moment than this," he said. "One day you'll bring your second child home and say to your wife, 'The *children* are sleeping.'"

Dr. Hird had lost his argument within the first twenty-four hours: the Boss, like Starling and myself, did not believe in one-child families. I spent a pleasant hour in the president's office, talking about the past and future. He was pleased with the Press and expected it to grow. He smiled at my earnest plea for Reed's sabbatical year; in time, he said, easygoing with connivers whose appointments filled the better part of his day. Perhaps a harder taskmaster never lived, for Clothier could fuss for hours over minute details while the staff despaired; and yet there was a place in his heart for others, a compassion that was deep and real, and in this respect he was a very gifted man. Since my trouble with Dr. Will he had stood behind me, firm in his belief that I could find a good life. What I was learning from Dr. Clothier became a rule of life: it is men at the top, men used to taking responsibility, who play down a disability and play up the human being. In contrast, a personnel director is likely to be far more critical of the physical limitations he can observe, but then he is himself a jobholder who feels his greatest security in playing proven averages.

᪐

Both Starling and I were quite unprepared for the tragedy the following year brought. Jack Wyckoff, Starling's brother, was barely in his thirties when he died. I watched Starling's parents, trembling with grief, implore within their hearts: "Why did this have to happen?" There was no answer. Nor had there been an answer when my cousin Herbert, who was less than ten, was killed hooking his sled onto the back of a car. In both cases, part of the parents also died. Starling came home from the funeral, quiet and shaken; she clutched our baby with a fierce tenderness and I prayed that God would allow him to grow and enjoy a full life.

Another blow awaited us within a month. Years of sporadic medical care began to tell on Father; often he was bedridden and wracked with pain and then he contracted a streptococcus infection in that time when so little was known about sulfa drugs. One bleak, wintry day, in his sixty-second year, the struggle ended.

You never forget a man like my father: not in your heart. He was buried in the old cemetery in Colt's Neck not far from where his baby LeRoy had rested all these years. There was no autumn mellowness as in those early days of my childhood when we had picnicked in this country graveyard and Father had hugged us all as the horses found their way back to the farm. On this sad day, the weather turned raw and blustery, as though heaven itself were heartbroken. I had placed in the grave a relic of my freshman year in college—a prayer that was set to music and sometimes is still sung at university functions:

> We, men of Rutgers, bow in prayer
> To ask Thy blessing, loving care,
> Provision for our many needs,

Thy guidance in our daily deeds.
Protect us, God, as we go on
To meet the challenge of the dawn.

We, men of Rutgers, turn to Thee
To make our hearts beat pure and free,
To see the glimmer of the light
That leads us into paths of right.
As we trod old Rutgers' sod
Keep us ever near Thee, God.

My faith, then and still, is childlike and unquestioning like Father's. I have never shaken the boyhood habit of talking directly to God, sometimes prayerfully, sometimes sassily.

⁓§

With time the dearness of memory healed the sadness of death and the flow of life resumed with all its old compelling insistency. Despite the short stories that I sold consistently to the Sunday School publications, we felt the pinch of Starling's loss of salary and came to understand, with a growing child, why drug stores prosper. We moved to one house because we needed more space and then to another house nearer New Brunswick to cut down on the cost of commuting.

We lived now within a stone's throw of where the Hall-Mills murder had occurred. The famous crab-apple tree under which the minister and his choir-singing mistress had loved and perished long since had been stripped to the ground by souvenir seekers, and the Pig Woman, whose testimony once had titillated America, had vanished. The house itself was one of those jerry-built constructions, vintage of World War I, that was depressingly without any semblance of charm. The stairway was in the dining room so that at meal time any excursion to the bathroom halted conversation; and the three bedrooms off the upper hallway were like freight cars abandoned on a siding.

Starling and I experienced real terror in this house, for here, one muggy summer's day, David became desperately ill. Dr. Hird could not hide his concern, muttering that the symptoms were similar to those of polio.

The torment of such moments leaves deep scars. Old superstitions, rooted for thousands of years in emerging civilization, suddenly come alive. Looking down at the suffering child, one thinks: What have I done? Why is he being punished? One looks at blank walls, at the stars, at the blackness of a sleepless night, wondering, confused, overwhelmed by a sense of guilt that is illusive and yet dreadfully close and real. The child's whimpering is like a knife thrust, and the ticking moments pulsate with a growing belief of personal unworthiness. Suppose this child should lose the use of his arms or legs . . . the terrible prospects stretch out, and prayer falls into a silent chant: Why? Dear God, why?

I thought of my father at the time of my birth sitting hour after hour between his wife and afflicted baby. Was this, too, how he felt? Years later when I would meet hundreds of parents seeking an answer to why through an accident of birth, highway or battlefield, their sons and daughters had been permanently crippled, these hours of David's suffering allowed me to understand intimately why their eyes could look so haunted. I would see that look in New York and California, in Minnesota and Texas. This searing experience was universal.

In time David's illness, whatever it was, passed away and we heard him tinkling the bell on his racing tricycle or romping with our mongrel dog which, like a devotee of printing, I had named Pi.

But this house was suddenly unendurable. We had to move even if I had to find some new source of income. Luck played into my hands, for the Westminster Press, which is the publishing name for the book program of the Board of Christian Education of the Presbyterian Church in America, offered me on a part-time basis the position of trade editor which meant commuting to Philadelphia two days a week. Yet my annual salary at Westminster would exceed that from the university. I was now thirty-one, strong and healthy; I saw no conflict in running an expanding university press, all the university publications, and the operation at Westminster, and, with these three jobs, I had no intention of giving up my writing.

The decision became Reed's to make. All his life outside work had made his existence endurable; he could comprehend my motives. Again he reached deep into the past, remembering those first two years at the college when he had commuted between Rahway and New Brunswick. He had ached to live on campus, for he was missing so much. Four newspapers had appointed him their Rutgers correspondent, but still he would have been short of funds if he had not received five dollars a week teaching junior and senior English at Miss Anable's School for Girls. Miss Anable required Lycidas in English IV, about whom he knew nothing, but he had learned as he taught. He also was an Alger boy born to fight his way from rags to riches. He consented to the Philadelphia experiment.

"The college will still be here for you, if it doesn't work out," he said. And suddenly he seemed to reverse his strategy: "It's good to take chances when you're young and strong." He fell into a reflective mood, puffing resolutely on that old corncob, and his thoughts, I knew, were of that sabbatical year he coveted.

Like Brooklyn, Philadelphia is more than a community: it is a way of life. People who joke, "I came to Philly on Sunday but it was closed," hit close to the truth. But on Monday, Billy Penn's "goode greene towne" awakens as west down the Main Line on the Paoli Local, north from Germantown and Chestnut Hill, south from Wilmington, across the river from Camden, the commuters pour in. Dutifully they alight at the same stations and walk the same paths to their offices, for Philadelphians like to cling to old habits: to eat year in, year out in the same restaurants and to live in the same neighborhoods until Gabriel comes blowing his horn, and to toil for half a century in the same business establishments and, more than likely, at the same desks. You cannot beat out of a Philadelphian his love for scrapple. Or for pepper pot soup. Or for the Mummers Parade on New Year's Day. Old-timers will tell you that the string bands in these parades are of recent origin and when you press them to explain what they mean, they'll tell you: "Well, the bands didn't appear until 1915."

To fall in love with the names of Philadelphia streets is one of the pleasures of Billy Penn's Holy Experiment, and in spring children prance along the sidewalks, singsonging:

> High, Mulberry, Sassafras, Vine;
> Chestnut, Walnut, Spruce and Pine.

Old ladies (doubtless in the same hats) have been coming in for the Friday afternoon concerts of the Philadelphia Academy of Music for as long as fifty years and Connie Mack, who joined the Athletics in 1901, stayed even longer. To meet in front of the eagle at Wanamaker's is a custom long established and as imperishable as the crack in the Liberty Bell or Ben Franklin's statue atop City Hall. The Witherspoon Building at the corner of Juniper and Walnut, where I worked, was by now another reliable Philadelphia landmark. The elevators were operated by a hand crank on a wheel and the shaft was open so that you could see from the top floor to the basement, a sobering experience that made you grateful the Presbyterians were laboring on the Lord's side.

A denominational publishing house posed problems not unfamiliar to one who had served an apprenticeship as a university myth maker. All sorts of taboos were placed on what could be published. Sex in any vital sense simply did not exist, the word "damn" amounted to blasphemy, and there was considerable confusion over where earthly ignorance and holy innocence divided.

This outward calm, however, was deceptive. A leading official and churchman thought it a huge joke to greet visitors with the sly comment: "Say, did you see in the *Inquirer* today a list of people who are not going to trade any longer with Jews?" With a burst of laughter he handed the puzzled visitor the obituary page. Yet one would have been the sorriest of fools not to sense the underlying prejudice against Jews, condemning them as a race for the crucifixion. Roman Catholics fared little better and "go kiss the Pope's foot" had the demeaning connotation of a longshoreman's lustier epithets. Drinking was a forbidden subject in the fiction we published, but the staff was not without those who liked to hit the bottle to the point of bordering on rum-dums. On racism as it affected Negroes these churchmen were militantly aligned with the blacks, and with equal vigor championed the right of the handicapped to escape from superstitions that so often were founded on the doctrine of original sin.

"This crowd," I told Starling, "invented ambivalence."

Like people who tell their friends, "You write such beautiful letters you should write a book," people who believe anyone can become an editor are misguided clowns. In most cases the letter writers are not really exceptional, and even if they were they would still lack the talent and technique that must go into the creation of a book. And good editors are even rarer than good authors, for this craft requires a marriage of bright intellect and personal humility. An editor who tells an author how to write a book is not an editor but a frustrated author, and there is a special lower circle in hell awaiting him. The true editor must take the time, though it may well exhaust his patience, to penetrate the author's stream of consciousness. On awkward passages he asks, "What are you trying to say?" and as the author explains his ideas, the possibilities are strong that he will automatically rewrite the troubling parts of his manuscript. But not necessarily all. Still, it is a tyrant and not an editor who fails to realize that no one paragraph should make or break a book.

Luckily the operation at Westminster was entrenched by the fact that the Presbyterians owned their own chain of book stores and numerous periodicals that appealed directly to this special clientele. In the children's field, in which we specialized, our authors were experienced and well-established, attracted in no small measure by the dividend of separate payment for serialization in the various church school publications that Westminster Press also issued.

The real professionals taught me more than I taught them, and quickly they clarified the distinction between the mechanics of editing and the craft of editing. After all, correcting grammar, punctuation, and spelling is stylizing and not editing; and checking names and dates is expertizing and not editing. Beyond these chores must rest that intellectual fellowship between editor and author which respects the author's right to be heard. Here comes the test, the stress, the exhaustion in the craft: here the editor must turn into the selfless catalyst, the unknown confidant, the sharer of dreams he cannot possess but only recognize. He guides, he encourages, he inspires, he coddles and virtually wet-nurses and, not infrequently, in seeking an explosive mental insight into his problems, he drinks too much.

These were some of the lessons I learned during my three years at Westminster. Pat Jenkins, the director of the press, seemed far more interested in church politics than trade publishing, which may explain why I was given a free hand. Clarke Hannaford, the sales manager, was a happy-go-lucky, roly-poly sort who, by simply changing hats, could peddle anything from pulpit chimes to books for beginners.

I grew to love Philadelphia and from the time the train rumbled over the bridge at Trenton onto the soil of Pennsylvania my heartbeat quickened. I became as habit-bound as a native, lunching at the same table at Henri's, eating pepper pot and scrapple almost without variation, drinking the same Scotch while staring at the same pornographic prints, and always waited on by Carl who stood by discreetly anticipating the same tip. Then came that walk to the wonderland of Leary's with its floor upon floor of secondhand books and I loaded my arms with classics bought for a nickel or a dime a copy. Or I haunted the extensive book department at Wanamaker's, where I would watch people buy books and eavesdrop on their conversations, trying to understand what impelled them to select the volumes they did. Evenings, when I stayed over to entertain an author, always were spent at the Warwick for the soundest of reasons for here also could be found my childhood pets, the Brooklyn Dodgers, whenever they were in town.

H. L. Mencken called Philadelphia "the most pecksniffian of American towns," but what did this old Baltimore curmudgeon know? How often did he stroll Rittenhouse Square on a sweet spring afternoon? How often did he sky gaze through a summer concert in Robin Hood Dell? True, Baltimore produced bawdier burlesque shows than the old Troc, but what can Baltimore put up against Philadelphia's claim to Chubby Checkers, who gave the teen-age world The Twist?

When my first list at Westminster was ready for presentation to the trade, Clarke Hannaford insisted that I accompany him on his sales trip to Chicago.

We caught The General at Paoli and sat up most of the night, drinking and talking. Just as clergymen are forever preoccupied with sin, which is their stock in trade, so do bookmen discuss endlessly their own products. I doubt if an accountant can talk for ten hours about double entry bookkeeping, but a pair of fuzzy heads in publishing can reel off this stint about a single book without killing more than a fifth of Scotch. Suddenly beyond the darkened windows showed orange-tinted belches of fire, as though, as Mother had warned, hard liquor had floated us into the depths of hell, but we were only passing the steel mills as we approached Pittsburgh.

I slept fretfully, caught up in part by the excitement of train travel, an intoxication that would linger with me for the remainder of life. But I was convinced also that Clarke was crazy-crazy: what, in God's name, was a nervous person doing on a sales trip? I was no Curley, given to glib humor and fast talk. A hundred strange people to meet, to put at ease without stuttering like a hapless idiot—why had I allowed myself to be bullied into this situation? Clarke lapsed into contented snores, but I saw the false dawn followed by the first glimmer of sunlight across the snow-covered Indiana farmland, and a loud-mouthed porter shouted at the conductor that it was a mite nippy outside. The temperature was ten below zero. At Fort Wayne I reset my watch, thinking that it was all right with me if time moved back twenty-four hours and I never boarded the train. Glumly, I picked at my breakfast, frightened and upset.

The approach to Chicago by way of Union Station is bleak and uninspiring. Somewhere after Gary, when glimpses of Lake Michigan begin to punctuate a dreary succession of steel mills, cement plants and smoke-smudged factories, Carl Sandburg's lines become discouragingly real: "Hog Butcher, Tool Maker, Stacker of Wheat, Player with Railroads and Freight Handler of the Nation" . . . from this view, Chicago is all of these. The old Ojibway word, *she-kag-ong,* whence the city derives its name, means "wild onion place," and speeding by the depressing dilapidation of the Negro slums on the South Side you well can wish that the onions were never uprooted. All at once Comiskey Park, where the White Sox play, looms beyond the window and you have a sense of shock: this is still America and no more drab than that ball park amid the slums of North Philly where Connie Mack held sway. Then you tumble out into Union Station, swallowed by the sea of restless commuters who daily flow through this vaulted terminus, and the enormous energy of the town hits you with staggering impact.

Thus—scared, disconcerted, overwhelmed—I stumbled into the Chicago that I would grow to love so dearly I call it my second home. We stayed at that hoity-toity hostelry, The Drake, where the wicker covers on the johnny seats jabbed my bourgeois conscience with a sense of guilt at even requiring to use a bathroom. But Chicago is full of contradictions like this. It is simply the damnedest, most lovable, deplorable, beautiful, decrepit, sophisticated, naïve, wonderful, crummy, unpredictable, mixed-up city in America. You can always take your choice in Chicago: it is only a five-minute walk from the Art Institute on Michigan Avenue with its world-renowned collection of French Impressionists to the country's dirtiest peep shows on South State.

To master the fact that the meandering Chicago River divides the city into a North, West, and South Side does not do too much good; with time and patience you learn that there is also a German Chicago and a Polish Chicago, an Italian Chicago and a Yiddish Chicago, a Greek Chicago and a Lithuanian Chicago. In this metropolis slums rub elbows with the gold coast, and never far away are those screechy honky-tonks that somehow cannot quite outgrow the loose morals of the Capone era.

Chicago is bums sleeping off a drunk on the sidewalks of Skid Row, and nutty orators haranguing a few hungry panhandlers in Bug House Square, and cops growing sore as hell when Cicero mobsters dump their stiffs across the city line, and the Moody Bible Tabernacle, and quiet parks and museums and university campuses, and the town that launched old Abe Lincoln on his way to immortality, and a lake front where yachtsmen cruise and lovers startle summertime visitors with their surrender to Aphrodite. To sum it all up, I guess that North Side politician was right when he took for his campaign motto: "Chicago ain't ready for reform." It sure ain't . . . not this open-faced, warm-

179

hearted, giddy-headed frontier town that, as the songsters pro-
claim, even Billy Sunday couldn't shut down.

The image of a city that lingers in the heart is not constructed of brick and mortar but of flesh and blood. An unaffected
friendliness combined with a toughness of mind gave the Mid-
western personality a spirit to which my own nature responded
instinctively. Those fears that had haunted me as The General
sped across the Indiana countryside were quickly dispelled as
Clarke introduced me to the giants of the Chicago book trade
in that age: shrewd yet gentle Papa Kroch, a legend in the
Windy City; that devoted cultivator of orchids and drawer to
inside straights, Wendell Goodpasture, who is no small part
of the genius behind the Kroch-Brentano empire; those incom-
parable gentlemen, Guy Kendall of A. C. McClurg and Ralph
Henry of Carson, Pirie, Scott; Heinz Werner, then of Mandel's,
who watched me with a birdlike intensity as he measured my
reactions in terms of his own cerebral-palsied daughter; Rose
Oller Harbugh, the female dynamo of Marshall Field, who gave
me a motherly embrace and chuckled: "Don't ever be fooled by
an old war horse like me—I can be had." What in a single day
these people did to give faith and strength to a very frightened
young man—and did so because it was the normal way they lived
and reacted—they could never know. For years, coming back to
Chicago, I no longer saw the drabness of the South Side as the
train rumbled toward Union Station: I saw these faces with a
feeling of eager anticipation.

If Fred Babcock or Fanny Butcher of the *Chicago Tribune*
ever noticed my handicap, I was never aware of that fact. And
there is a special place in my heart—as I believe there is in
heaven—for the Tribune's Kelsey Guilfoil. Officially Kelsey was
Fred's assistant, but Fred and I and everyone else knew better:
Kelsey was the conscience of the *Tribune's* book section. He was
a pitiful little hunchback to behold, this sweet-tempered man;
he felt pain that he rarely admitted, most of all commuting. But

Kelsey's philosophy of life was to be found in an old Hindu proverb: "I had no shoes—and I murmured until I met a man who had no feet."

Kelsey was a bookman of sensitive tastes, a friend of unyielding loyalty, a drinking companion of respectable staying ability.

Another among Chicago's fourth estate who won my quick affection was Dave Appel, then book editor of the *Daily News* and later of the *Philadelphia Inquirer*. Dave was a victim of polio with a dragging leg and a twisted arm; he had a round, benign face with curly, upended hair and you half expected him to spend his days in a synagogue studying the Torah and Talmud for he was a Jew who looked like a rabbi, and like Kelsey he bore the nuisance of his disability with a disarming graciousness. Two men for Reed to ponder, I thought: men unafraid of the rough and tumble world beyond a campus.

꿏

As my second home, Chicago continued to capture me, the more so after Paul Angle came up from Springfield to be Director of the Chicago Historical Society (but I shall hold Paul off-stage at this moment, for once he puts his foot into these pages, he will be hard to get out). Meanwhile, my circle of friends grew. Huyler's then was across from The Drake, and here Lloyd Lewis, whose *Sherman, Fighting Prophet* was a classic and who now was embarked on the research for his definitive life of Grant, would keep the table spellbound as a knowledge of the Civil War spilled out of him. Lloyd made no secret of why he had turned to history. "My God," he said one day, "being editor of the *Daily News* was terrorizing. Each morning I dashed out trembling with the fear that one of my editorials may have agreed with something in the *Tribune*!"

Another afternoon could be given over to the charm of Wright and Zoe Howes with their rare books, tea and cats; the

Howes were living encyclopedias of American bibliography. Or I could ride the elevated through the Loop to the South Side to see Era Bell Thompson, whose *An American Daughter* was a truly sensitive autobiography of a Negro girl; and together we would see Johnny Johnston, who was making a fortune from *Ebony Magazine* by teaching advertisers that Negroes represented a luxury market despite their ghetto homes.

My friendship with Ralph Newman goes back a quarter of a century to that time when, in partnership with John Valentine, his Abraham Lincoln Bookshop stood on the floor above Cook's Travel Agency on Michigan Avenue. From the start Ralph was called by detractors a pusher looking for a fast buck, but these persons mistook Ralph's wild enthusiasm for bluff whereas this quality in Ralph was exactly what it pretended to be: wild enthusiasm. If Ralph were not a genius he was at least the genius-type, and the one can be as wearing as the other on the less imaginative. But the reward for those who understood was a friendship that wore like an old shoe.

Of course, trying to fathom the many sides of Ralph was like seeking one's way through a maze. He was a dealer in books, manuscripts, and autographs, a part-time literary agent, an occasional author, editor, and newspaper columnist, entrepreneur of a book club and the only quarterly specializing in the memorabilia of Franklin D. Roosevelt, intimate friend of Carl Sandburg, Adlai Stevenson, Bruce Catton, Allan Nevins and God knows who else, appraiser of private collections (including the Truman manuscripts), accoucheur of every important Lincoln and Civil War enterprise during the past twenty-five years, innovator of radio and television programs, lecturer, politician, and the despair of those who misjudged him as a hopeless scatterbrain.

He spent money like a prodigal, and would have starved years ago if his two faithful co-workers, Margaret April and Dick Clark, did not exhaust themselves tying up "the loose ends." He has helped so many historians with contracts, research, subsidiary rights, cocktail parties, and an occasional loan that no one keeps count any more. I never know where next Ralph will be encountered: at a luncheon at the White House ("They've changed this place around," Ralph will say, indicating that he has been here before); in cap and gown on a commencement platform where I was receiving an honorary doctorate (he is also a college trustee); at Statesville when Nathan Leopold of the Leopold-Loeb murder was judged rehabilitated and deserving of a pardon (he is likewise a humanitarian); and at celebrations in the nation's capital sitting in the front row of the speaker's platform (for he is incurably a ham).

At last count he operated one bookstore in Chicago, one in the state capital at Springfield and two in New Salem, where Lincoln rounded into manhood and may have cast calf-eyes at Ann Rutledge. There is a cavern under the Lincoln Memorial in Washington that only needs an entrance and shoring up to make a curio shop, but at last report Ralph had not exploited this opportunity.

There, in thumbnail, stands the Ralph Newman I first met in shirtsleeves, moving like a ferret among the book cases on the floor above Cook's Travel Agency. In a way he symbolized the city that had spawned him: ambitious, generous, opportunistic, earthy, urbane, unafraid—a Rush Street sucker combined with the North Side builder of dynasties.

So grew the city in my heart . . . this city of Papa Kroch and Guy Kendall, of Lloyd Lewis and Ralph Newman, of Kelsey Guilfoil and Dave Appel. It had more for me emotionally than Philadelphia, much more than New Brunswick. I know that most Midwesterners feel they have not arrived until they reach New York, but I was born backward and so, quite naturally, went the other way.

≈§

But New Brunswick was home base, family, my fundamental job, and much was happening here. In 1941, Reed was round-ing out at long last that so coveted sabbatical year. He had summered in Maine and was now wintering in Florida, having borrowed $2,500 from a generous alumnus. Part of his dream came true: the story about the mother he had sent home to a lonely lunch on the 12:17 train became *Stars in the Sky* and was published in *Good Housekeeping*; the same periodical published *To a Brown-eyed Girl*, the story inspired by Lou Rubin, whose father had owned the neighborhood candy store and who had edged out Rahway's boy poet for the captaincy of the Grand Street baseball team. "We learned that this one free year was not an entity in itself but rather an integral part of other years," he wrote afterward; but I am not sure either he or I fully understood why.

He was glad to come back to the college, to take up former tasks, to work off the $2,500 he owed, and to embrace again the security of the old campus. The life of the full-time writer is one of hard self-discipline; it is a way of life without prescribed hours, for the subconscious mind must keep on working while the body slumbers. It is a lonely and sometimes desperate existence best pictured by a man and his typewriter sitting at the bottom of a deep well. Reed had tasted the adventure, in part, and had called the experience "stimulating and worthwhile"; but deep down he *knew*: if this was the life he truly wanted, he had waited too long to make the change.

His loyalty to the institution would not have permitted him to break free anyhow, for soon he was needed acutely. That December brought Pearl Harbor and leaning on the counter in Hop Brill's campus bookstore Reed and I listened to the radio as F.D.R. spoke soberly of "a day which will live in infamy." Reed turned away quietly, his lower lip caught in his teeth; his thoughts were of his son, Sam, who would soon be called to action. "God knows what will happen," he said, and he walked back to the office, like so many millions of parents that Monday, lost in his own silent prayers.

Gas rationing and price controls were the least of the disloca-
tions that those war years produced. The university fell apart
momentarily, then was patched-up on a war basis and seemed
more vital than ever. My nephew, LeRoy Danks, came down to
Rutgers that fall, but like so many his heart was not on books;
the war, the war was what he saw on every page; and he was
one of several who soon was gone to his ultimate destination of
flying the Hump.

LeRoy Danks and Sam Silvers were only two . . . the office
mail was filled with hundreds of letters from youngsters whom,
it seemed, we had seen only yesterday on campus and now were
in boot camp or on their way overseas. Clark Lee of the AP on
Bataan and Martin Agronsky, rarely more than a step ahead of
the advancing Japanese as he broadcast the news from the Pacific, were Rutgers boys we knew, and their dispatches, their
voices above the crackling static were poignantly personal.

From the start we decided to publish in the *Alumni Monthly* every letter that expressed the experiences and emotions of
these fighting men, and one day some perceptive historian will
be grateful for these columns of material reflecting how a group
of soldiers drawn from a common cultural background responded
to this many-sided war. Thinking of Sam, Reed wrote his heart
out in support of these valiant lads. When all America was
stirred by the four chaplains aboard the sinking *Dorchester* who
gave up their own lifebelts and, joining hands, went down with
the ship, I was deeply affected. One of that quartet, Clark Poling,
had been a classmate. Vaguely my memory recalled a quiet,
mild-mannered boy with a shy smile walking to class with books
under his arm; he was no hero fashioned on the football field
(as the myth makers were forever proclaiming in those days in
defense of intercollegiate athletics). The Clark I remembered
had locked the courage of a principle and a faith within his
private heart.

Cynics rather scorned the war then: it was a bitter war,

they said, fought without compelling spiritual conviction; but the letters that poured into the office, even when the censor's razors made them look like lace doilies, belied the cynics. What these years of anguish meant required a perspective that neither Reed nor I possessed, yet the magnificence of its significance tantalized us; and later a historian of the stature of Arthur M. Schlesinger, Jr., would capture completely the mood for which we groped when he characterized John F. Kennedy as "the first representative in the White House of a distinctive generation, the generation which was born during the First World War, came of age during the depression, fought in the Second World War and began its public career in the atomic age." And Schlesinger continued:

> This was the first generation to grow up as the age of American innocence was coming to an end. To have been born nearly a decade earlier, like Lyndon Johnson, or nearly two decades earlier, like Adlai Stevenson, was to be rooted in another and simpler America. Scott Fitzgerald had written that his contemporaries grew up "to find all Gods dead, all wars fought, all faiths in man shaken." But the generation which came back from the Second World War found that gods, wars and faith in man had, after all, survived, if in queer and somber ways. . . . Instead of reveling in being a lost generation, they set out in one mood or another to find, if not themselves, a still point in the turning world. . . .*

Too often, friends of only a few years ago on the campus did not return. We heard of their deaths—shot down in an air raid over Germany, riddled by Japanese machine gunners on some God-forsaken beachhead in the far Pacific—and the sunlight of the day paled, the laughter of the workaday world sounded hollow. One of our office favorites was Dotty Smith, a pert, intelligent, affectionate blonde who was engaged to marry

---

*Arthur M. Schlesinger, Jr., *A Thousand Days.* 113.

186

a likable, rough-and-tumble athlete named Vinnie Utz. Vinnie had been one of the heroes of the victory over Princeton in the stadium dedication game and it was said that in scrimmage he jumped in the air and landed on his head in the belief that this exercise strengthened his neck. "Utz is nuts," Reed would giggle with a special fondness, and no one should have been surprised when Vinnie became a paratrooper. We declared that Vinnie would breeze through the war—dumb luck would spare him—but underneath we fretted, for his sake and Dotty's.

The blow came unexpectedly during the Battle of the Bulge: Utz had lost his right arm. "But he's alive," Dotty said with savage intensity. One arm less, what did it matter—to her. And to him? None of us talked nonsense. We knew this girl and her courage, and we knew Vinnie and his pride. When you were born with a visible handicap, as I was, you inherited a way of life that seemed normal to you because you never knew any other experience. But an acquired disability was like a semi-colon dropped into a sentence; henceforth the meaning could change. Resentment and sensitivity and self-pity could be much deeper, much more destructive of the whole person.

Dotty nodded. She understood. How did a proud man with only a left arm readjust to a right-handed world? She studied every room, every life situation in these terms; her love was strong and beautiful and selfless. She knew that they would have their quarrels, but they would endure and have kids and make a life together that would be rich, and who had a right butting into their business, anyhow? I smiled, remembering the busy-bodies who had gossiped over Starling marrying a man with cerebral palsy.

🦢

Life seemed especially precious to Starling and me when late in 1943 our daughter Meredith was born. David grew like a healthy weed. We lived now in a pretty little house in Milltown, a sleepy, residential community that dreamed of its commercial importance before the Michelin Tire Company had moved away. There were still farms on its main street; and an old French box-car in a nearby field was a relic from the First World War that amused the local airplane spotters as they took up their vigils in this second conflict that had demonstrated the world was still unsafe for democracy.

The Press that was supposed to wither began to flourish. Our selection of titles revealed a war-consciousness: *Price Control: The War Against Inflation, Home Vegetable Gardening* (which in a joint edition with Pocket Books was touted as the helpmate of more than 600,000 Victory Gardeners), *Backyard Poultry Keeping* (a cheap reprint edition was available through the World Publishing Company).

I must have believed I had the strength of an ox during this period, for along with running the Press and handling all university publications I still was commuting to Philadelphia for my two days at Westminster. I told myself that I needed a long vacation all by myself, and went off to a little town called Evergreen in the mountains beyond Denver. It was a goofy idea, but possibly cheaper than hiring a couch and a psychiatrist.

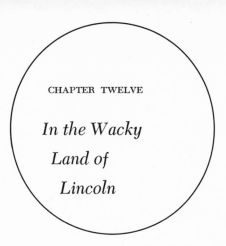

CHAPTER TWELVE

In the Wacky
Land of
Lincoln

*O**nce upon a time,*
or so local legend insists, all of Evergreen, Colorado changed
hands in a poker game and when dawn spread over this mountain resort and the lucky winner gazed upon his newly won domain, he could see in the far distance the snowy crests of the
Continental Divide. In 1943, when as a jittery, exhausted young
man filled with self-pity I alighted from the one bus a day that
connected Denver and Evergreen, the terminus was convenient-

189

ly the town's only saloon, appropriately called the Round Up since the sheriff also hung out there. A fine old lady, who slugged down straight gin without a blink, was also a real estate operator willing to rent me a "furnished" cabin for ten dollars a week.

There were two restaurants in Evergreen, one in a shack that reeked of deep fat, and a rather attractive place recommended by Duncan Hines. The proprietor of the nicer establishment was a cold fish in a ruffled shirt who greeted me with a gritty manner: "Get out, get out, we don't take your kind here."

In anger I demanded an explanation.

"Look at you," he said, "you're shaking. Get out, get out, get out."

I looked like one of my mother's hot flashes. "You'll hear from me," I threatened, but later when I consulted a lawyer in Denver I was told there was not a thing I could do even though I wanted to instigate a test case in behalf of all physically disabled persons. Colorado law gave a proprietor the right to turn away whomever he chose for no better reason than the fact that he disliked their nervousness or the color of their eyes or skin. I surrendered grudgingly; I could not fight the whole state of Colorado any more than I could fight New York City's Fifth Avenue Bus Company because often when my hand trembled handing its drivers a fare, they hissed nastily: "Buddy, why don't you go home and sober up?" For years I sulked over both injustices, then admitted that there was no profit in fretting over the nutty fringe of humanity. Still, unjustly, I continue to feel uneasy entering any restaurant recommended by Duncan Hines.

My Evergreen recuperation developed other difficulties. The cabin the gin-drinking old lady had rented me perched just below the timberline; two lumpy beds, a broken chair, a wobbly table, and a leaking oil stove were its principal accommodations; an ice box on the back steps could not be used because of a restless bear that wandered around at night, slapping apart such contraptions in its search for food. The two rooms, which became steam baths under a broiling sun, turned into arctic mortuaries with nightfall. I tried horseback riding on which I had counted for my chief recreation. Whereas I possessed no horse sense, the mount I hired possessed considerable people sense, knowing a sucker five miles down the road, and once out of sight of the stable he stopped and went to sleep for all I could tell. I shouted, kicked, and sweated away ten pounds before he moved with a peculiar gait that sent the saddle cutting like a knife through my middle. A week later I healed.

So, in the end, my Evergreen recovery settled into the monotonous picture of a brooding young man sitting on a rock in the middle of a mountain stream and admitting that he was a homesick fool who had better return to his wife and children before he died of ptomaine poisoning eating in that shack of a beanery. The answers I sought were not in Colorado but in New Jersey. I was no superman, capable of serving two masters: either I worked full time at Rutgers or Westminster or found another job that would pay the bills. I thumbed my nose at the cabin, the horse, and my gin-drinking landlady and caught the bus to Denver and the airport.

In my heart, I knew I was going to stay at Rutgers for many reasons: the Press was growing and the real opportunity was here; I was fond of Reed and Dr. Clothier and trusted them both; and my family was better protected. One of the true curses of my cerebral palsy was the fact that no company would give me life insurance since there were insufficient actuarial statistics to calculate the risk involved. At least at the university I could be covered by group insurance—I was, at any rate, after a bitter fight with Cy, who had no heart for this type of human relationship.

"My condition"—damn Cy, he alone was forever needling me about "my condition" and using it against me! He set $3,000 as the limit of group insurance which I could carry and I stormed into the president's office where the figure was raised to $7,000—

little enough to protect a wife with two growing children. Cy did not surrender graciously. Quite clearly, he did not approve of handicapped people marrying: he must have been filled with ancient superstitions. He left a ragged wound on my spirit that festered.

President Clothier guessed this conflict. Whenever there was a blowup, and we ended in the president's office, Cy always addressed the boss as "Bob," as though emphasizing the higher level on which they operated. It was a wheedling kind of infighting, and I said so when Dr. Clothier and I were alone.

"Call me Bob if you like," the president said, putting an arm around me.

"No, sir," I said. "You deserve the respect of being called Dr. Clothier by the younger men." His smile had a kind of wispy thoughtfulness that sometimes gave him an elusiveness. But in 1945 when I was named director of the Press it was he who made me responsible only to the president, a status equal to that of a dean. It was he who pushed through the plan to give the Press its own building on the corner of College Avenue and Hamilton Street. It was he who raised my salary steadily and rather quickly to $9,000 a year, which at that time was a good university income. And it was he who stood squarely behind me when I decided that I was going to invade the wacky Land of Lincoln to work out a cooperative publishing agreement with the Abraham Lincoln Association in Springfield, Illinois.

Even the two trains that the Gulf, Mobile & Ohio runs between Chicago and Springfield are called the "Abraham Lincoln" and the "Ann Rutledge." Over three hundred miles of prairie stretch between these two points—most of it planted in corn—and after a while the fleeting landscape casts a hypnotic spell. Small stations flash by, almost unnoticed until one reaches

Bloomington, once famous as the site of Lincoln's "lost speech" but in those mid-1940's immortalized as the home of "Gee Whiz— the best candy bar that is." Lincoln and Nana, I thought—somehow I had the feeling that my genes had predestined this pilgrimage to Springfield. I had a strange sense of confidence: I belonged here.

Springfield is a mood, a glorious experience: the more so, I suspect, to a visiting Easterner who happened to be Nana's grandson. Here stands the home where Lincoln "passed from a young to an old man"; in the heart of town is the old State Capitol where he awakened the nation's conscience with his "house divided" speech and thereafter moved irresistibly toward "a task . . . greater than that which rested upon Washington." Close by is Oak Ridge Cemetery where Lincoln's body finally rests well-embedded in concrete after God knows how many vandals have tried to run off with his corpse. Not far away is the reconstruction of New Salem, that log-cabin village on the Sangamon where a younger Abe wrestled first with the bullies from Clary's Grove and then with the intricacies of frontier law.

I emerged into this heartland of the Lincoln country with a throbbing excitement and sought out the officers of the Abraham Lincoln Association. We met in the bank where Lincoln once had deposited his money, for its president also ruled the destinies of the Association.

In a time when bankers were suspected of having saddled the country with the Depression, Gib Bunn defied the popular stereotype. His was the warm and immediate charm of the shy, unobtrusive gentleman-scholar. When he hesitated in a discussion, he was searching for a felicitous phrase and not calculating a new twist for foreclosing a mortgage. He loved books and Lincoln and among his avocations was the Hobby Horse Press in the basement of his home. Long years before, after graduating from Princeton, he had coveted a literary career. He had moved in those circles where Sinclair Lewis was struggling to emerge and had suggested the title *Main Street* for the novel that since has become a fixture in the nation's literature. Family duty had called him home to Springfield and banking; but the old love lingered—in the gentleness with which he opened a finely made book, in the twinkle in his eyes at a good turn of phrase, in the spirited tone with which he talked of his dreams for the Association. I fidgeted at our first meeting but I was unafraid: gentle men were my refuge.

Our other luncheon companion that day has ever since been so intimately a part of my life and thoughts that it would be folly for me to attempt introducing him objectively. Biographical data about Paul Angle means very little to me. That he came from a small-town, modest Ohio family background and had worked on an ice wagon and in a steel mill and had been a football star at Miami of Ohio before turning to historical scholarship do not portray Paul to me. I know too much about how this fellow thinks and works to recall how he looked that day. I daresay that his pants were buttoned and his face clean-shaven, for he is a meticulously neat man; I daresay that he spoke sensibly and well, for there are no fuzzy edges to his mind; I daresay that he was straightforward about the fact his relationship as executive secretary of the Association soon would end and he was becoming director of the Chicago Historical Society, for he liked all the cards on the table, explaining why he is not much of a poker player; and I daresay that the occasion rang with laughter as bawdy as Gib's sensitivities would permit.

We agreed that the Press would publish in a cooperative arrangement with the Association *A Shelf of Lincoln Books*, which Paul had edited, and shook hands all around. None of us guessed we had made a climactic decision that would change the course of many lives.

"The best of all reasons for studying Lincoln's life is the fact that he was a truly great man," Paul wrote in the introduction to *A Shelf of Lincoln Books*. "He not only influenced the course of history; he also exemplified those virtues to which civilized man has given his highest allegiance—steadfastness, faith in righteousness, humility, and the forgiving spirit. At the same time his humor, his earthiness, his utter lack of pretension made him one with common humanity. To spend time—much time— in such a man's company can be one of life's privileges."*

With those words an idea began to germinate. In *A Shelf* Paul provided a skillful and authoritative analysis of the eighty-one books that seemed essential to a fundamental understanding of the life and times of Lincoln. What, I wondered, would result if Paul extracted the best in each of these books and blended the selections with appropriate editorial comment into a single volume?

A book idea like this frightens an editor. It is too obvious, once he sees it. He asks why it has not been done before; and he is terrorized by the fact that anyone with a sound knowledge of Lincoln literature—or even with average intelligence and a copy of *A Shelf*—could do it. I fretted over this possibility all the way home.

I sought out Curley, who dashed to the phone to summon his old friend Harry Dale, an officer in the Book-of-the-Month Club. Harry came into the University Club with his usual appearance of owlish wonderment. He had known Curley too long not to view this old friend warily: on a boat trip to Hawaii hadn't Curley kept the ship in an uproar by hanging around the slot machines and posing as a journalist investigating gambling in the islands? "He complains," Curley grumbled. "After I get the best suite in the Royal Hawaiian and a car provided by the chief of police!"

Curley was not satisfied with simply explaining my idea to Harry. Had the Book Club ever selected a Lincoln book? Harry thought not.

---

* Paul M. Angle, *A Shelf of Lincoln Books*, XVII.

"Well," Curley exclaimed, slapping Harry's shoulder, "there you are!"

"Where am I?"

"You've got one!"

Harry half rose in self-defense, a reflex he had cultivated around Curley. "The judges pick the books, I don't. You know that. Nothing can be promised . . ."

"Ah," Curley interrupted, "forget the picayune details. Miers, order us another drink and then get off your tail and sign Angle to a contract."

I flew to Chicago and met Paul in his new office at the Historical Society. Within three months Paul had put together two chapters to see if the idea would work. It did. We toiled hard that second meeting, outlining what we intended to call *The Lincoln Reader,* a best seller hand-tailored. The first printing, I promised Paul in a burst of wild enthusiasm, would be 25,000 copies. The possibility of the Book Club was not all popeyed silliness, I insisted. Paul tried not to be bitten by the same bug that had afflicted me but only partially succeeded. He could not, he thought, finish a manuscript in less than a year and a half, and who could tell what might transpire meanwhile? It was now about midnight, we had signed a contract and deserved a celebration.

We were both younger then: we closed a Hungarian cafe with a fiddler who played with a gypsy's heart; we outlasted a couple of strip joints on Rush Street; and sometime around dawn, wandering around Lincoln Park for reasons never explained, almost hailed a police car for a taxi. A historian and his editor ducking behind a privet hedge and waiting for the police to pass without noticing is an act that has a sound sobering effect on both; and a call from Paul two or three hours later completed the process: "I've lost the contract and outline."

Paul's tone reflected my glumness for upon occasion the Land of Lincoln is wacky, untrustworthy country where the woods are full of wolves. At the turn of the century Ida M. Tarbell was the terror of that country and stories are told of how whenever she appeared to carry on her researches into the life of the Great Emancipator other writers "frequently secreted their Lincoln manuscripts in mattresses or cubbyholes."* Since publishing people tend to congregate in the same places, Paul and I both feared the quickie that might result if that lost outline fell into the wrong hands. Paul reduced to five months the time necessary to complete his manuscript; we would produce our own quickie.

Among historians, Paul ranked with the unsanctified, meaning that he neither had undergone the academic drudgery of graduate school nor earned his livelihood by teaching history. In the Lincoln field, however, the unsanctified long had flourished (nor did they do poorly as students of the Civil War if Lloyd Lewis and Bruce Catton are selected as representatives). Not until 1945, when Professor James G. Randall of the University of Illinois published *Lincoln the President,* could the professional historian lay claim to a contribution of any appreciable general interest. A Johnny-come-lately in discovering both the appeal and importance of Lincoln, the professional tended to turn up an academic nose at the unsanctified, a snobbery quite unjustified by his accomplishments then and later. And if the mark of a professional was his resort to original sources, thorough documentation and complete objectivity, he had more to learn from Paul than he had to teach.

No one but the finest of Lincoln scholars could have achieved so quickly and so well what Paul produced in *The Lincoln Reader.* He was an editor's delight: willing to accept criticism graciously yet ready to stand his ground when he knew he was right. His reactions to my comments on his chapter entitled "Romance and Marriage" were a typical Angle response:

---

*Benjamin P. Thomas, *Portrait for Posterity,* 183.

. . . Hundreds, if not thousands, of pages have been written both about the Ann Rutledge affair and Lincoln's marriage, but all of it is either trash or superseded by the work that [Carl] Sandburg and I did [the reference is to Sandburg and Angle, *Mary Lincoln, Wife and Widow*]. I will see what I can do in working over the chapter again, but I am not promising anything that will make the *Ladies Home Journal* audience sit up and gasp.*

As the manuscript neared completion, my conviction grew that we had a potential best seller unlike any in university press history. Cy fell into a fretful mood; we were over our heads, he argued, but the Press Council never wavered. Then Curley pouted because Paul would not consent to an introduction by Carl Sandburg. "Dammit," Paul said, "this is going to be all my book or no book." He was right, I declared: Lincoln books with Sandburg introductions were commonplace.

In November the bound galleys went to the Book Club and Cy moaned that the total cost of the work would run upward to $30,000. Harry Dale was our underground contact at the Book Club and if I wanted a real baptism into the war of nerves professional publishing became at this level I was thoroughly immersed. One day we learned that *The Lincoln Reader* was on the "A" list, the next that the judges were meeting, the next that *The Lincoln Reader* and John Steinbeck's *The Wayward Bus* were tied, the next that we were definitely out, the next that Steinbeck had agreed to delete certain offensive Anglo-Saxonisms, delaying his novel until March, and we were definitely in. We shouted a hurrah for four-letter words, collected $100,000 from the Book Club, increased our first printing to 50,000 copies and received by special messenger an orchid from the staff at Princeton.

A blurry two months followed. I dragged Paul to press

---

*Earl Schenck Miers, "Lincoln as a Best Seller," *Abraham Lincoln Quarterly,* December, 1948.

interviews and radio programs and to a reception at "21" that cost the Press $1,100. Paul's smile grew thinner as the rounds of autograph parties wore on and one day handed me a copy of his book, passionately inscribed:

Miers,
Kiss my ass!
Angle.

But in three months, Book Club and trade editions combined, *The Lincoln Reader* sold over 500,000 copies and we topped every major best seller list. Reprint rights were sold around the world and there were as well other editions in paperback. But Cy complained over the extra work of auditing the sales receipts. I couldn't win.

❧

Late in the year 1947 B. M. (Before Medicare), I had my first of seven hospital experiences when I left my appendix in Chicago. Up from Springfield to see me came Ben Thomas, who said: "I want to join your writing stable if you'll have me." Ben knew I would do anything for him I could: I had no doubt with time and patience he would emerge as one of the leading literary historians in America. It is difficult, knowing the tragedy that awaited Ben, to write objectively of this chubby-cheeked old friend who then was so exuberantly alive.

To appreciate Ben one had to understand Springfield, a funny town in many ways. Despite its flood of tourists and legislators, Springfield remained provincial and back-bitish: if not a Peyton Place on the prairies at least a Main Street. Springfield had its circle of prosperous business executives who took a heady pleasure in the money they had made and Ben did not quite fit their pattern. True, the Thomases were reported to be well-to-do—Sally's money, they said, invested in livestock breeding farms that Ben ran capably—but Ben, a professionally trained historian from Johns Hopkins who dreamed of becoming a successful writer, was still somehow out of step in Springfield. Ben never would confess this attitude in so many words, but he conveyed the feeling intensely nonetheless; by God, his manner said, some day he would make Springfield sit up and take notice.

As Gib Bunn was a rare personality in this capital city of Illinois, so also were Ben and Sally Thomas. Sal could always twist me around her finger: she had a personality and a sense of values that reminded me of Starling. Her faith in Ben's ultimate triumph was only one trait we shared in common. Sal liked bawdy limericks, gay conversation, good books. She was without affectation: if I forgot to bring a straw, Sal could always improvise one from a piece of macaroni.

As a historian, Ben was a superb craftsman. My own professional training in the field, squeezed into the early years of marriage, had lasted through one term of graduate school. At the time I had been fascinated by the colonial history of the Connecticut Valley about which I was writing a novel, but the head of the department had a personal interest in other subjects which he wished researched. This lackey system in graduate work may have merits that I could not appreciate. I know that it stifled enthusiasm and turned excitement into drudgery, and so I joined the ranks of the unsanctified. Yet no graduate course ever could have taught me so much about the joy and methods of historical research as I absorbed working with Paul and Ben. Moreover, unlike most department heads in history, they knew the technique of skillful writing so that they possessed the full resources of the literary historian. Perhaps Allan Nevins could beat them: I have watched Allan working in a library and where the average scholar works from sources to notes to manuscript Allan could, if so inclined, eliminate the middle step. His massive output was neither an accident nor the result of a graduate student chain gang.

Where both Allan and Paul possessed an advantage over Ben was in their sense of what made a book commercially appealing. In the early books on which I worked with Ben this judgment was lacking, yet both these works—*Portrait for Posterity*, a masterful study of Lincoln's biographers, and *Theodore Weld: Crusader for Freedom*, a fine biography of this publicity-shy Abolitionist whom Carl Sandburg called "a storm-bird in the making of American history"—were grooming Ben for his ultimate victory. Allan, like Paul and Carl, was a native son of the Midwest into which Ben had migrated; yet in spirit and personal friendship they were a close quartet, sharing a common love for an original turn of phrase that so often provided a penetrating insight into historical reality.

Carl was the elder statesman of the group, almost as great a legend as Mr. Lincoln. Off-the-record stories abounded about Sandburg: one friend swore that "this Swede" still owned the first dollar he ever had earned, another that he had never forgotten anyone who ever had given him a caustic review. Perhaps it was true that a Chicago hotel clerk who once greeted Sandburg, "I know you—you're Robert Frost," put Carl into a two-day sulk; certainly the Sandburg-Frost edginess over who was America's foremost poet was well-known. Only affection inspired Ralph Newman to joke that he had invented the all-time best-selling curio for the Lincoln collector—he was going to package locks of hair belonging to Sandburg, Lincoln, and John Wilkes Booth, all for five dollars—but Ralph understood what Carl had achieved as the silver-haired saint of the Land of Lincoln.

Carl was "show biz," the personality who vitalized the Lincoln-consciousness into a public property, and his talent benefited all. Carl's six volumes about Lincoln were unique, if uneven. The first two, *The Prairie Years*, were both history and poetry, causing some professionals to wince and an admiring critic to sneer, "To hell with the professors of Lincolnology!" But his four concluding volumes, *The War Years*, were, as Paul said, wholly objective and if orthodox historians were sometimes confused by this "gigantic piece of reporting" they would still have to learn how to live with it. Ben Hecht recalled Carl from his early newspaper days in Chicago when lesser mortals on the staff grumbled: "I understand this fella's a genius. You got any idea what a genius can do?" Carl taught them, as he taught the orthodox historians, that a genius can do what he damn well pleases. The reputation was gold to him, like his white hair and deep, sonorous voice: each made the image of Sandburg as much a part of the Land of Lincoln as the Great Emancipator's Tomb in Oak Ridge Cemetery.

Perhaps Ben did not aspire to equal the legend of Sandburg, but he believed that Paul's success with *The Lincoln Reader* was within his grasp. Despite a charm that was outwardly self-effacing, Ben's ambition had a driving intensity. Yet he was a tremendously significant figure for quite another reason.

Properly, the story of how *The Collected Works of Abraham Lincoln* matured into one of this generation's indispensable gifts to our national literature begins in 1924 when the old Lincoln Centennial Association was reborn as The Abraham Lincoln Association. From the tales that are told, Logan Hay, its first president, must have been a wonderfully imaginative, energetic man with a booming voice which, when he was aroused, could reach to Chicago if nudged by a favorable prairie breeze. Hay conceived of the project to compile and publish the *Collected Works* as the Association's final objective, a responsibility that now rested upon Gib as president and upon Ben, who for a time followed Paul as executive secretary.

Why the University of Chicago Press or any other principal university press was napping and leaving this landmark in American history unclaimed was none of my business; I wanted our young Rutgers Press to have this massive work and so become a permanent patron of our national literature. Gib, Paul, and Ben were willing allies and a cooperative publishing agreement was arranged. Ralph Newman told me I had stolen the jewel of the Lincoln field. Datus Smith, who had followed Joe Brandt as director at Princeton, described the arrangement as "wizard."

From the start Cy was against a venture of this magnitude. My God, I was getting as bad as George Little who, not satisfied with a stadium and crew, was campaigning for a field house behind the gym. But since the success of *The Lincoln Reader* Cy tended, at least temporarily, to handle me with kid gloves. A number of Rutgers books which had seemed dead had been revived by sales to various reprint houses. Cy did not know what to make of me or the Press. "It is Dr. Clothier's decision to make," I reminded him and on that status of a grudging armed truce, we let the matter rest.

In human enterprise all men tend to dwell in ghettos: the brokers in their Wall Street warrens, the lawyers in their court-rooms, the professors in their ivory towers, the politicians in their smoke-filled caucus rooms, the doctors in their offices and hos-pitals. Even private clubs tend toward ghetto-like patterns: the petty gamblers monopolize the card rooms, the bone-weary the steam baths, the young Ivy Leaguers the squash courts, the uncertain executives the bar. As an inmate of the bookish ghetto, I haunted the library and so inevitably grew to know Douglas Southall Freeman, who lived at the University Club whenever he came to New York from Richmond.

Freeman, another of the unsanctified, was at the height of his literary fame. His four volumes of *R. E. Lee* had created a romantic image that left the United Daughters of the Confed-eracy swooning with delight on their Southern piazzas, and in the three volumes of *Lee's Lieutenants* he had confounded the orthodox historians by writing both romantic and analytical history within the soundest traditions of their craft. In appearance, he was the epitome of the old Southern gentleman, even to the massive gold watch chain across his vest and, yet, the early morning energy which prodded him to predawn labor always seemed more of a Yankee quality. A room on the fourth floor invariably was saved for him so that he could pad in bedroom slippers into the Club's library, perhaps one of the most beautiful in America since it is modeled after the Vatican Library with its frescoed domed ceiling. His approaching visits could always be detected by a rising excitement within Mark Kiley, the finest private club librarian ever sent from heaven to glorify the human race. Freeman was Mark's pet. Quite shamelessly, the Club had accumulated one of the best Civil War collections in America, and it did not bother Mark's conscience or mine or Freeman's that the unbookish heathens in the bar were being well taxed through their dues for this extravagance.

Upon rare occasions Freeman could be led from his work to a conversation in the Fifth Avenue Room where there was absolutely no truth to the rumor that among the early morning duties of the staff was sticking pins into the members to determine if they were still alive. Here, fiddling with his watch chain with its dangling elk's tooth, Freeman talked about Lee and the Civil War and the world of the middle 1940's faded away. As he talked, Jefferson Davis still lived in Richmond, intrigue enlivened the dull routine of that war in this beleaguered city, and the invincible Lee with his loyal and ragged columns was rolling through the lush farmlands of Pennsylvania toward Gettysburg.

"A book should be written about that battle," he said, suddenly interrupting his own narrative. He fixed a steady gaze upon me and said, more a command from Lee than a suggestion from Freeman, "You do it."

I did, not wishing to be shot at sunrise on one of his future visits to New York. I engaged Richard Brown, a cerebral-palsied youth who recently had graduated from Rutgers, to assist me in the research. But the literary labor of putting together this story as a documentary of those who had lived through the three bloody days in July of 1863 was entirely my own. How much I had learned through my association with Paul and Ben became evident. Historical research grew into a joy, the book an enchantment. At times Mark Kiley seemed to be working as hard as I, turning up sources.

Every free moment I could find, I slipped away into those weeks of 1863 leading up to the famous battle. Others could talk about such trivia as Truman and his Fair Deal, my heart and mind dwelt in another reality. 1863 was in an age when twenty cents bought an excellent pamphlet on "Moustaches and Whiskers in 42 Days"; when doctors were unnecessary since Ayer's Cherry Pectoral cured coughs, colds, hoarseness, influenza, bronchitis, whooping cough, croup, asthma, and incipient consumption; and when salesmen for Oriental Burners could earn $60 a month. It was an age when Grant was stuck in the mud behind Vicksburg's entrenchments; when inflamed ladies wrote letters to *Harper's Weekly* about the loungers on Fifth Avenue who interfered with proper church-going on a Sunday; and when New York was agog over the marriage of Barnum's General Tom Thumb to petite Lavinia Warren, who stood thirty-two inches in height, weighed twenty-nine pounds and possessed "a well rounded arm and full bust." It was an age of "bread riots" in Southern cities with bacon selling at a dollar a pound, coarse shoes at fifteen dollars a pair, and apple brandy at fifteen times its prewar price. In Washington, Lincoln was up to his old trick of commuting army death sentences and received General Butler, the "Beast" of occupied New Orleans, at the White House on the day the armies clashed at Gettysburg.

Such is the historian's luxury to wander far afield, hoping that some little of the spirit of the times into which he has escaped will trickle into the pages he is writing. In the case of

Gettysburg (1948) the process somehow worked, for it received front page reviews in all important media and climbed quickly onto the best-seller lists. In a glass case in the University Club Library stood a set of first editions of Bret Harte, a gift from Phil Brett. Whenever I fondled these books, I remembered the man who, as acting president at Rutgers, one day had stopped a frightened boy and told him to have faith until he found the right way ahead. "Doctor," I whispered to myself, "perhaps I've found your corner."

CHAPTER THIRTEEN

Years of

Wine and

Rose Thorns

*A*s *Mama Stollman*
might have said, how by me could life be sweeter? What I
should have remembered was Mama's warning that troubles
hatch like eggs, but I was living a giddy life between New Brunswick and New York, Chicago and Springfield, to which I would
add intermediate stops in Pittsburgh and Washington, D. C.

The success of *The Lincoln Reader* and our identification
with the *Collected Works* gained the Press a prominence that

reached far beyond the campus. A former colleague at Rutgers, Stan March, was responsible for my invitation to address the students in the Department of Printing at the Carnegie Institute of Technology. Stan now was director of public relations at Carnegie, but I remembered the happy-go-lucky harum-scarum who had surpassed even George Little in exuding enthusiasm for football; but Stan must have outgrown this passion, for Carnegie had so deflated football that only a few ragtag young engineers ever romped around its stadium playing a pickup game.

"Make a speech in public?" Starling said. "I'd drop dead."

But I was stubborn: my handicap was not to set limits on where I went or what I attempted. Some hesitancy—or stuttering, if you prefer an old-fashioned term—marked the speech of most athetoids. It was a problem to be thought through and conquered, I insisted. In later years when I knew Wendell Johnson from the University of Iowa, a stutterer who so mastered this handicap that he became one of the world's outstanding authorities in speech pathology and psychology, I realized how sound my instincts were. Jack Johnson—the nickname went back to his Kansas childhood—always stressed the fact that stuttering was a disability of the listener since hesitancies in speech were normal, and only when a person was made conscious of these hesitancies so that he became his own listener did his stuttering grow pronounced.

Curley thought it would be fine if I put a glass with a straw on the speaker's lectern and paused now and then to take a sip, thus winning the audience's sympathy, but Curley missed the point. The handicapped speaker, Jack Johnson could have told him, must never emphasize what he *is* or *has* but should talk about what he *does*.

In these terms, I made my first appearance at Carnegie Tech. My subject, "The Printer and the Publisher as Craftsmen," sounded more pretentious than it was, for I simply discussed my experiences from the time I had met Carl Rollins to the present development of the Press. Halfway through I became aware of the stillness in the auditorium and realized that the audience was listening with genuine interest rather than courtesy. I had made a speech as an isolated adventure, I told myself, never suspecting that soon I would be embarked on a speech-making crusade which, before I finished, would carry me across tens of thousands of miles.

Nor was my association with Carnegie ended. Quickly its president, Robert Daugherty, became a personal friend. That Stan loved this fellow who had kicked Carnegie out of bigtime football was in itself a memorial to Daugherty's magnetism. He was as fidgety as I and when we were in a room together the way you told the handicapped from the unhandicapped was by the fact that Daugherty used a slide rule when he talked. In Pittsburgh he was a figure approaching a legend: the man who had come down from Westinghouse in Schenectady, New York, reputed to be the equal of the hunchbacked dwarf and genius, Charles Steinmetz; the man who mated the humanities with technology, believing that an engineer building a bridge or any other structure without understanding the social consequences of his act was out of step with the modern world; the man who walked into offices of industrialists like the president of United States Steel and said: "See here, you employ x number of Carnegie graduates in top positions who cost us y amount of dollars to educate, so I figure that is what you owe us in endowment this year." At home he was also a legend: the man who complained his wife was too easily sold by trinket peddlers at the door and who, to demonstrate the technique of sales resistance, responded when next the bell rang and bought a baby grand piano.

Across the gully from Carnegie rose that "university in a skyscraper" which was the University of Pittsburgh, the pride of Chancellor John Bowman, who was Clothier's old boss. Beyond this massive, phallic, univied academic hall—known locally as

"Bowman's Erection"—stood the University Club where one happy weekend a cooperative publishing agreement was worked out between Carnegie and Rutgers. The Scotch had flowed freely before Daugherty reached for his slide rule.

"Put it away," I begged. "Take my word for it. You assume all the risk and we make all the profit."

He said: "That fact I can work out in my head. I'd just like to know how much."

Daugherty was like that: straightforward, quick, an objective idealist, practical, good-humored, one of the easiest men with whom I ever have dealt. He was not interested in technical books for Carnegie. He was zealously intent on emphasizing the importance of the humanities in technological education and wanted this side of the Carnegie program stressed.

At the time the Press was also publishing a little book by Dr. Bowman and the contrast between these neighboring educators, both towering men in America, was interesting. I met Bowman in a two-storied, vaulted room that seemed like a cathedral; where Daugherty was an informal lounger, Bowman was stiff and erect and precise, but his mind too had a far range.

Yet Daugherty to me was the warmer; I never did learn whether Bowman drank Scotch or bourbon. Daugherty, though outwardly shy, was inwardly an intensely passionate philosopher. His mind, like John F. Kennedy's, constantly sought new definitions for ideas that had lost value because they had sagged into political clichés.

و§

Pittsburgh and Carnegie were a convenient stop on the journey to Chicago and Springfield. In Lincoln's old home town stability at last was brought to the small suite of offices in the First National Bank Building occupied by The Abraham Lincoln Association with the appointment of Roy P. Basler as editorial factotum of the *Collected Works*. In lankiness Roy had the look of old Abe, but the red hair did not fit the Lincoln image. A practicing scholar of literature before he entered the field of history in 1935 with the publication of *The Lincoln Legend,* a remarkably able study of the hero myth Lincoln had become, Roy was an amiable fellow, filled with the bedevilments of raising a family which he took with that kind of exhausted bewilderment normal to a parent, and he and his wife Virginia added to the fun of an evening with Ben and Sally.

That red hair of course stood for spirit—Roy was like a match which when scratched would fire—but he was surrounded by a task that must have approached chaos. The size of the project constantly was being revised upward: from six volumes to eight, not counting a separate volume for the index. The search went on for Lincoln manuscripts in libraries, private collections, and the hands of dealers; hundreds of writings for which no text could be found, forgeries and spurious items attributed to Lincoln were identified, and a mountain of paper was consumed in compiling the necessary annotations. The labor frayed nerves and tested personalities and took more time than Mr. Lincoln had required to win the world's bloodiest civil war.

Since the project was a terminal enterprise, Roy and his assistant editors, working on one of the most exacting historical assignments imaginable, would finish their labors out of a job. Living with this double-edged worry required a dedication that only a steadfast personality could provide. The money that the task paid was no inducement: there was enough to hold skin and bones together but little more. Yet there was always an undeniable responsibility nagging at everyone's conscience: the *Collected Works* must stand for at least fifty years when published and very likely for a century or longer.

If Roy was sometimes a colorful cusser in the privacy of his own office, I could not blame him. He would stick till the job was completed—he would see it done right, by hopping Godfrey—

he was a man to admire for his toughness of mind and character.

Ben could understand Roy's worries, both in the office and for the future of a growing family, and Roy needed a warm friend like Ben. They were an amusing pair together, the lanky redhead and the somewhat squat cattle breeder with his heart set on becoming a famous literary historian.

To watch Ben mixing a drink was an experience: the ice flew in one direction, the whiskey in the other, while the glass rolled in the sink.

"For God's sake, let me do it," Roy said. He had suffered a hard day and was thirsty. Ben winked, then giggled. Hell, why was Roy fretting over the future? He could always be a bartender.

᠍ᡈᢅ

Luther H. Evans was Librarian of Congress when in 1947 I was summoned to Washington. A limousine and chauffeur met me at the airport and whisked me to the Library of Congress so that I should have been alerted to the possibility of having more to lose than to gain. Luther possessed both Texas-style energy and enthusiasm: even the eyes beneath his bushy black brows could flash with a certain hypnotism, and I always half expected to find him busting broncos in the Library's main foyer.

The specific problem we discussed had been created by the Inter-American Conference for the Maintenance of Peace held in Buenos Aires in 1936. One of the recommendations of this conference charged each American republic with the responsibility of issuing a quarterly bulletin giving notice of recently published books of a scientific, historical, literary, or artistic nature to be distributed and exchanged among the republics by suitable government agencies.

When this political ball stopped bouncing in Washington, it landed in the lap of the Library of Congress at the request of the

Department of State's Interdepartmental Committee on Cultural and Scientific Cooperation. The result was *The United States Quarterly Book List*, a substantial and important periodical that Luther's staff prepared and which he now sought to have the Press publish.

My business judgment failed me and I became more romantic than analytical. I liked calling the Librarian of Congress by his first name. And, God knows, any youngster from the New Brunswick outlands could feel flattered sitting on an advisory committee that included Detlev Bronk of the National Research Council, Frederick N. Cromwell of the American Library Association, Olcott H. Deming of the Department of State, R. R. Hawkins of the New York Public Library, Cornelius Krusé of the American Council of Learned Societies and a dozen other persons of equal prominence.

The editor of the *Book List* was Joseph P. Blickensderfer, who had been a dean at the University of Oklahoma during Joe Brandt's presidency of that university. Blick had the jolly appearance of Humpty Dumpty before his fatal fall and, clearly, he was obsessed with the belief that the *Book List* was the kind of touch-and-go governmental burden that at any moment could tumble him into oblivion. His quarters were in the attic of the Library, where you were dropped out of the elevator like a cube from a dice box to roll among the congressional page boys who swarmed all over the place. The consultant in poetry also had his aviary here.

Blick worked with the finest scholarly talent in America to put together the *Book List* and as an editorial achievement no apology was ever required for this enterprise. The trouble was that I had put the Press into the magazine subscription business for which we were not geared. The harder we tried to rise above this blunder, the more we became entangled. Forcefully, the *Book List* taught me the truth in the adage that no man knows what he can do until he tries to undo what he did.

✒

In 1944 Reed Silvers finally escaped as a myth maker and became dean of men, permitting him to indulge all the fatherly impulses that were so basic to his nature. To the students he was never a stiff-necked disciplinarian but an indulgent friend and adviser talking about the ancient virtues that had filled his twenty-seven books for youngsters. In a magnificent tribute Dr. Clothier once said: "He has been called Rutgers' Mr. Chips. He was far more than that. He was Rutgers' Reed Silvers."

Reed moved from Rahway to the dean's house on College Avenue. His study was like a model in a magazine, but for Reed's creative spirit the place seemed sterile. He talked bravely of the books he still cared to write, but his words were strangely unconvincing. He needed the clutter of the old attic room in Rahway, the stutter of the antiquated Oliver typewriter, if he wished to go on recapturing youthful dreams.

From year to year, toward the end from month to month, I could see him aging. A hard siege of pneumonia weakened him frightfully and he went to Sarasota, Florida, hoping to recover. How long he had suffered with an ailing heart no one can say— perhaps from as long ago as those days when as a skinny youngster he had run the longer distances on the college track team— and on a night in late March of 1948 a heart attack killed him. He was only fifty-seven.

We devoted an entire issue of the *Alumni Monthly* as his memorial. In a portrait entitled "Father Silvers," I wrote compulsively of the man I loved:

> I wonder if Cy Johnson ever knew of the great campaigns that were plotted against him on the first floor of Old Queen's. We would need a new typewriter or $1,000 more in the budget for "cats. & bulls.,"* or

---

*"catalogs & bulletins"

a part-time stenographer, and Reed would say a little grimly, "We'll have to get the money out of Cy." Now I daresay Reed could have walked straight into Cy's office many times, stated his case, and that would have been the end of it, but perhaps not (you hear so many stories). Reed would say, "I'll handle Cy—at the right time," and the game was on. From day to day the tension mounted, and Reed bore himself with a quiet mastery at the art of tactical retreat: "He was too occupied today, fellows"; or "I planted the seed in his mind, but let it germinate." So you waited. You watched Cy covertly to see if you could detect some clue to pass on, like "Cy's in a pretty good humor if you can judge by his smile" or "Better keep away today, Boss, for Cy looks as though somebody's just given him hell." As you waited, Reed explained that Cy was really a fine fellow—no better friend in the world, no loyaler servant of Rutgers anywhere—but you thought darkly that if Cy didn't hurry up and get himself in a mood to be handled you were damn well going to run him down on College Avenue. What gloom penetrated the inner ranks when the Boss was in retreat; and when the case at point was another youngster coming along and the need for a raise to feed the little brat, your wife also became entangled in the tension and you fretted over the problem both at home and in the office.

Henceforth Cy was icily hostile toward me. Almost immediately he refused to execute four contracts that had been approved by the Press Council. Aside from my senior-year interview with Dr. Will, I never have encountered such a meeting. Cy purposely unnerved me, laughed when I burst into tears, stormed that every penny invested in Press inventory was wasted, mimicked me when I replied. I fled, finally, shattered physically and emotionally.

But by morning I had regained my composure and the battle resumed in Dr. Clothier's office. It is not nice to see any man cut down as Cy was that day, the more so since Clothier, never raising his voice, said: "You needn't sign those contracts, Cy. As president I can sign them." We were alone when he handed me the executed documents. He spoke in a strangely husky voice about principle and how difficult it became, as a man grew older, not to make compromises—the difference, he said, between a true Quaker and a sporting Quaker—and he added: "I envy young men—it's so much easier for them to take the risk of standing by what they believe."

My ordeal was not over. Soon the rumor was current that I was afraid to hold a Press Council meeting. I sloughed off this falsehood. Then the word circulated that a special trustees committee would investigate my operation of the Press.

"All right," I told Starling, "if that's what they want that's what the bastards will get."

◆§

We now owned a house in an old settlement of faculty families in the nearby community of Stelton. Starling, heavy with her third child and edgy from shouting some semblance of obedience into David and Meredith, complained testily: "Just once I wish we could have a baby without having Cy Johnson mixed up in the process!" I nodded sympathetically. The youngster was expected almost any day; it was a rotten time for this sort of upset.

Our next-door neighbors, Walt and Mabel Peabody, were a wonderful couple. Walt, much older than I (and wiser, gentler, less impulsive), was a professor of economics at Rutgers, which meant he was one of those experts who knew everything about money except how to hold onto it. Walt threw himself unselfishly into helping prepare a sound presentation of the Press as a business. Every type of book we ever had published was analyzed in terms of its sales performance and sales expectancy.

Under Walt's instruction, I drove the Press staff crazy preparing charts that made clear the peaks and valleys of our sales performance and how we could project with reasonable accuracy the gradual liquidation of our inventory.

In human and financial dimensions we had a compelling story to tell, for in less than a decade we had built the Press from a one-man operation into a going enterprise that grossed over $100,000 a year. We had built a sales staff of commission men who gave us trade representation across the nation. Unlike the average university press, we received no direct subsidy for Press salaries even though in the case of Research Council books, which could never pay their way but were an essential part of the university's academic apparatus, we absorbed at least 30 percent overhead on every dollar spent. Certainly we had made mistakes, of which our involvement in the publication of *The United States Quarterly Book List* could be called a conspicuous example, and we were willing to say so. But the story in its preponderant details was sound and optimistic; nor did we intend to yield in the matter of the *Collected Works,* which was to be our monument.

The Trustees met then in Atlantic City. I loaded the car with all the exhibits we had prepared and appealed to Starling: "Don't have the baby before I get back."

"Tell it, not me," she said.

I am no devotee of Atlantic City under normal circumstances. On a chill January day, not knowing at what moment my wife would be whisked off to the hospital, my mood was excessively glum. The Trustees assembled at the Hotel Dennis, whose owner was a board member; in addition, he was no sporting Quaker and there was not a drop of liquor served on the premises, which meant that if I wanted to meet anyone socially, I had to dash across the street to the hotel where there was a bar. A nasty Atlantic northeast wind gusted along the deserted boardwalk, but at least the screeching honky-tonks and concessions were mercifully silenced as a result.

The meeting, like the city, was disjointed. I was speaking not to men with backgrounds in publishing and literature, but to lawyers, merchants, small town businessmen. They glanced at my charts and looked away, not comprehending their meaning or caring to be told. Possibly some read a book occasionally, but there were others clearly who had not touched anything so unclean since leaving college. The Republicans made no secret of the belief that writers were intellectuals, who, as a group, leaned toward the pale pinks and since the days of F.D.R. had nearly ruined the country with their ideas. So the graphs, my figures, my arguments were brushed aside. The bookkeeping plainly had turned unfriendly. In the future, they decided, persons representing their group should decide what, if anything, should be published and under what circumstances. Someone muttered that if we did not hurry up and finish before the full board meeting he'd never get across the street for a drink.

I grew calm and indifferent. I listened listlessly, knowing that as far as *my* profession was concerned I was talking to children who wanted the recess bell to ring. They were good fellows within the limits of their abilities, but there was no Gib Bunn here or a Curley Wilhelm or a Paul Angle or a Ralph Newman: no man burning with an inward fire. I knew, in good time, what I must do. Meanwhile there was no advantage for me in playing the role of Lear roaring at the wild storm, bareheaded and helpless.

Dr. Clothier tried earnestly to talk me out of resigning.

"No, Doctor," I said. "There's little I may know but of this much I'm certain: a clean break heals faster than a wound that is being constantly salted."

Like the perfect little gentleman he instinctively was, our third child, named William Holmes after his two grandfathers, waited until after the fiasco in Atlantic City before making his January entrance into the world. Starling accepted my decision cheerfully and, I suspect, subconsciously over the years we both had realized that this moment must come sooner or later.

"Do you know what you are going to do?" Starling asked.

"I'm going to work for Alfred A. Knopf."

"Does he know it?"

"No," I said. "But he will."

CHAPTER FOURTEEN

Lord Alfred

There are probably

as many Alfred Knopfs as there are human emotions. There was one Alfred known to his wife Blanche and another known to his son Pat; there is the Alfred known to professional people like Curley who attend the weekly luncheons for which Alfred is celebrated and another known to those scores of eager academic people who crowd into his out-of-town soirees and are wise not to tipple his alcoholic beverages too generously; there is an

Alfred who is a craftily packaged myth in the pages of *The New Yorker* and there is an Alfred known to the working staff that comes and goes but rarely remains permanently in the Knopf offices at 501 Madison Avenue. And there are a great many other Alfreds, but no matter. It is really no surprise that Alfred and H. L. Mencken struck it off like two bedbugs in a mattress (or two employees in the crowded back editorial room I knew); Gerald W. Johnson's description of Mencken—"Into that medium-sized body was packed the vitality of twenty ordinary men"—could have applied to Alfred, give or take a moustache.

I can only write about my Alfred. In no small way the impact of his genius upon the American consciousness influenced all the years of my intellectual awareness. In 1915, when I was five years of age, Alfred began his publishing career and hardly a dozen years later, when I was finishing high school, I was familiar with his Borzoi books. Such authors as Sigrid Undset, Knut Hamsun, Thomas Mann, and that chilly pessimist, Oswald Spengler, appearing under the Knopf imprint, were a profound part of the life of any young intellectual as the late 1920's drifted toward the Great Depression. The green covers of copies of *The American Mercury*, edited by Mencken, cluttered my room. No one can tell me that Alfred and Mencken did not know what they were achieving: a large segment of a rising generation was being conditioned to appreciate good taste, brilliant literary judgment, and romantic publishing energy; and if Mencken did not realize that a volume like his *Treatise on the Gods* (1930) had enormous appeal to the awakening agnostic in college or college-bound, then his cunning was overrated.

My first contact with Alfred came in 1938 after Thomas Mann addressed a special convocation of the Rutgers students and faculty. Mann's remarks, calling upon America to "stand forth in an abandoned and ethically leaderless world as the strong and unswerving protector of the good and godly in mankind," was filled with the moving power of this mysteriously creative person. We published the address in a handsome pamphlet and sent Alfred a copy. Back came a snappish letter inquiring how dare we issue any statement by Mann without placing it under copyright? I replied, in effect, that we had the finest reason in the world: we were too stupid to know better; moreover, this snippet of Mann's work falling into the public domain was of small moment in an "ethically leaderless world" and we wished an end to Alfred's popping off over the incident.

My instincts were right: this was precisely the way to deal with Alfred, who could be outrageously sassy in unrestrained moments. Sometime during or right after the war (my recollection is hazy), I asked Curley to arrange an appointment with Alfred. I wanted a book about Alfred for the Press as the one man in America who had vitalized the significance of the arts in our generation. Alfred received us graciously, and called in an editor named Follett who looked exhausted with other details, and a fine idea fell through.

I remember Alfred saying, "Such a book should show the bastard side, too," but he said it, I didn't.

After *The Lincoln Reader* appeared, Alfred made gracious references to it that were printed in *Publishers Weekly*, a fact that I very much appreciated. I had come now to know Pat, who was apparently a happy example of how to exist on the edge of a perforating ulcer, and Roger Shugg, who was Alfred's textbook editor and combined the ambivalence of a New England conscience with the tough, single-minded instincts of an Assyrian merchant. Alfred had given me a contract for my next Civil War book—one of those massive documents that run to several pages of legal exuberance and come to you tied in black ribbon and stamped with a red seal so that you have an impression of being knighted by Lord Alfred.

So I was not unknown to Alfred when, hat in hand and asking for a job, I sought him out at the Harmonie Club, an all-Jewish establishment on East 60th Street. Alfred sat with an injured leg propped on a cushion, the victim of a recent skiing accident, and looked like an aging man who should have had better sense. And so we met, and quickly reached an agreement: Alfred would pay me $10,000 a year and see how "we" worked out. Even as a casualty of the ski trials, Alfred was an impressive, dynamic personality. His mind was quick, penetrating, witty, and his laugh was distinctly a fine and warming sound. I liked his eyes, which were filled with an explosive fire, and with time, I suspected, I would grow accustomed to that silly moustache which seemed to be a compromise for a full rabbinical beard in the sense of sparing the hair but not the impulse for expressing opinions as though they were enunciations of The Law.

That Alfred was a personality, carefully groomed in loud shirts and sporty tweeds, even he must have known, but the production was artistry and a pleasure to both actor and audience. I admired this man immensely—and still do—and had my friends kept their mouths shut everything would have worked out better.

"You're going to work for Alfred, for God's sake? . . . Have you lost your sense, throwing yourself into that old lion's den? . . . My God, the trade is full of Alfred's alumni, who escaped with their souls if not always their sanity!" The chorus was general. I spent a night in the apartment of a fellow toiler in the Knopf vineyard and awakened to find him sitting upright, moaning.

"What's wrong?" I asked.

"Jesus, what a nightmare of a dream!" came the half-strangled answer. "About Alfred! When I think what I have to take from that man I could spit in his eye!"

On this reassuring note, my friend fell back onto the pillow and groaned at the wall. So, day by day, the fear grew in me. I cannot quite explain what happened: the result, in any case, must have been psychotic. I tried to conceal this feeling of Alfred as a monster image, but it was always close to the surface and any ease I once had enjoyed in his presence was replaced by a constant tenseness that kept my scalp crawling and my neck itching. Nor did it help to be told that his father, Sam Knopf, had been a gruff old bird who bawled out employees for loitering too long at his expense in the johnny; old Sam, my informants said, also wore one of those silly damn moustaches.

ৠ

The job was like Alfred himself; there were as many sides to it as human emotions. I began by attending the spring sales conference the season Alfred published John Hersey's *The Wall*. Hersey was there to explain how he had written and rewritten this book, seeking the proper frame for his story. He was a modest, soft-spoken man as he spun this tale of an artist caught in the web of his craft. We met in the library at 501 Madison Avenue where the walls were lined with the books the Knopfs had published since 1915. The room was crowded but almost breathlessly silent. My glance swept over shelves containing, I thought, good-bad books because the quality of Western civilization was itself good-bad. My gaze rested here on the name of Willa Cather, there on the name of A. E. Coppard, elsewhere on the names of W. H. Hudson and A. E. Housman and H. L. Mencken and Julian Huxley and others who stood for the stars in this generation's literary firmament. And then my attention came back to John Hersey, speaking quietly and earnestly about the story behind *The Wall*. A chill of excitement crept over me.

For a day the magic of John Hersey touched almost everyone, but next morning the house of Knopf was back to normal, which meant that the majority of junior executives had returned to the cloak-and-dagger intrigues that were their favorite pastime. This game never stopped. X and Y, meeting in the elevator on the way to their departmental offices, agreed that Z was an untrustworthy bastard; at lunch, Y and Z exchanged the private opinion that X was an incompetent, a lush and possibly a fairy; and over cocktails that afternoon Z and X, blabbing out what Y had said, muttered that Alfred should be wised up to this slob who everyone knew was Blanche's confidential informer. The principals in the firm—Alfred, Blanche and Pat—were common property. Everyone gossiped about them, with a considerable range of originality and shifting opinion, and within one work week a single source could be responsible for this astonishing variety of intelligence:

Monday—Alfred was a genius; Blanche was going blind, hadn't been able to read a manuscript for years, and wouldn't understand one if she could; and both regretted the fact that Pat ever had been born.

Tuesday—Alfred was aging and might well be dumped at the next board meeting; Blanche's intelligence held the firm together; and Pat should drop dead.

Wednesday—Alfred was loyal, generous, a martyr to his staff; Blanche was being sent to Paris to get her out of the way; and Pat was the white hope of the firm.

Thursday—Alfred had instructed the telephone operator to listen in on conversations and report all disloyal remarks to him; Blanche's headache was really a monumental hangover; and Pat was pulling the house out of the red because he loved his father and hated his mother.

Friday—All the Knopfs were thicker than thieves and they could go to hell.

Half of Alfred's office overhead was consumed in supporting this nonsensical rot; it was no wonder he often glowered at everyone. Pat owed no apology for his presence in the firm. Perhaps he was sometimes excitable and a wild-eyed enthusiast and even an irresponsible chatterbox, but he worked hard, knew sales and promotion and had inherited from Alfred and Blanche those incorruptible instincts for publishing that would carry him to brilliant success as a partner in Atheneum. And people who made a great to do over the famous authors Blanche had brought to the list, as though trying to strike a favorable balance with Alfred, fell for the old Knopf cloak-and-dagger game. If, as often was said, Alfred and Blanche were slave-drivers, the slaves they drove most unmercifully were them-selves, and it was part of their mutual genius that each respected the other's individualism.

Blanche was an unusual personality. A tough-minded old gal, many said, and that she could be; but she was as well an intensely feminine being, in a warm, compelling way and one of the brightest intellects I ever have encountered. To some her eyeshadow looked swabbed on with a paint brush and her fingernails grew into oriental talons, but Blanche had an exotic quality that she wore well. I found her an enjoyable luncheon companion and a woman of great emotional depth. I might, occasionally, launch a barb at Alfred, but Blanche was not subject to that kind of pettiness as far as I was concerned: to me she was the lady of the house.

The weekly editorial meetings were scheduled in the same library where John Hersey had held us enchanted. In a way, I suspect, we should have paid Alfred and Blanche for attending these meetings for what we were receiving was the only bona fide graduate course in publishing in America. The temper of those occasions varied, depending on how they opened. If early in the session Alfred turned to Blanche and inquired, "What do you think, Mother?" the moments were going to speed by on golden wings; if, on the other hand, Alfred barked: "Blanche, will you for God's sake stop tapping the table with those nails!" a kind of galvanizing electricity charged across the room and hung statically above our heads.

Alfred sat imposingly at the head of the table, the week's choicest correspondence before him. Letter by letter the drama unfolded. In the course of the year correspondence from the great and near-great would be in that pile. Alfred knew them all with keen insight into their idiosyncracies as people and as literary craftsmen. He could tell a story with charm and penetrating selection of detail, a master of the labors he peddled. As a college professor he would have been a marvel of the academic world, for he could teach. His was a whole philosophy of publishing, reliable and full-bodied. There was no compromise with niggardliness of talent and effort here (except to make a quick buck, which was only sound business sense). His mind was so civilized that it could give as well as take and in this spirit his editorial meetings were conducted. I stood in awe of the man. Even his prejudices were genuine.

Aside from the tensions my friends had ingrained within me when I confronted Alfred, my first months at Knopf were spent in a state of euphoria. I was given a free hand, and perhaps benefited from the Jewishness within the Knopf organization that could not resist messianic expectations. Ultimately, I knew, I would take my place as X or Y or Z in the old cloak-and-dagger pastime, but I was willing to await that day and deal with it when it came.

Meanwhile, I sank luxuriously into the excitement of midtown New York. I hung out at Michel's, for the old Philadelphia habits were difficult to shake, yet with time I learned to appreciate the romance of this part of the city where within a short walk any culinary taste could be satisfied: French, German, Italian, Spanish, Persian, Japanese, Chinese, or on-the-run Brooklynese. The walk along the East River, the water bright with sunlight and the tugs plying to and fro beneath the 59th Street bridge, had an irresistible appeal. Window shopping on Park, on Madison, on Fifth, along a dozen side streets was an endless wonderment for a gawping country chap. The theaters, the museums, the clubs, Rockefeller Center, the little bars in the mid-fifties with their special four o'clock clientele (and the big ones on Second, with their good Irish smell of corned beef and cabbage) . . . so grew midtown New York in my heart.

And there was a particular fascination I discovered: on summer evenings New York suddenly turns tranquil. All at once the commuters are gone. Late sunshine splashes along the pavement, the street noises are muted, the people come out of apartment caverns to walk their dogs, the taxis cruise listlessly by, and a kind of rustic hominess descends on this teeming metropolis. An echo from the past haunted me: I was back again in Brooklyn, roaming city streets and looking, looking—for what? But there was what I sought: a little girl on a porch, hugging a doll. Unhappily the cobblestones were gone along with the clop of horses hooves, the rumble of an ice wagon.

I wanted to write a good book for Alfred and as an indication of my euphoria during these months I completed two: one serious, one partially a joke. Among Civil War generals none ever had fascinated me more than William Tecumseh Sherman with his nervous temperament, his early hallucinations rendering him unfit for command, his mental rehabilitation under the patient Grant, his brilliant campaign against Atlanta and his subsequent march to the sea. In my research for *The General Who Marched to Hell* (1951), I was determined to cover in person every foot of the country Sherman had traveled on his journey to fame and infamy. This redheaded warrior who once had threatened to send every Southern woman to the washtub was far from forgotten below Mason and Dixon's Line; houses that had burned to the ground in the Carolinas and Georgia the week before still were blamed on Sherman; and an old gentleman in Raleigh, North Carolina, pointing with a cane to the gold cock atop Christ Church, exploded as though the war had never ended: "See that? That's the only damn chicken Sherman left in the South!"

By now the South ignored the fact that it once had for-given Sherman and, indeed, had embraced him as a friend for his hostility to the postwar policies of Andrew Johnson; but then Sherman's *Memoirs* had appeared, ridiculing Southern general-ship and political leadership, and the old hatreds had revived with a new fury. But Southerners, including some historians, possessed a trick of conveniently forgetting whatever clouded their myths.

My first of many journeys into the South was both a delight and a disturbing experience. Jim Crow laws were then a matter of habit, and any criticism of the grievous housing conditions of Negroes or the disparity in educational and economic opportu-nity drew the same rejoinder—"You don't understand the South." I bit my tongue, repressing the comment that perhaps North-erners were beginning to understand the South too well. A classmate who stood high among the executives at Rich's in Atlanta told me the store had recently featured steel bars for front and back doors as a protection against housebreaking and had struck a bonanza, but Negroes and not whites were the pre-dominant purchasers. Tensions existed.

Later, on a trip to Birmingham, I looked down from a hotel window when the factories let out. The streets were filled with Negroes who surged like a marching army toward the miserable ghetto in which they were confined. At the time they were good-humored and peaceful but, I wrote Starling, my blood chilled at what could happen if ever they determined to throw off their shackles. And in the museum that was part of the Cabildo in New Orleans I stared, sick at heart, at the various instruments of torture that had been used to subjugate Negro slaves in Louisiana. I had a sense of dread: these were still the symbols of a subjugation that had not disappeared. They remained ugly, repulsive, and shameful, not as relics of history but as the crude progenitors of more subtle modern weapons of repression—the press, local law, political power, ruthless custom. Had the struggle for a new birth of freedom truly been won? Or was this why persons like myself were driven back to the Civil War, seeking the reason why the promised victory had been unfulfilled?

The quest for the sources of a book is a high-hearted adventure. The joy is in discovery: the journal of a seventeen-year-old girl who lived through the burning of Columbia, South Carolina, found in the Library at Chapel Hill; a file of *The Loyal Georgian,* a newspaper published by Sherman's troops during the occupation of Savannah and found in the library there; the wise and incisive diary of an eight-year-old child kept during the siege, occupation, and destruction of Atlanta and found among the archives of that city's historical society.

One of the finest historical minds in Atlanta at this period was Wilbur Kurtz, a splendid old gentleman whose expert knowledge had guided Margaret Mitchell through the pitfalls in the writing (and later the filming) of *Gone With the Wind.* Why, Kurtz asked, had Sherman burned most of Atlanta but carefully guarded some homes? Why had some Atlanta families recovered so quickly during Reconstruction? What kind of double-dealing had gone on? "If you could lay your hands on the amnesty papers in the War Department I think you might find the answer," Kurtz said. In this bright prospect I traced, crabwise, the route by which Sherman had led his armies from Tennessee to the boundaries of Atlanta. Bud Case, then a Representative from New Jersey, tried heroically to help me budge the amnesty papers from the War Department, but after almost ninety years they remained classified as a top secret. Nor was the Adjutant General in any mood to rake over old wounds and scandals; and I suppose it was the sheerest happenstance that he had graduated from The Citadel, one of the South's leading military schools. A historian has his silent griefs.

The fun book that I wrote for Alfred was *The Christmas Card Murders* (1951), and the three names of our youngsters,

David William Meredith, made an impressive pseudonym. Starling was the mystery fan in the family; I thought I owed her the courtesy of writing one book she might enjoy. Our own neighborhood was the setting for this whodunit and it won quite some local fame, or rather notoriety. My main character and his wife were quite a gay, lecherous pair. Neighborly eyebrows raised. Were we really like that?

"I'd like to know what to tell them," Starling said.

"Make it sound worse," I suggested.

～§

In these euphoric months at Knopf, I brought to the house books that were a credit to the list, but my wildest enthusiasm was for Ben Thomas. A one-volume life of Lincoln based on modern research was long overdue; here was Ben's chance to score his triumph.

We met in Springfield, Chicago, and New York as Ben threw himself into this labor with the will of a man possessed. The manuscript had a lilt from the first page. Ben became Lincoln. Almost a lifetime of scholarship supported every word he wrote; the result was rich, alive, glowing—biography in the grand manner.

But Ben needed a succession of pep talks. He could all but taste the victory that would arouse Springfield to a respect for the writer who lived there and could make a pail of dough; yet Ben was a fellow with deep worries and repressions. A friend's autobiography that recalled the sounds of his parents making love in the next bedroom flabbergasted Ben. "How could anybody write about their parents like that?" he inquired, startled by what he considered an impropriety. Not that Ben was a prude—far from it. He could tell with relish what occurred in some of the sideshows that were part of the cattle-breeding fairs he attended; but there were complexities to the human animal

231

that shocked him. There was a simple goodness in Ben, the same simple goodness that was in his hero, and it brought to his *Abraham Lincoln* a success such as few books enjoy.

It was a joy to see Ben basking at the top of the historical heap: there was Old Ben heading the best-seller lists, and excerpted in *Look Magazine,* and grinning impishly from a television screen, and speaking at commencements and piling up academic honors, and running off his legs to autograph parties—Ben was living. Old friends like Paul Angle and Ralph Newman and Gib Bunn were warm in Ben's happiness. Springfield had not produced such a celebrity since Lincoln had walked down to the Great Western station in 1861 to catch the train to Washington!

The years immediately ahead were filled with kudos and continued success for Ben, and Sal glowed in his deep inward satisfaction. Alfred reissued one of Ben's previous books that had gone out of print, *Lincoln's New Salem* (1954), and the sales were extremely good. He edited with equally good result the following year *Three Years With Grant,* the recollections of war correspondent Sylvanus Cadwallader which had been known to a few Civil War experts since that day years ago when Lloyd Lewis first came upon this remarkable manuscript.

But Ben was seeking a subject for another major biography, and I was one of his close friends who urged him to turn to Stephen A. Douglas, not only as "the man who made Lincoln" but also as a pivotal political figure at a time when democracy was falling apart in America. Other influences, never clearly identified, turned Ben from this figure with whom he was richly endowed to deal, to Edward M. Stanton, Lincoln's Secretary of War, whom Ben would never completely understand. He was tense with the assignment. Stanton was a mysterious mixture of quirk and human contradiction: a man who for months carried around the coffin containing his daughter's corpse. "How could he do that?" Ben asked. "How do you probe that kind of mind?"

I could not answer these queries and wished that Ben would chuck the whole business that so plainly had dulled the edge of his creative drive.

Ben never did complete the manuscript. One day Paul called me from Chicago: "Ben killed himself yesterday afternoon."

I walked to the library at the University Club, put my face in my hands and burst into tears. Why? my mind asked dully. Why had this incomprehensible tragedy occurred? I tried to reach back to yesterday, to feel what Ben had suffered, but I was helplessly alone in this room with its vaulted ceiling and frescoes.

But Ben had been composed within his own mind on that fatal yesterday. He had said good-bye to Sal, who was going to a luncheon and a meeting for one of the Springfield civic activities in which the Thomases always were interested. Alone, Ben sat at the desk where he had written his *Abraham Lincoln* and for months had been toiling on the Stanton manuscript. He drew forth a sheet of paper, took up his pen and began his letter:

Dearest Sally:

I'm going to the basement to do what I feel I must do. It will be a terrible shock to you and also to the kids, I know, but it is the best way. Otherwise, it is virtually certain that I would be facing long and hopeless agony of body, possibly with disfigurement and that, for you, could only mean a long-drawn-out agony of mind.

I love you. Life with you has been wonderful. It couldn't have been more so. And you are brave, and *will* be brave, too.

I love all our kids also, and I count Nettie one of them. Don't let them take it too hard. I hate to do this on Sarah's birthday, and just when so many of our friends are looking forward to Margie's wedding, but I don't know when I'll have the courage or the chance again.

233

I hope you will understand and forgive me, if forgiveness is called for.

> Yours,
> Ben

Rereading these sentences, he could not feel reconciled to his decision. Time passed as Ben pondered his problem. He wanted so desperately for Sally to realize his motive. He added a paragraph:

P.S. You'll understand this better when I tell you that Bob Patton thinks this thing is already down in the lymph glands in my neck so you can see how widespread an operation like that would mean. I can't bear to leave you but I must. Good-bye.

> Ben

Still he was not satisfied. He wrote the word "over," twice underlined, and turned the leaf of paper. He thought of his wife by a pet name such as a man locks within the intimacy of their love. Time now was running out, but the courage prevailed. He resumed writing:

Cancer in its later stages is a hideous, putrid thing to have to live with and I don't want you to have to do it, nor to remember me that way. I'd be nothing but a burden to you. And if I wait until it gets me down, I won't be able to do anything about it and will have to go through to the end.

As you can see, this has been written at various times throughout the day as I thought of things to tell you. It is now 3:30. You'll be coming home soon, so I can't wait any longer. So long, Took, and thanks for everything.*

I flew to Springfield for the funeral and Paul met me at the airport. "God," Paul said, "if we could only have talked to him it might not have happened." Friendship can be an aching thing when the miles between become whole destinies apart.

---

* Used with the permission of Mrs. Benjamin P. Thomas.

We went into the Leland bar for a drink, needing it badly. But the place was full of memories: of Ben principally.

The interment was in Oak Ridge Cemetery on a knoll that looked down on Lincoln's eternal place of rest. Nearby was the grave of the poet Vachel Lindsay. Shadows played among the trees in this sanctuary where, with Lincoln, all men belong to the ages.

❦

By now long, busy years had passed since I had left the Knopf organization. My life had changed so radically, I had been cast so intimately among so many people who in varying degrees had despaired as Ben had done, that I was stirred with a sense of mystical communion with the man who rested on the knoll in Oak Ridge. The plane flight home was a succession of reveries of how this recasting of my life had come about.

I remembered the day when Alfred had signed the contract for Ben's book, muttering something about how poorly Mid-western historians wrote. I smiled, understanding Alfred—a cuff with one hand went generally with a pat of the other. As I recall, this was the Yuletide season when the scuttlebutters insisted that Alfred expected no more Christmases. We were in one of those publishing valleys between peaks like Hersey's *The Wall* and Ben's *Abraham Lincoln,* and the spirits of management were depressed.

Quickly thereafter I realized that my Knopf honeymoon had ended; indeed, I was rather in the position of the bride whose trousseau has worn out and who cannot afford a whole pair of drawers with winter coming on. Nothing I suggested satisfied the house. I wanted very badly to approach Herb Block, the brilliant cartoonist for the *Washington Post,* to do a book around his cartoons, and was told tartly that Washington was Alfred's territory and no one else need decide what were its book possibilities.

I came back from a luncheon at the New York Democratic Club dreadfully excited over a meeting with Frank Costello, one of his lawyers, and Meyer Berger, among the most brilliant reporters of *The New York Times*. The fact that such a meeting took place within these portals was in itself significant; Costello's complicity in crime certainly was no secret and, I must say, waiters and others at the Democratic Club treated him with respect. Costello himself was a fascinating contradiction, more a kindly Italian patriarch than a gang lord. He talked softly of how much he admired Steinbeck's *Of "Mouses" and Men,* and how he had sent bathtubs to his relatives in the old country. My notes are lost: they ran for pages. At the office even the possibility of a book about Costello was called ridiculous. But I wondered then and I wonder still.

An editor's morale is not strengthened in this manner. Then all at once my desk was moved to another floor, away from the stream of the trade department and I was left to stare by myself at a blank wall. I am not made to endure in a mole hill; any creative personality needs at least a small window on the world. I could sense, too, by the manner of many around me that I was either X, Y or Z in the old cloak-and-dagger business, but that did not break me. No matter how well lacquered the veneer of old-fashioned manners surrounding it may be, the voice of insult and provocation was not a Knopf staff invention: the same voice sounds in counting houses and diplomatic corridors and African jungles and wherever primitive defenses are needed for personal frustration.

Perhaps I was being caught up in what later Allen Sherman, the comedian, recognized as "the Madison Avenue Game" wherein an executive never is fired but forced to resign. To defeat that game would have been simple: I would have told Alfred how deliriously happy I was to be placed alone, against a wall, away from the mainstream; I would have heaped lavish praise upon his genius in divining this secret side to my per-

236

sonality. Of course, I cannot say for sure why I was being treated so shabbily, for no one told me anything, but I knew I was not wanted.

I went around to Michel's and hooked my feet behind a bar stool. A number of television people stopped by here, personalities you could see on the screen if you turned on that idiot's box. A drugstore down the block specialized in making up actors for television appearances and occasionally a face drifted by the window looking like a ragamuffin left over from Hallowe'en. These were the days of paid tattletales who harried networks and advertisers with lists of who was or was not a past, present or future Communist and a mild hysteria shook the pavement of Madison Avenue like the subways hurtling below.

It was a Friday afternoon, I remember, and the mood in Michel's was relaxed at another week gone by. Everyone was friendly and, upon occasion, a bit giddy-headed. All at once I realized that I had solved my problem. To hell with hanging onto any job: the sea was too full of other fish to fry. But I was not making a move until May; I liked warm weather for starting new ventures.

But mysterious forces had been working within me. Suddenly I was going to be asked to turn inside out everything I ever had experienced, thought, perceived, or believed. And to do it all for free. If I were a prophet, I would have said my life was finding a purpose. But purposes are easy to find in a midtown bar on a Friday afternoon.

CHAPTER FIFTEEN

Physician,
Heal Thyself

The Industrial Revolution
was still very much on the move in the early decades of the
twentieth century. In 1910, that year of Haley's Comet and my
arrival on earth, a wayfarer who braved the old stagecoach
road from Bristol, Virginia to cross the mountains into the hill
country of northeastern Tennessee came eventually to a log
cabin, a meadow, a river, the single track of the Clinchfield
Railroad and a boxcar that served both as a post office and tele-

238

graph station. Dreamy-eyed investors, leaning against the boxcar, told the wayfarer that he had reached Island Flats or Boat Yard, whereupon the investors returned to their speculations. Tracts of virgin timber covered the hillsides. Shale, limestone, silica were plentiful. A short haul away on the Clinchfield were the coal fields of Virginia and Kentucky.

In 1917, with counsel from the Rockefeller Foundation, the charter for the city of Kingsport, Tennessee was adopted. Industries sprang up: a cement plant, a brick company, a tannin-extract plant, a pulp mill. Logically a local pulp mill should supply a local papermaker who in turn should supply a local printing plant, a chain of events which explained the appearance of the Kingsport Press in the abandoned building of a defunct harness and saddle business.

The hill people of this Cherokee country, direct descendants of the Scots-Irish who had escaped over the mountains from Charleston during the closing years of the American Revolution, were sturdy farmers of such steady habits that their speech retained traces of Elizabethan English. Old Sam, the town undertaker, stood guard at the door of the Kingsport Press, collecting the guns as these farmers came down from the hills to learn the printing business for ten cents an hour. The Bible was the first publication of the plant; as rapidly as the books passed through the bindery, they were carted back into the hills as gifts to relatives, for these farmers turned craftsmen were as proud of their new handicraft as they were of their hills that linked the Blue Ridge with the Great Smokies.

In time the Bible-snatching ended and from sufficient paper to manufacture 100,000 copies an eventual 25,000 copies were shipped to market. Thereafter, the Kingsport Press hummed more profitably to the splash of tobacco juice in the buckets scattered around the plant. By the time Colonel E. W. Palmer came down from the old J. F. Tapley bindery in New York to take over command of the Kingsport Press, the beginning wage scale had soared to fifteen cents an hour. Palmer shook up the plant, for he was full of drive, organizational genius, and homely platitudes that made good business sense. Friends whom he badgered into buying Kingsport stock for a dollar or two a share long since have profited handsomely as Kingsport blossomed into one of the country's leading book manufacturers with sales offices in New York, Chicago, and Los Angeles.

The Colonel was an extraordinary man. When we became friends in the late 1940's he was both Curley's boss and a fellow member of the New York University Club. He was one of those energetic short fellows, bald as an eagle and almost as bright-eyed. His head had a way of tilting alertly like the head of an inquisitive terrier. What more than anything set the Colonel apart from his colleagues was the fact that he was, selflessly and tirelessly, a do-gooder. His pet interest was the National Society for Crippled Children and Adults which, over the years, he had helped raise from obscurity to one of the nation's leading voluntary health agencies. Since the Society's convention in 1949 was to be held in New York, the Colonel was determined that, as a handicapped person, I should speak on its program.

The Society, meeting at the Hotel Commodore, overran the place. My mouth felt dry when I faced the largest audience I ever had encountered. I looked down at parents, doctors, therapists—all devoted servants of the crippled in America—and wondered what, in God's name, I could say that would be meaningful. I stumbled on, overwhelmed by a sense of inadequacy, but my remarks brought a standing ovation and the *Ladies Home Journal* gave special emphasis to my concluding paragraphs:

> Actually, of course, no one is set apart; we all belong to humanity; and the real goal we would achieve is the goal that everyone wishes to achieve. It is a goal of many perplexities—a goal of normal living. It requires that we attain dignity as human beings, that there is some God-given reason for our existence, some purpose for us to ful-

fill. It requires that we be worthy of love—both the giving and the receiving of it.

I must live the day as it comes to me, and if I am wise, I will live it tenderly, for when it is gone it is a day that has escaped into eternity. Perhaps here is the key to the real goal we would seek: to see the world clearly as the only world that ever will be given to us—at least within this planetary system—and to see it for what it is: a world that gives us each day to live but once.

That was the crude beginning as I began to grope for an articulate philosophy of life that would be helpful to the handicapped and their parents. It would be a quest of more than fifteen years and I would never be sure that I succeeded. It would be a quest that carried me across New Jersey and into New York, Connecticut and Massachusetts; a quest that turned into Pennsylvania and West Virginia, Maryland and the District of Columbia; a quest that moved south into Georgia, the two Carolinas and Florida, swept along the Gulf coast to Louisiana and Texas and then northward to Oklahoma and Kentucky; a quest through Missouri into the prairies of Illinois and Iowa and north to the peninsula of Michigan and into Canada; a quest that turned westward through Wisconsin and Minnesota into North Dakota and across the high Sierras into California.

It would be no idyll: nothing is lonelier than a hotel room at night far away from wife and family; nothing is more wearying than waiting in railroad stations and airports where the coffee is poisonous, the whiskey raw, the recreational facilities idiotic; nothing is more depressing than the end of a speech and the burst of applause followed by the audience disappearing, leaving you in a void to contemplate whether all this effort and sacrifice and bone-tiredness has amounted to anything worthwhile.

No matter how ridiculous the fact may appear, I was almost forty years of age before I learned that the medical terms for my condition were cerebral palsy and athetosis. I had grown up thinking of myself as a "nervous child," but there were lots of nervous people in this world where misery simply adores company. Occasionally, a family doctor would call me "hypersensitive," which was all right too. The world abounds with what Hop Brill would have called sensitive monkeys.

But now I was thrust into the specialized realm of the professional; I was now a "CP" or an "athy," and I very deeply resented this tendency to cage me in a human zoo. I felt like a bug under a microscope. My affliction had taken dominance over my wholeness as a person. If I hitherto had been hostile toward medical men, I became more so. Perhaps I was unreasonable and yet if doctors could look at me impersonally, then I could return the compliment. Doctors were no special breed of cats: some of them were homosexuals, some alcoholics, some rotten mates at home, and outside of a hospital or office, where they ruled like little potentates, they were often dull bores. But not all: there are men of epic vision in the medical profession too imaginative to say to a fellow practitioner: "Doctor, I want you to meet Miers, a CP." Try that as a snappy opening for a conversation. There is only one reasonable answer: "Miers, CP, greets you Jones, MD. My underwear is BVD, my shoe width E, and I always unzip my fly when I get up to P."

Starling sensed my fretfulness, the exhaustion I felt after these treks. "Why do you do it?"

"I have to."

"Why do you have to?"

"I don't know why, but I do."

Really I did know why: I could not run away from what I considered the most valid challenge of my life. It would have been cowardly and shameful to do so, especially when I understood how slight was my disability compared to others who were giving cheerfully and unstintingly of themselves to the same quest. They restored my humor and revived my strength and I decided that if, truly, God had created a Chosen People, I was in their presence.

I would never meet anyone who for valor and charm surpassed Ann Carlson. I first saw her at a reception in New York. What God had intended for arms were pitiful stumps that she pressed together to hold a cocktail glass. Unobservable was the fact that she stood on artificial limbs for Ann had been born without arms and legs.

When next I met this remarkable woman the place was a United States Senate committee room where we both were testifying in behalf of an education bill designed to provide special equipment for handicapped children. Ann spoke unaffectedly of her early years. Another child in the neighborhood had been stricken with polio, overprotected by her parents, kept from school and other normal activities, and as a result had remained a lifelong, ineffective invalid. In contrast, Ann's parents had mounted her on artificial legs and said, "Go meet the world." Ann had learned to write by holding a fountain pen in her mouth, a skill that had permitted her to earn her doctorate at one of the best state universities in the Midwest and afterward to serve as an educational administrator in North Dakota. Senator Lister Hill from Alabama presided at this hearing. His eyes looked fringed with tears: Ann had that sort of impact on people.

Perhaps the Reverend Harold Willkie was her equal. Here was a minister of sweet and even disposition, whose religion was founded not upon dogma but upon the overwhelming compassion of Christ as the Savior. Harold had also been born without arms, but had decided that legs could do double duty as arms and feet as hands. I have seen him at banquets eating with his feet and making the incident seem perfectly normal; he can tie a bow tie with his feet; and once Starling and I watched him in the crowded lobby of the Hotel Fontainebleau in Miami Beach writing a check at the main desk—so swiftly, so naturally could he handle a pen between his toes that not one in a hundred saw anything unusual. Once when Harold wanted his church painted and the consistory decided it lacked sufficient funds, he resolved the problem by doing the painting himself—a man on his back on a scaffold. By numbers alone one cannot measure the good Harold did as a counselor to wounded veterans of the Second World War.

One can argue that Ann and Harold adjusted so well because they were "born that way" and life gave them no other choice if they wished to live in the world around them. I agree. It is easier to meet life never having legs or arms than to lose them suddenly. A friend I cherished when I worked at Knopf was Betsy Barton, who went around in a wheelchair as the result of an accident. Betsy lived close-by in one of those city mansions that came to a family whose head was a business phenomenon like Bruce Barton, a driving spirit behind the advertising empire of Batten, Barton, Durstine & Osborn. Betsy at birth had been endowed with many bounties: wealth, social position, intelligence, beauty. Had this very abundance somehow made paraplegia harder to bear; could the anticipations of life, if too great, become a handicap when the physical blow struck? In a brotherly way I loved Betsy: she was so handsome to behold, so bright a conversationalist, so warm and honest as a human being. Yet at times I thought there was a lingering pain, even a lingering resentment, in Betsy's eyes that would never fade completely, but I could not be sure and the impression could have been a product of my imagination.

No such question ever crossed my mind in those old Knopf days when my journeys carried me to Yellow Springs, Ohio where Antioch College and Louise Baker were then that community's claim to renown. Anyone who has read Louise's two delightful books, *Out on a Limb* and *Party Line,* knows how she lost her leg. She was a gay and vibrant woman now who no

244

longer startled unsuspecting friends by calmly sticking thumb-tacks into her artificial leg. But the imp remained in other ways: in a defiance of life that had been far from easy, in an impudent cynicism toward human vagaries (including her own).

Like Betsy, Louise was a beautiful woman, strikingly so, and among her lasting contributions to the world of fashion were crutches of varying colors to match the ensembles she wore. By her writing she had supported a husband through a trying illness. Now she worked in a research institute connected with Antioch and later went to Chicago to become a principal officer in the National Society for Crippled Children and Adults before marrying Howard Wilson, president of a life insurance company.

It was difficult to fluster Louise, and only once did I see her at a loss for words. We were standing in a hotel lobby in Springfield, Ohio, and Louise was easily the best dressed, most prosperous appearing woman in the place. But the drunk who stumbled over, extending a quarter, was too bleary-eyed to notice such distinctions.

"Here, lady," he mumbled, "take it. I never pass a cripple without offering to help."

Louise hesitated and I hissed: "For God's sake, take it. We can put it toward a drink."

And we did, before Louise drove off in the bright red sports car that I jokingly called her brothel on wheels.

Ann and Harold, Betsy and Louise . . . there were hundreds like them who crowded upon my consciousness: a tap dancer on a peg-leg, a one-armed pitcher in professional baseball, children who could not control their hands and so were learning to typewrite with their feet, a concert pianist who had lost both hands in an explosion during the Second World War and had taught himself to play beautifully with a pair of artificial hooks. I needed to be told by Jack Johnson of the University of Iowa that an affliction could exist more in the minds of others than in one's own mind. I needed Henry Viscardi's story to illustrate this same point—dynamic Henry, who as director of Just One Break, Inc. drove himself unmercifully to build an organization for hiring the handicapped into a model copied around the world. One night on one of his far-reaching journeys, Henry scrambled into an upper berth too weary to take off his shoes. He simply unfastened his artificial legs and rolled over to slumber. The porter, coming through the car to shine shoes, saw Henry's oxfords and gave a yank. Out came shoes and legs. The porter's scream awakened the car.

Then came that day in a hospital in Columbia, South Carolina when I was observing clinical procedures. A colored couple brought in a baby in their arms. The child's movements were listless, his eyes dull, his lips mute. The tenderness with which the Negro man and woman handled this helpless creature during the examination was a touching sight; their fingers clucked the chin indulgently, in loving voices they cooed encouragement.

"They possess the adoration of a madonna for that baby," I said. "That baby," the therapist told me, "is more than thirty years old."

I turned away, too affected to reveal my emotion. Who was I to have any claim to self-pity? My quest would continue.

৵

In working with the handicapped there are two problems—the parent and the child. Under most circumstances, the child is the easier of the two: nature and society are on his side and, if only left to his own instinct for survival, may manage rather well. But the parent stands alone, overwhelmed by that unanswerable question: "Why did this have to happen?"

With how many of these parents have I spoken? Some have been shy, some regretful, some shamed by guilt feelings, some bitter toward God, some reasonable, some lost to my powers of communication (and perhaps to any power in this lifetime). I have looked into eyes and seen tears and defiance, love and hatred, forgiveness and bitterness, petition and the pride that goeth before a fall . . . it is not always a pleasant experience. I have known parents who have chained their deformed children to beds or locked them in secluded rooms, seeking an out-of-sight, out-of-mind approach to their agony. And I have known parents who have modified this rejection into absurd overprotection as they respond to an impulse to prove to society they are not at fault for all that has happened.

All, I have tried to understand by seeing beyond the present moment to what went before. Once there was just a boy and girl in love building the dream castles of courtship and finding the courage to marry. Once there were those nights of the deeper union, two persons locked in an embrace, their passions blending. Once there were those weeks of waiting, hoping, praying, and parrying the awkward jokes about the bulging front; and then there was the labor, that frightful struggle a woman makes which sensitive husbands find all but unendurable; and at last the sweet, relaxing miracle of the birth itself—this reward for which millions of years ago humanity crawled out of the sea and stumbled across the earth.

But to some more is given than to others if physical perfection is the measure. What then? Is it not human through the long day and longer night that follows to cry out against this injustice and even to doubt if heaven itself exists? What could be more natural than to give voice to the inward torment: Why, *why* did this have to happen? To my mind often has come the memory of the travail suffered by Agrippina, condemned to death by her own son, the Emperor Nero. "Do you forget that nine full months I carried you in my womb and nourished you with my blood?" cried Agrippina in her misery. And the superstition that smote Agrippina yet endures: "It may be that the just gods were angry at my excessive love of you and used this way to punish me."

As one professionally untrained in medicine, psychology and sociology, I was often baffled and sometimes terrorized at the questions asked by these people.

A tiny, fiercely intense little woman with her hair twisted into a topknot like a handle on her head inquired insistently: "Shall we move our family to a city where the services for our handicapped child are well organized?" I could only answer as common sense dictated: "Do what is better for the family." Some people are happier in the freedom of country life, some respond to the fast pace of a city. The handicapped child, after all, was born into the family and should live their way rather than force them to live his. Can families uproot their natural habits for one child without harboring resentments which may be far more detrimental to the child than any lack of specific treatments?

After a speech in Battle Creek, Michigan, a husband cornered me in a hotel bar. His voice was husky. "You know," he said, "I ain't laid my wife since we had our CP kid. She won't take no chances on having another one like that."

"There are contraceptives," I said.

"We're Catholic."

"The chances that you'll have another child with an affliction can be very remote," I said. "Your doctor can advise you."

"Not her," my bar companion croaked. "We got two rooms upstairs—one for her and the kid, the other for me. But I know a place in Chi; it's twenty-five bucks but the girls are clean. Say, if ever you're in Chi—"

"No, thank you," I said, trying to break away.

My confidant followed me to the door. "Look," he said, "I ain't proud about that Chi business. It makes me love my wife more. I've just gotta do something to keep my sanity. So it's better for everyone, do you see?"

"I see," I answered. But I wondered what was happening to the child, deprived of a home founded on a healthy, normal love? Women especially liked to talk about how much they loved their handicapped children and seemed almost desperate in their desire to impress this fact upon society. But was not love subconsciously given? Nature, not law or society, afforded parents this right, this capacity. The reaction should be the same, whether or not the child was visibly disabled. But try to convey this philosophy tactfully to a woman who secretly resents her child's outward imperfections or whose husband has found solace in a Chicago sporting house.

It was in Iowa, I think, that Robert's mother assailed me. Her boy was eight, a spastic with legs that wobbled, hands that were twisted and a mouth that drooled when he attempted to speak. "Robert writes poetry," she said proudly. "Would you like to read one of his poems?"

"Of course," I replied.

The composition she handed me was entitled "To My Mother." I never read beyond the first two lines:

> I brought you pain instead of joy,
> The day that I was born . . .

Dear God, how could a parent root into any child this guilt-consciousness!

A very dear and understanding friend, one of the foremost persons on the American literary scene, wrote me a warm and mildly scolding letter about all the time and strength I was pouring into this quest. "They will drown you in their winey appreciation," she warned. "For you will have made them feel good, warm, human. They will give you something that the reviews of your books will never give you. But they give it to demagogues, too. . . . They give it, and the speaker wants more, and more (I am writing you my own autobiography) and then one day, you will suddenly feel drained in a way that no writing has ever drained you. It is as if you have poured your blood into the loose sands and all of it has slipped through the crevices. Has it nourished those sands? You do not know; you will never know. You beg yourself to believe that here and there in those audiences there are a few gentle minds, sensitive and good, who will keep what you have said in their memory and someday give it back in another form to the world. You make yourself believe that this is a way of group-growth and a good one (and it is). But it is a terrible expenditure of time and body; and I still do not know, after eight years of doing it from one end of the country to another, how much it counts. I like it; I like the shining eyes, the warm handclasps; I like to hear myself outwit the hostile questioner and I like the laughter from the audience that comes after witty sallies. All this is wonderful. And the old man who comes up and says, 'This is what I have waited my life through to hear someone say.' That is sweet. Bouquets are so nice, and wilt so soon and then throw off a stench to heaven. . . ."

I pondered this letter and its author, who was Lillian Smith.

Lillian had a vital claim to my time and energy. After leaving Knopf I determined to establish my own publishing organization and Lillian was the shining star among the authors I had under contract; as a literary property she could mean to me what Joseph Hergesheimer had meant to Alfred in his early years. Yet I never thought of Lillian in these commercial terms. She was too vibrant a human being for maudlin judgments.

We exchanged visits, she to Stelton and I to her home on Old Screamer Mountain in Clayton, Georgia. No one truly knew Lillian until they met her in the environment of her beloved mountain top. A letter would begin: "The old mountain is beautiful today with clouds and mists boiling up from its little coves and valleys"; she lived in a timeless place, beginning on another occasion: "Thursday. October—I don't know the date!" Once she and her father had run a summer camp on Old Screamer and Lillian, who never married, carried the memory of those children in her heart like a lonely mother. She could sit for hours, arms folded around her knees, recalling the stories she used to tell them about the Buss-Eye Ha'nt that lived in the trees. The old camp lodges, scattered across the mountain, were now her home so that you walked to one building for meals, to another to sleep, to another for a long evening's conversation before a roaring fire in a book-lined room. At night the stars were close; in spring the flowers bloomed gloriously.

Lillian's place in American literature had been secured by her novel, *Strange Fruit* and, in my judgment, by a later book, *Killers of the Dream*. Her love for the South was that of a mother for a prodigal child: so many failed to realize how pure and all-wise her devotion was. "I am neither popular nor unpopular," she once wrote. "I am hated by some, actually revered by some; hated as much by Negroes as by whites because I am not 'for' Negroes and they know it; I am for human beings and they (some of them) don't like that." She was insulted by a college that awarded her an honorary degree "because of her courage," adding almost snappishly: "I should have been given one because I write well or not given one at all. I certainly am not a brave gal. The world's scariest, probably. I am just too scared not to write, not to say these things that hurt inside."

Her letters were filled with sharp comments on publishers, editors, authors, Southern luminaries; frequently, in a sentence, she could destroy a person. In some future day, when enough years have rolled by, a fortunate literary historian will find rich treasures in her correspondence. Her life had been dedicated to her beliefs in a new South that could rise, splendidly crowned in social justice, and what wealth had come to her from *Strange Fruit* had been poured back in many ways to support and to ennoble that conviction.

So Lillian knew intimately the cost of a cause: how the years slip away and strength ebbs and friends forget or become absorbed in other interests. Loneliness is not the worst of what can creep around a mountain top, or the knowledge of resources that have dwindled away: it is bone and muscle weariness that touches the night with a sudden chill. And time running out. She talked of putting her Buss-Eye Ha'nt stories into a book, but that dream was hard to hold. She started a little Christmas story for our three children, but that too was never finished.

Frequently her faithful amanuensis, Paula Snelling, would write that Lillian had been ill. Or Lillian would tell of visiting the Clayton hospital into which had gone part of the earnings of *Strange Fruit:* "The hospital is so beautiful, so simple, so right —if the spirit can measure up to those softly tinted walls, the slabs of glass, the chromium, the operating room, the X-ray lab and so on. I roam around wistfully, admiring but troubled too . . . wondering." The cancer she feared cost her finally the removal of all the frontal chest and side muscles on her right side. "When I had Paula phone you," she wrote, "I didn't even know all my muscles were gone! They told me, little by little."

It is difficult not to wince when a dear friend is hurt so deeply. Tears were made for these moments. Yet even if Lillian had been able to foresee the future, this sensitive woman would have pursued her cause with the same dedication, for such was the sum of her spirituality. And, in time, I knew that I must continue my quest. But with a change. No matter what the revelation might cost me I intended to know exactly what the words meant when I told an audience: "My name is Earl Miers and I am afflicted with cerebral palsy."

◆§

For a mentor I found the first doctor I ever had admired. Meyer Perlstein is a rotund, rather squat fellow with a sunny disposition, a fondness for salami and kosher corned beef, a lively curiosity over the nuttiness of mankind and an inexhaustible capacity for work until a cardiac condition slowed him down. He was as typical of Chicago as The Loop, which, when viewed in profile, he somewhat resembled. His father, a bookseller, often operated his business more for pleasure than profit and as a result Meyer's boyhood years frequently were short on cash. But when Meyer lacked bus fare he could walk. He could endure between classes on sandwiches in a bag which gave him more time to study and to meet Min, his future wife. And so, in this hustle-bustle way, he completed his courses at the University of Chicago and the Rush Medical School, established a flourishing private practice and joined the hospital staffs at Cook County and Michael Reese.

One day, early in these professional years, Meyer's absorbing interest in pediatric neurology led him to a lecture by Dr. Winthrop M. Phelps, medical director of the Children's Rehabilitation Institute in Baltimore. For the first time Meyer heard the subject of cerebral palsy discussed with probing insight, and the experience was as though, like Alice, he had slid down a hole into his own medical Wonderland.

I doubt if in the world today there exist two more knowledgeable authorities on cerebral palsy than Meyer and Min Perlstein. Patients travel thousands of miles to visit their examination and treatment rooms on Chicago's west side. Meyer and Min live upstairs in the kind of neat but cluttered apartment that fits their personalities. Min, tall and a bit mannish looking and endowed with an incisive Jewish sense of humor that explodes into a tender understanding of life, is an irresistible force whether collecting china cows (she must have come close by now to cornering the world's supply), or collecting grandchildren (fewer than the cows), or telling her mother: "Mama, for God's sake, don't point here and then there and tell me you have cancer. Stick to one spot and we can make an examination."

Meyer has a little room where he turns semiprecious stones into costume jewelry for his friends, largely a post-midnight hobby. There are a pair of yapping dogs that nip at your heels. Meyer and Min shout at the dogs, but the canines know softies when they meet two.

I suppose it was the books I wrote that first attracted Meyer to me: no Jew of Meyer's disposition can resist even a spark of creative ability. His mind was the kind to which I respond instinctively—a mind that seeks strength through truth, courage through compassion, tranquillity through objectivity. Unlike many professional people, he neither discouraged nor disparaged my quest; rather, he was willing both to teach and to learn in this association where I, the cerebral palsied, was the explorer and he, the medical man, was the explainer.* Thus I brought him the experiences of a lifetime spent in large part among the disquieting shadows of ignorance and superstition, doubt and fear, and his guidance, patiently given, was like a sweet, refreshing wind blowing across an arid spirit. Not weeks and months but years went into this colloquy; Meyer possessed a gift for reaching back into memory and quoting the precise illustration I needed, using now a case study or the experiences of old friends like Winthrop Phelps or Dr. Howard A. Rusk, the director, and Dr. George G. Deaver, professor of clinical rehabilitation and physical medicine at New York's Institute of Physical Medicine and Rehabilitation.

There was only one point at which to start: what is cerebral palsy? These words were a ghost term wandering through our language like the words "lung trouble," which could mean tuberculosis, pneumonia, asthma, lung cancer or a cyst on the lung. Rather, it was the effect of cerebral palsy that had to be

---

*From these discussions came *Cerebral Palsy: Dr. Meyer Perlstein Answers Questions Parents Ask,* a pamphlet published by The National Society for Crippled Children and Adults; the observations about cerebral palsy that follow are based on this collaboration.

identified: where did the involvement reside—in the legs, arms or speech; were convulsions involved; were emotional problems a factor; a hearing or visual loss apparent; or some other sensory defect indicated?

Meyer spoke like a diagnostician, inventorying the effects of the disability, for the doctor's task is to treat a patient rather than a disease.

As a husband and parent, I wanted a straight answer to what was the life expectancy of the cerebral palsied. Meyer smiled; I was posing a question without a specific answer. He could generalize and say that the cerebral palsied have shorter life spans than normal individuals. He could even cite statistics of a sort: in the so-called normal population the death rate is 3 to 4 percent during the first six years of life and 25 percent among the cerebral palsied; at birth the life expectancy of a cerebral palsied child is about thirty-three years and after the age of six that life expectancy advances to about forty-five years. But there was an obvious flaw in these statistics, he added quickly: "A large group of successful, long-lived cerebral palsied people, who never think of themselves as handicapped, are not included in such surveys. They're just living, raising families, holding jobs, running their own businesses, getting along quietly and happily—and no statistical research agency, or no voluntary health agency, knows anything about them." Since I was then about forty-five, I thanked him for this addendum; I was not yet ready to start living on borrowed time.

It is not my purpose to detail the far range of our discussions which covered such general subjects as how the cerebral palsied child should grow, good and bad relationships between child and parent, home training, whether or not cerebral palsy is hereditary (if so, the chance is less than 1 percent), whether or not drugs could help, when surgery was advisable, the occasional necessity and cost of institutionalizing the child, education and intelligence expectancy, helping the child to make friends, and God knows what else. Meyer loved to turn his mind to a term like "IQ," which was used glibly and loosely at meetings involving the handicapped. In such moments a twinkle would light his eye, for he enjoyed debunking professional clichés:

"A child with an IQ of 80 is technically 'mentally retarded'; but if his father or mother have IQ's of 80 to 90, he isn't necessarily handicapped to them; and if he takes care of hogs or chickens for a living he may not be seriously handicapped in his work. But a child with an IQ of 110, which is above average, may be a misfit with parents and brothers or sisters whose IQ's are 160. Thus a handicap cannot always be defined in terms of the physical or mental characteristics of the individual; more accurately it reflects the social reaction of a particular environment to these characteristics."

Whatever Meyer told me I never quoted, for to do so would have been to pose as a professional. I had only one valid approach to parents and their children: I could talk subjectively as handicapped and objectively as a parent. I spoke more kindly and, I believe, with a great deal more sense, and Meyer was a powerful crutch upon which to lean.

◆

Just as moral propaganda is wasted on happy sinners, so is it utterly futile to exhort resentful parents to love their afflicted children. They don't, they can't and they won't; that is their handicap. These people, as Maupassant said, "reach the age of life with a bandage over their eyes and reason"; thus, like children lost in a forest of shadowy emotions, they stumble from one reality to the next, feeling cheated and mean. They have taken too seriously those fairy tales that ended: "And they lived happily ever after." So the joy of finding solutions which under the circumstances are possible and satisfying passes them by, and the sooner they can be separated from their children the better. Fortunately such people are a small minority.

Parents who can ask, "Why did this have to happen?" and then put the question aside, for seldom has it an explicit answer, I found to be an increasingly receptive audience. The real questions could be faced then: what has happened, how complicated is the resulting problem, and how do we compensate for these disabilities in acquired skills, in developing a wholeness of personality, in understanding the nature of human nature?

The story of Elizabeth Barrett, I discovered, had a profound impact upon these parents, for they could look upon it impersonally and still see its dramatic meaning. At fifteen Elizabeth had suffered a spine injury; at thirty-nine she was still an invalid. All hearts reached out toward this enormously sensitive and intelligent woman who understood every subtle nuance of the part that mind and body and spirit and emotion played in human experience. Her defeat could have been so pitiful, imprisoned as she was by the excessive domination of a severe and possibly incestuous father. But Elizabeth Barrett possessed within her frail body the blessed gift of spirituality and through her dog Flush, whom she called "Loving Friend," she clung to her dream someday of living a full life. Other dogs tracked the hares on moor and meadow, but Flush:

> Roses gathered for a vase,
> In that chamber died apace,
> > Beam and breeze resigning—
> This dog only, waited on,
> Knowing that when light is gone,
> > Love remains for shining.
> This dog only, crept and crept
> Next a languid cheek that slept,
> > Sharing in the shadow.

Elizabeth's lonely vigil ended tempestuously with the appearance of Robert Browning, the buoyant courtship, the years in Italy. The woman who once had described herself as "a little person loving little things" grew almost robust; at forty-three she gave birth to a son. Secretly, through these years of escape, she wrote the story of her love for Robert. When the manuscript was finished, she crept up behind him, stuffed the pages into his pocket, then fled from the room. He could, she whispered first, destroy those pages if what she had written was worthless. Because Elizabeth was dark complexioned, Robert often called her "My Portuguese," and the story of her love, which he now read, was presented to the world as *Sonnets From the Portuguese*, among the finest sonnets written since Shakespeare.

"You mean," parents would say afterward, "that I must think of my handicapped child finding his ultimate fulfillment beyond his own home?"

"I mean your child with a handicap," I would answer, "not your handicapped child."

After all, the world divides between two groups—those with handicaps that show and those with handicaps that do not show. I watch two men coming down the street. One propels himself on crutches, the other strides along on a sound pair of legs. What I know—all I know—is that both men are in motion. My eyes cannot tell me which of these two is more severely handicapped. Were I to trust some remnant of a ten thousand-year-old superstition lurking in our culture, I might choose the cripple. But Abraham Myerson, a truly gifted psychiatrist, has told me that "a man may get bald early in life and so have 'unfit' hair, but the brain is not affected by the baldness of his skull"; and so I smile with Dr. Meyerson at the absurdity behind all theories about the survival of the fittest insofar as those who do survive in any specific environment by that fact are the fittest and this "high-sounding statement . . . ultimately proves nothing."

So I come back to my two men in motion along the street and speculate over which is the fitter to survive in the specific environment that we share. Which is the more courteous? The more likely to smile? The more aglow with a warmth for life? The more responsive to another's need? The more willing to render faithful service to his employer, his community, his family? Which is better trained in his work and thus more capable of bringing insight and imagination to his labors? Which is less filled with prejudice, less consumed with conceit?

What is the greatest gift a parent can give to a child—any child—whether or not his disabilities are visible? I answer: give him an open mind, a tutored mind, an interested mind—a mind at ease with human endeavor everywhere—a mind that agrees with Judge Florence E. Allen: "They who wait upon the Lord shall renew their strength"; and with Louis L. Austin, a West Virginia innkeeper: "There exists within every human being an unlimited capacity for joy, achievement, love and peace of mind"; and with statesman Aneurin Bevan who believed that imaginative tolerance is "among the foremost virtues of a civilized mind"; and with comedian Eddie Cantor who said that the sum of happiness is "work—family—faith"; and with Dr. Charles W. Mayo who contended that "there is a definite purpose behind the inanimate and the animate, and the birth, life and death of all living things."

Parents have wonderful experiences preparing their disabled children to meet life courageously and exuberantly! A mother goes through her day finding all around her opportunities to help her child mature. In sounds like the splashing of water, the buzzing of a bee, she aids the development of his speech. Gaily, almost like giddy playmates, they imitate the noises of a teakettle, a barking dog, a moving steam engine, all speech helps. Or they sing. And other games fill their day— games to help normalize the child's breathing and chewing patterns. A sense of balance grows within the family, and if there are other children, then, sensibly, they should be made to share the extra work that the care of the handicapped child requires.

I look back upon the almost primitive clinics of my Brooklyn childhood and shake my head in wonderment: how changed today is the America of my childhood. Then there was nowhere for a nervous little boy to turn and now there are special clinics almost everywhere, and schools with specific equipment for his needs, and summer camps, and research organizations working on his problems. "Crippled children," Howard Rusk has said, "who in the past would have died early in life, now survive. They want to grow and work and love and be loved."

And America intends that they shall. What in little more than half a century I have observed has been a social revolution. Why and how all this came about stems from the fact that the do-gooder is as germanely a part of the American scene as the crack in the old Liberty Bell. Indeed, he has been around a great deal longer.

CHAPTER SIXTEEN

The Do-Gooders

*E*ven in those
turbulent years that preceded and followed the American Revolution, the do-gooders were as busy as beavers at a new dam. The range of their interests was almost limitless: Philadelphia had a society for assisting distressed prisoners; wherever the Scots, Welsh, Irish, English or Germans settled, societies sprang up to aid fellow immigrants; New York sponsored the Society for the Relief of Distressed Debtors; both Boston and Phila-

261

delphia were concerned with rescuing those suffering from "suspended animation," a term covering such afflictions as drowning, hanging, sunstroke, lightning and drinking cold water when overheated; and the Massachusetts Humane Society possessed a unique instrument, a "fumigator," that was used "for pumping tobacco smoke into the rectum of a person supposed to be drowned." As early as 1769 a Charleston society collected funds for "the deplorable maniac" and in 1786 Boston proposed building a hospital for disabled seamen. Huts stocked with food and firewood awaited the shipwrecked along the Atlantic seacoast.*

Doubtless from the first appearance of the do-gooders there were grumblers who complained that these societies were increasing like fleas in a henyard and someone should "get up a law ag'in' 'em"; but no one ever has found the will to risk such legislation. From time to time organizations like the United Fund have tried to scoop up armfuls of voluntary movements and have often found the effort similar to catching raindrops in a sieve; usually while the rain falls a dozen new societies blossom. With God's good help may it ever be so, for in a democracy everyone should be free to expend his charity on whatever need touches his heart.

Certainly the nervous little boy who recalls those Brooklyn clinics when there was no help for the cerebral palsied could not plead otherwise. Without the National Society for Crippled Children and Adults there might never have been an American Academy of Cerebral Palsy, and through that Academy's program of brain research came the enlistment of the National Institutes of Health and the Armed Forces Institute of Pathology into probing the problems of people afflicted as he was.

Nor, in all likelihood, would that nervous little boy have sat in 1960 as an invited guest and participant of the Eighth World

---

*Merrill Jensen, *The New Nation*, 140-2.

Congress of the International Society for the Welfare of Cripples and gained so clear an insight into how the peace of the world depends on more than guns and politics. The news from South Vietnam at those sessions struck a far happier note than it would six years later:

> In just a few short years, South Vietnam has built up an impressive Center located in the Military Hospital at Saigon. . . . There is an adequate prosthetics shop which uses local wood and leather. Work in plastics has also been started. . . . Training of local technicians has been proceeding well under the direction of the United Nations expert. . . . The vocational rehabilitation set-up through ILO [International Labor Office] advice and help is also adequate. A physical therapy expert has started work and teaching and is doing well but is overloaded with clients. Although the orthopedic department in the Center itself has not been developed, they have noted that it is less pressing since orthopedic services are available in neighboring hospitals. To benefit more fully, however, from the physical therapy expert, they feel it would be desirable to have a French-speaking expert working with the Vietnamese. Vocational rehabilitation work needs to be intensified at Cap St. Jacques, at Tu Dhuc, and at Vung Tau, with a supplementary purpose of developing sheltered workshops. A large children's hospital exists and a crippled children's program has been considered. . . . To tie all these developing services with possible sources of facilities and services in existing set-ups for able-bodied civilians, a rehabilitation administrator should be trained, possibly with the help of international experts. . . .*

Someday when the military men and diplomats have quit the scene, the do-gooders will come back—not only from the free world, but also from places like the Central Test and Work Organization Institute of Disabled Men in Moscow, for rehabilita-

---

*Eugene J. Taylor (ed.), *Rehabilitation and World Peace*, 32–3.

tion has penetrated the Iron Curtain. The report of how, voluntarily, men reach out a helping hand to the less fortunate—not only in southeast Asia, but also in every corner of the globe—thrilled the nervous little boy, now grown a half-century old. And he looked back eleven years to that first meeting in the Hotel Commodore and to the one person who more than any other had shuttled him around the country in his quest to assist others by discovering himself.

꧁

Larry Linck, leader of the do-gooders among whom I plunged, was as bald as Curley, but Larry's pate was more distinctive since under duress it turned red like an overheated stove. Larry must have been born somewhere at about the year of my own earthly appearance, but I recollect only that he attended Northwestern where he accumulated a degree, which presumably did him some good, and a wife, who was the more valuable acquisition. Barbara Linck came from Green Bay, Wisconsin, where her father was a merchant and an early sponsor of the Green Bay Packers, which by Midwestern standards gave her status and a certain holiness, and this delightful, robustly good-humored woman deserved at least these crowns. To dance to the tune that Larry piped required inexhaustible energy and faith, and Barbara, happily, possessed both. Among Larry's early crusades were years devoted to awakening Chicago to the fact that venereal disease existed and he took considerable satisfaction in having persuaded the *Chicago Tribune* finally to use the word syphilis in print, though I doubt if he realized he thus had inspired one of the Midwest's favorite jokes:

> *Joe: Gee, am I happy! My girl has syphilis.*
> *Moe: Is that good?*
> *Joe: It must be good—the* Tribune *is against it!*

264

The Lincks lived in Hinsdale, Illinois in a Dutch colonial home which was itself a refreshing indication of good taste amid the architectural extremes the newly-rich sometimes inspired in the suburbs surrounding Chicago. It was a home I frequently visited: a home with books, and the glass bottles which Barbara collected almost as passionately as Min Perlstein pursued cornering the world's output of china cows, and two lovely growing youngsters, Gail and Jeff, who kept their parents terrorized in the subtle ways that come naturally to youth. Jeff was perhaps the more richly endowed demon: he could acquire great leg gashes falling out of trees and slipped four-letter words into his spelling lists to make certain his mother was not napping when she reviewed his lessons.

As executive director of the National Society, Larry had an office in downtown Chicago at 11 South LaSalle Street. It was a delightful location: with the proper introduction any corner newsstand operator would place a horse bet for you; and a ticker in the men's bar in the hotel across the street clacked out stock market quotations if you preferred that kind of risk. But Larry was unaware of these amenities. From the moment Colonel Palmer had persuaded him to take over the Society and lift it from a small Ohio operation into one of the nation's foremost voluntary health organizations, he had lived, slept and thought nothing but the problems of the crippled.

Soon after I drifted into the Society's awareness with my little speech in 1949 at the Commodore, I was elected a trustee-at-large and four years later a member of the executive committee, which was the governing body of this multimillion-dollar operation. For the next dozen years, in one capacity or another, I would share in the administration of projects which in no small measure were revolutionary in their impact upon the social structure of America.

My first executive committee meetings were held in New Orleans where the Society was joining in the dedication of a

Crippled Children's Hospital soon to rise along the banks of the Mississippi. We were given the keys to the city, a boat ride and dinner at Antoine's, and our sessions were held in the *Vieux Carré* where the charm of the French Quarter architecture blended with the quackery of an old riverboat medicine show. The narrow streets and the ancient buildings with their iron-trellised balconies and myriad-shaped roofs cast a spell that was undeniable. It was not only believable that the ferocious Lafitte once strode Pirate's Alley en route to some deviltry in Absinthe House, but also quite likely that most of the shops in the *Vieux Carré* were managed by his descendants.

Among the staff members who attended the New Orleans meetings was Jayne Shover, a legend among the devoted professionals toiling for the betterment of the crippled. A beautiful woman and wealthy, Jayne worked because the needs of the handicapped filled her heart. Nothing could shatter her dedication. We tried to do so one night when we took her to see that astonishing attraction of the *Vieux Carré*, the Cat Girl, who could stand with tassels dangling from each breast and simultaneously twirl them in opposite directions.

"Goodness!" Jayne sighed, enraptured. "If only I could teach that kind of muscular coordination to cerebral palsied children!"

The personalities who congeal into an executive committee manage to live together because they share a dedication somewhat like Jayne's. Usually each in his home state was a prominent organizer of facilities for the crippled: the president of a state society as I was in New Jersey, or the builder of hospitals, clinics, summer camps, and sheltered workshops for the tens of thousands of crippled people directly serviced by the Society.

At the meetings in New Orleans each person held a special interest. The dominant personality, aside from Larry, belonged to Dr. William T. Sanger, then president of the Medical College in Richmond, Virginia; he was rather a troll-like man who sat through meetings with his fingertips pointed on his chest and his eyes closed, giving him not only an ethereal, airy appearance but making an observer believe that if his dreams vexed him he might vanish into thin air. Judge J. Raymond Tiffany was a fellow New Jerseyman, attorney for the Book Manufacturers Institute and a warm friend of Colonel Palmer. Davis E. Geiger of Ashland, Kentucky was in the hardware business but the greater measures of his ability were his gifts of diplomacy and his devotion to sour mash Bourbon. Edgar Kobak was a former radio and television executive who drank Alka Seltzer as though he had discovered the secret that had eluded Ponce de Leon.

And there was Theodore H. Wegener of Boise, Idaho, an attorney and Republican Party power, a bundle of nervous energy and devoted sportsman, unique in my experience as the only man who could drive a golf ball and beat it to a sand trap; and Paul Dietrich, who owned theaters in Los Angeles and Elwood M. Brooks who ran a bank in Denver and Harry B. Kelleher, a New Orleans attorney, and Tom B. Medders with his batch of oil wells in Wichita Falls, Texas.

There was Dorothy Houghton of Red Oak, Iowa, a Republican committeewoman who, it was whispered, was in line to become ambassador to The Netherlands and who touted Governor Harold E. Stassen as the coming man in America; and Harry A. Mitchell of San Francisco, former chairman of the board of the Western Pacific Railroad; and Mrs. Bruce Schaefer, wife of a doctor in Taccoa, Georgia, which was not far from where Lillian Smith lived on a mountaintop with her Buss-Eye Ha'nt; and Howard S. Wilson of Lincoln, Nebraska, the insurance company president who married Louise Baker.

Under a system of automatic rotation some of these people would leave at the end of the year, and among the annual replacements would be an occasional fathead. Governmental luminaries, though they added newsworthy names to the group, were a risky lot. Intrigue was so deeply ground into their habits that they drifted into cliques and encouraged rivalries. Academicians

267

generally grew peevish when crossed, for they were more accustomed to teaching than learning. The socialites were a distraction with their knitting and embroidery (or else they compiled reams of notes for purposes never disclosed); and the medical men tended to withdraw to Olympian heights and hurl thunderbolts at the discussions. There was usually a great amount of politicking for the presidency since traveling around the country during a fund drive with some celebrity like Bob Hope or Lucille Ball and being photographed shaking hands with the current occupant of the White House not only was satisfying to the ego but good business publicity at home.

One might conclude that this was a hell of a way to run an organization that today grosses better than 20 million dollars annually, but remarkable results were achieved. The drive of a Larry Linck, the dedication of a Jayne Shover willing to learn from even the Cat Girl were responsible for this happy circumstance. The Society maintained separate organizations in all fifty states, Puerto Rico and the District of Columbia; more than 1,600 local chapters supported hospitals, clinics, special schools, sheltered workshops and summer camps where some 200,000 persons received care and treatment for such crippling disabilities as arthritis, cerebral palsy, poliomyelitis, muscular dystrophy, multiple sclerosis, other orthopedic conditions, cerebral vascular accidents and speech disorders.

But statistics could not tell the story. One had to stand beside the doctor and therapist to appreciate the intensely human drama that was taking place beyond the board room.

A six-year-old child unable to utter the lively thoughts locked within his mind sits before a speech specialist. Between them is a communication board—simple pictures that can be translated into sounds—and a bell to ring when the child is ready to speak. Time, patience, devotion, struggle—and the result: a human mind set free.

Or observe an eight-year-old boy, a victim of a rock thrown

up by a lawn mower damaging the nerve centers in the brain controlling all motions of arms and legs and the power of speech. Science here must be marshalled on several fronts—doctor, physical, occupational and speech therapists working together as a team—and the result: a badly hurt little boy begins to speak again, to feed and dress himself, to stand upright and learn anew how to walk.

Or consider the Indiana part-time farmer and industrial grinder operator, age thirty-eight, with both his arms and legs so badly damaged when he tried to repair the clogged mechanism of a corn picker that amputation became imperative. To fit this man with prosthetic arms and hook hands only began the work of the physical and occupational therapists; everything had to be relearned from opening doors and turning on lights to slipping coins into vending machines—and the result: a man back driving his own car and holding his old job as a grinder operator.

Hundreds of case studies, covering the whole range of crippling disabilities that can befall a human being at any moment, were the compelling force that drew people voluntarily from all sections of the country to executive board meetings of the Society once every two months. Yet important though these individual achievements in rehabilitation were, they did not by themselves produce a social revolution. A great deal more was needed: imagination, courage, a reshaping of public attitudes, a willingness to engage in battle with the self-interests of a wide variety of narrow personalities, lobbying in legislative halls, and a boundless faith in the essential intelligence underlying the democratic process.

⁓ঌ

Again I return to that nervous little boy in a Brooklyn clinic and remember what America was like then. The night watchman at the company gate was usually a cripple injured on the job. I can remember Broadway in Brooklyn: a blind man with a tin cup played a fiddle on a street corner, another man without legs wheeled himself along on a platform hawking pencils. And then, almost so quickly that the phenomenon passed without comment, they began to disappear: the blind beggars, the crippled night watchmen, the pencil hawkers without legs. Through rehabilitation and public education a different America emerged. An "Employ the Handicapped Week" was instituted; an office of vocational rehabilitation became an important adjunct of the Federal Department of Health, Education, and Welfare; and White House conferences devoted long sessions to the problems of the visibly disabled. Now hundred of thousands of these persons go to jobs for which they are specially trained. Instead of depending on family charity or public welfare, they retain the dignity of self-supporting taxpayers.

The voluntary health agency was the motivating force in reshaping these public attitudes. And that so often scorned do-gooder likewise was responsible for taking the drooling child out of the secret back bedroom and unlocking his mind and putting him in school, where he always belonged. In place of the fear and the fantasies of suicide that so often haunted the handicapped when I was a child, a new America concedes his right to be different. We know today that a certain percentage of our people will, for one reason or another, become crippled. They are in the main as normal as anyone else if we give them the *right* to grow and learn and work and prosper and love and be loved.

At National, in those Board meetings, one of the major decisions we made was to change public attitudes toward architecture. A simple question was asked: "Why in a true democracy should there be back-door citizens?" Yet a great many buildings with long flights of stairs leading to their entrances are unavailable to persons on crutches or in wheelchairs. Revolving doors are a similar menace, and escalators, and self-service elevators with doors improperly timed, and public toilets that do not consider the problem of wheelchairs. In short, a good part of America had been designed only for those who walked on strong legs with stout hearts. Could public attitudes be changed and the face of American architecture with it?

We said it could with what we called the Architectural Barriers Project. A campaign of behind-the-scenes education was launched—the type of imaginative salesmanship for which a Larry Linck and a Jayne Shover were created. We talked, we pleaded, we argued, we set examples. In New Jersey, I worked where I could be effective, persuading friends at Rutgers to eliminate architectural barriers from the design for the entrance to a new university library, and, as a member of the local library commission, insisting that a proposed new township library be made equally accessible to all residents.

Other board members across the country were finding that an intelligent presentation of the case met with both sympathy and enthusiasm. Active support for the elimination of architectural barriers came from many sources: the Vocational Rehabilitation Administration, the Council of State Governments, the Committee on Hospital Architecture of the American Institute of Architects, the National Park System, and national hotel and motel directory publishers. More than half the states in the Union now have adopted or have started legislative action toward adapting public and business buildings so that they may be freely used by the crippled and the infirm.

At those executive board meetings another project always found Dr. Sanger fully awake and shuffling his papers. He was as near-sighted as my old friend, Carl Rollins, had been and like Carl always read with a paper pressed to his nose. But all the arguments as to why the Society should establish a national research foundation were so well fixed in Dr. Sanger's head that he could have expounded them eloquently in his sleep. Even the knitters put away their needles when Dr. Sanger stood, looking no taller than a toadstool and fingering the lapel chain on which he wore his Phi Beta Kappa key. He put heartfelt questions to the board. Can we prevent crippling? Can we reverse or retard the process of crippling? Can we unleash the biological and psychological potential of the physically disabled? What is our model of the rehabilitated person? Can we accelerate the process of rehabilitation? Can we improve the education of physically handicapped children? Can we help the handicapped live full lives in the community?

Noises rose from the canyon of South LaSalle Street: the honking of taxis, the high-pitched squeak of a whistle by which a Chicago policeman could be identified anywhere around the world. But within the board room only the voice of Dr. Sanger mattered as he spelled out this vision of the future that we all wanted to see fulfilled.

Yet I understood well the obstacles that must be overcome. To establish a national research foundation would mean placing a tax for its support upon the local chapters, which would stir up trouble. The old argument that money collected by a community should be spent at home would be vigorously expounded. "We know what is best for our own children," people would say, a reflection of the kind of parental possessiveness that made so difficult freeing the handicapped child to live a full life. I would see a crippled child having a wonderful time tumbling around on his own in summer camp when suddenly a parent—or, more likely a grandparent—would appear and snatch back the child. "I can't bear not knowing what is happening to him," they would declare, sometimes bordering on anger, sometimes on tears; and, with a sad sigh, I would watch the poor kid dragged away, his spirit and his self-confidence sagging. What good did it do to unlock a child's mind if you were going to chain him to the fears of unknowing adults around him? It was not enough to place a child on crutches or in a wheelchair—you must take as well a responsibility for the life into which you propelled him.

Why could not wings grow on these appliances of motion? Why should not a crippled child born in New York go to school in Illinois, marry a girl from California and settle in Texas? The purpose of a national and international society was to afford a crippled person wherever he went, across America or throughout the world, facilities for care and treatment and social attitudes that would accept him for the dignified, self-respecting human being he could be. And if research could help this person, then the resources must seek the talent no matter where it resided.

Unhappily where emotion is involved logical arguments still produce tempests. Yet we knew, listening to Dr. Sanger, that we were going to weather these howling winds and establish a realistic research program. The Easter Seal Research Foundation since its establishment in 1953, has spent more than two million dollars; in round figures, its grants have exceeded two hundred in support of over one hundred research projects in some seventy universities, medical schools and rehabilitation centers. Slowly and yet irresistibly, in charting future help for the crippled, the foundation has begun to close the gap between individual effort and massive effort. But scars were left before the battle was won.

It may seem ridiculous that a crippled person can become a bone over which rival dogs quarrel, but so he does. Philanthropic organizations in America are a big business, probably grossing some ten billion dollars a year. The National Society for Crippled Children and Adults, raising in excess of twenty million a year, ranks fifth among the voluntary health agencies.*

---

*The top four: Cancer, over 40 million; Tuberculosis, about 30 million; Heart, the same; March of Dimes, about 24 million. United Cerebral Palsy and the National Association for Retarded Children both gross above 10 million.

The symbol by which the National Society raises its funds, the Easter Seal, has been imitated by organizations competing for philanthropies in behalf of the crippled; the dates of its national campaign, when radio, television and press media have been mobilized in a common effort to "Help Crippled Children," likewise have been usurped by competing campaigns; and the United Fund has waged at least a cold war threatening the security of many of the Society's facilities.

The basic cause of such damaging conflicts scarcely can be called a mystery: where big money is involved so are large salaries and in the struggle to hold onto them few care who may be hurt along the way. Yet the National Society, or any professionally orientated voluntary health agency, cannot honorably surrender its independence. Its campaign, alerting the public to the needs of the crippled, is an educational force in shaping social attitudes, attracting young people to the highly satisfying careers provided by its services, awakening institutions to the research opportunities it offers, and insuring its elasticity in adapting quickly to new fields of care and treatment.

No one can fully appreciate the irritations that arise until he attends a meeting of the board where the complete national situation is reflected. A volunteer worker, no matter how firm his dedication, must live in his home community. Neighbors devote weeks to pressuring him to merge his appeal for help into the United Fund; sometimes the talk grows tough and even a little nasty; his nerves become frayed. To yield at home can mean losing a national charter and sacrificing all the professional assistance that association implies; not to yield can mean not only social umbrage but recrimination from local press, politicians and industries. "Lump all charity under one campaign—clear your conscience with one gift" . . . so runs the local argument that is so appealing. But in his heart the intelligent volunteer knows he must cling to his independence: his pledge as a trustee is to exploit every resource that government and the generous heart of mankind affords to the crippled. Sometimes, though not often, the volunteer resigns, worn out from fretting over the double-edged sword suspended above his head; sometimes he yields at home and the National Society starts anew, recruiting other volunteers who will fight the battle for independence, and very rarely is the public itself aware of this dogfight that disputes the right in a democratic society for individuals to exercise a free choice in the charities they wish to support.

Often I wonder at this do-gooder, this volunteer. His existence certainly has bettered America in a way that I have experienced personally. His motivation may be a disabled person within his own family, but just as often no more than a sense of duty to the less fortunate leads him to give of his time and fortune and physical strength to the common cause. He is, generally, a wonderfully resilient person; he is almost invariably a man of success, a believer in triumphs, a person who shares with my old philosophy professor a world of epic visions where men become heroes of the spirit.

It was at a convention in San Francisco when Starling and I first met Harriet Griswold, a gay, charming woman who wheeled her way into the room at the Top of the Mark. Poliomyelitis had stricken her in midlife, a staggering blow for a woman whose husband was Dean Erwin N. Griswold, of the Harvard Law School, with pressing social obligations and requirements for travel. But Harriet possessed what Larry Linck called "a ramrod spine"; she had no intention of being brushed aside from a bountiful life by this silly adversity. "You will be pleased for me that I travel with Erwin a great deal now," a recent letter told me. "I went to law meetings in Nigeria in '61 and returned to Nigeria last April when we visited their four new law schools. We were in Liberia in '63 . . . (and) last July we were sent to East Africa. I told them how to get me on a two-engine Piper plane so that I could fly from Tanzania to Zanzibar, a fascinating island."

Like so many others, Harriet proves that a pair of crutches, a wheelchair can sprout wings.

꿎

On a sunny October afternoon in 1957 when I reached the thriving city of Kingsport, Tennessee, it was difficult to realize that only forty years before the place had consisted of a log cabin, a meadow and a boxcar serving as post office and tele-graph station. We sped along a beautiful highway to the hand-some new building that I was to dedicate as the E. W. Palmer Memorial Center. More than twenty-six hundred persons had donated to the fund that had made possible this completely modern care and treatment center for the cerebral palsied chil-dren of northeastern Tennessee. "The old do-gooder," I thought affectionately, "had touched more hearts than he ever suspected."

Hundreds of grateful parents were in the audience: parents no longer afraid to face the problems of a visibly disabled child. I recalled how modestly Colonel Palmer had dismissed his role in helping to achieve a social revolution: "I'm only a darn old businessman—give the credit to the staff and the trained profes-sionals." And to the parents, I should have added. For I knew what it had cost them to meet the world as bravely as their children. They were, in the end, the core of the victory. Perhaps it was true, as a favorite pupil said of Leonardo da Vinci, "Nature cannot again produce one like him"; but of men as heroes of the spirit there need be no end.

And the same thought was in my heart on a May evening three years later in Pittsburgh when I gave the dedicatory ad-dress at the opening of the Pioneer School, especially designed to serve children with physical handicaps. The school was mag-nificently equipped, gay in decor, a place where any child could be happy. Pittsburgh had contributed only one-fourth of the cost of this building; the remainder had come from private donors.

I remembered my mother, marching her child off to school in Brooklyn. It was her spirit and not mine that had won. No Colonel Palmer, no Larry Linck, no National Society or United Fund or do-gooder could succeed without this surging strength of those headstrong parents willing to live with whatever fate hung onto their Trouble Bushes.

CHAPTER SEVENTEEN

The Amenities
of Living in
a Well

*T*here seemed
to be no middle ground with editors: either I liked them very
much or tossed in bed at night scheming over new ways to dispose of the corpses after slitting their throats.

Phil Vaudrin spoiled me; he was the editor with whom I
worked on *Web of Victory* (1955), the story of Grant's campaign
against Vicksburg, and *Robert E. Lee* (1956), a short biography.
He had arrived at 501 Madison Avenue following my departure

and we shared an admiration for Alfred and Blanche and an amusement for the childlike vendettas that were constantly ruffling the ranks of lesser officers in the firm.

Phil possessed the Ivy League appearance without the vacuous intellectual veneer that often accompanied this presence, and though he had lived for a time in Greenwich Village he had escaped without a trace of the "lit'ry" light-headedness that sometimes was engendered in that rarefied atmosphere of walk-up apartments. Perhaps it was his marriage to Pres that knocked so much good sense into his head, for she was that sort of girl. Phil knew books, good writing, the nature of an author, the limits of his own responsibilities. He was not an editor who demanded outlines before committing himself to an idea, for he understood his authors as craftsmen and could gauge their mental capacities. An outline, if valid, can be almost as much work as writing the manuscript; and if an outline is simply thrown together to protect an unimaginative editor, then its essential service is to reveal those personalities who do not belong in publishing. Nor was Phil a quibbler over words or a frustrated author seeking to impose his genius upon his charges. He toiled with good humor, intellectual honesty and a genuine compassion for the poor devil who was trying to achieve a result that would make them both successful; and, understanding his writer, he was satisfied when that lonely fellow, working in his deep well, emerged with the best manuscript of which he was capable.

Phil was an editor Lillian Smith would have liked. "For God's sake, Earl," Lillian once wrote, "let's work out our editorial problems only with each other and not discuss them with other people, with agents etc. I cannot work that way and never have with any other book. My agents did not see *Strange Fruit* from the time I finished it, sold it, and it was in final form—probably in galleys. George Brockway and I did not discuss any point of my book *Killers of the Dream* with my agents. It is nerve-wracking enough simply for two people to thrash the little points out;

it is just too much when everybody begins to get in on it and 'votes' for titles and so on and on. . . . You know and I know nothing creative ever came out of such discussions. It is always silly compromises where the original brilliant idea is vulgarized finally by numerous little demeanings and cuttings. . . . I sometimes get the idea but see it in the wrong costume so to speak, trail around with it, get disgusted, strip it, redress it, and well . . . so it goes. A good editor can be patient, can see what you are aiming at without hurting you by telling you what he would do. But other people always tell you what they would do, although they don't write and can't write and well—why slow down a piece of work by putting the author through such agony and hurt!"

What made a writer? How did his mind function when it teemed with ideas that he tried to sort out and put in order much as a child might play with a pile of blocks? Monica Mann, watching her famous progenitor who had given the world so priceless a literary bounty as *The Magic Mountain,* understood the process perfectly:

> My father's work consists of linking life which he experiences—and he does have some experiences—with that which he does not experience so that it becomes art. He hardly knows how to distinguish one from the other. At times he thinks he has invented something but has really experienced it, or believes he has pictured something he lived when he really invented it. This matter of invention is not very clear at all because it may represent a probing or prophesying of something that exists or will exist, or because one might have experienced it before birth. Creative writing is extremely mysterious.[*]

Phil Vaudrin perceived in his authors what Monica Mann observed in her father. Even a historian—the orthodox or the

---

[*]Monica Mann, "My Father," *The Saturday Review Gallery,* 431.

unsanctified—can employ methods of research that are clinically exact yet when this material passes from his mind onto paper that process becomes subjective; he may deny this flexibility between the library stacks and the printed page but the mystery is there nonetheless; and when its existence can be appreciated, a Churchill gives posterity the magnificent emotion and reality of his *Life of Marlborough*.

What made Phil Vaudrin dear to me, quite apart from his editoral ability, was his wonderful capacity for personal friendship. Spiritual communication between two people may seem an obtuse suggestion—like faith healing, for which I am far too faithless—but somehow we had this kind of quiet, easy-going relationship. Phil comprehended why I had hardly determined to become a publisher when I wearied of the enterprise: the creative spirit and business drudgery mixed poorly. Later I went back to New York as an editor for the World Publishing Company but when the firm moved to West 57th Street I was put in a room with four blank walls and a door. I knew then the association was ending: the old creepy feeling returned and for want of a window an editor was lost.

"It is a reasonable psychiatric reaction," Phil said. He worked in an office with two windows: across East 51st Street I could see Ed Murrow at his desk in CBS and down Madison Avenue was the old mansion that Random House shared with the Archdiocese of New York and where, it was rumored, Bennett Cerf had threatened to put up a six-pointed star to startle those who came calling on Cardinal Spellman.

Phil was my confidant when I decided to give my full time to writing. I had $1,500 in the bank: it was a risky business with a growing family of three kids, but I had a sound knowledge of the book business and a study at home with six windows.

"What does Starling say?" Phil asked.

"She says go ahead."

"Then what's the problem?"

So I burned my editorial bridges, so to speak. I had learned this much from Reed Silvers: if I waited too long I would be trapped by body aches and the onslaught of the years.

I could talk to Phil about my drinking, the only source of irritation that ever disturbed my relationship with Starling. Meyer Perlstein had been perfectly frank about my athetosis: in times of extreme tension the only drug that would relieve it was alcohol.

"It's a hell of a risky crutch," I said. "If you lean on it too heavily you land on your face."

"Is the increased tension physical?" Phil asked.

"No," I said. "It's emotional. But the drinking can become an emotional problem. I can end up with two afflictions—cerebral palsy and alcoholism."

Phil's smile was gentle. "My friend, you have a struggle."

And, off and on over the years, I have struggled, sometimes desperately.

Unexpectedly one day Phil Vaudrin dropped dead of a heart attack. I never again published a book with Knopf, but not because of any diminishing of my respect for Alfred and Blanche. I simply avoided 501 Madison Avenue, Michel's bar, or Pierre's where we used to lunch richly on Alfred's expense account.

I missed Phil too much.

⇛

Among the old friends who rallied around, anxious to help me succeed as a freelance, was Carl Haverlin, president of Broadcast Music, Inc. Carl worked in New York and voted in Los Angeles and had he concentrated on any one of his ten thousand projects he might easily have developed six ulcers. BMI was constantly involved in a legal war with the Music Corporation of America over the control of the country's musical talent, and each rival supported a legion of lawyers, but this extravagance was the least of Carl's worries. He was Damon and Ralph Newman was Pythias in God knows how many enterprises, for if anywhere in the United States there was an event or rare book or manuscript involving Abraham Lincoln, Walt Whitman or the Civil War, Ralph and Carl were somehow mixed up in it.

The energy that scientists released by splitting the atom Carl long since had released through sheer human exuberance. He both looked and bounced like a rubber ball and landed where he pleased. People worked for him without knowing it: Ralph, Carl Sandburg, Allan Nevins, congressmen and, I daresay, an occasional occupant of the White House. And yet who could resist a man who, coming from a performance of Archibald MacLeish's *JB* and being accosted by a ragged panhandler, peeled off a ten-spot and said gaily: "Here, take it—I'm so depressed I'd like to see someone completely happy"? Or, buying all the roses from an old woman in Grand Central Station, would go through the car of a commuting train, handing a rose to each woman passenger and saying impishly: "Compliments of the New Haven Railroad"? Those two ageless stalwarts in the Men's Bar in Washington's Statler always keep me apprised of Carl's latest forays into the nation's capital. "You missed Mr. Haverlin last week," one of them said not so long ago with a sad shake of his head. "Too bad. He bought champagne for everyone."

Within character Carl decided to do something sensible in the presentation of history on radio and the allies he enlisted in this venture, through Allan Nevins, were the members of the Society of American Historians who already had enjoyed flexing their muscles as cofounders and cosponsors of the magazine, *American Heritage.* These were no silly, cops-and-robbers dramatizations Carl wanted, aimed at an audience of semimorons; serious historians wrote honestly and intelligently about their fields of special interest. Bruce Catton discussed Grant and Lee, Carl Carmer the building of the Erie Canal, Arthur Schlesinger,

Jr. the age of Andrew Jackson, Dumas Malone the world of Thomas Jefferson, Elting Morison the wacky days in the White House when Theodore Roosevelt lived at 1600 Pennsylvania Avenue, Quincy Howe relived the Jazz Age . . . in all, more than sixty members of the Society participated. Better than four hundred radio stations carried these half-hour shows distributed by BMI, and discovered that millions of Americans could enjoy history without guns popping in the background and bogus Indians grunting "Ugh!" Carl dumped the whole mass of scripts into my lap and said, "Make a book out of them!"

The assignment called for combining editorial imagination with diplomacy. After all, these scripts had been written to be spoken and not read. But revising the scripts, or even appending the appropriate editorial introduction to each of sixty selections was the least of the chores imposed. To give the work proper continuity the manuscript had to be divided into eight sections, and each of these required its own essay that must be lively in style but sufficiently profound in concept to satisfy some of the most sophisticated historians in the country. Luckily the final judge was Allan who, as an editor, followed the style of Phil Vaudrin: he was no word quibbler, no imposer of his own will upon another man's labors; he suggested no more than a half dozen minor line changes.

Carl was so happy with the outcome that, like a French general, he kissed me on both cheeks, a rather ridiculous spectacle since we were dining at the Netherlands Club. "We've got something," Carl declared exultantly; and, indeed, we did for *The American Story* (1956) was not only a dividend selection of the Book-of-the-Month Club but also distributed by the Literary Guild and overseas and paperback editions followed.

About this time, too, I was laboring on a book about the Civil War in which I was passionately involved. I think by then I knew considerable about Abraham Lincoln and how his mind worked. I wanted to project him as the leading figure who had glimpsed, perhaps unconsciously, the emergence of a national conscience in the North that led irresistibly to war and was not unlike the present emergence of conscience in the struggle over civil rights. I knew that the Southern myth makers would try to howl me down, for they had a theory about the war that more or less blamed the great American conflict on Lincoln, who apparently had kidnapped Scarlett O'Hara, forced her to do a belly dance in the East Room of the White House while a darky band strummed "Dixie," and this outrage so inflamed the Southern gentility of old Jeff Davis that he blasted the hell out of Fort Sumter.

Since World had published six successful books for children for me, I signed with them for the publication of *The Great Rebellion* (1958) and was assigned Donald Friede as my editor. There were those who declared that Donald had been associated with publishing since Gutenberg perfected printing with movable type, but I always regarded this rumor as an exaggeration; moreover, Donald lived in the memory of a Paris-oriented background and a later fling in Hollywood, which did not necessarily square with a solid background in American history; and whereas I appreciated his gift for working with novelists which made Mac-Kinlay Kantor admire him, I differed from Mac in ways quite apart from the fact that he played the guitar and I could not.

Donald was an editor who had other ideas of how this book should be written. He pressed hard for his way and the experience became distracting. I kept my dignity in conference, but swore a lot in private. Carl Sandburg could appreciate my intensely personal involvement in this book, and in an address at the Library of Congress said: "I admire the remarkably vivid style, the colorful sweep of Earl Schenck Miers' thick book, *The Great Rebellion*. It possessed him and he couldn't help writing it." But, unfortunately, Donald was not Carl Sandburg. The book was finished in an atmosphere of hostility, and I wept anew for the untimely passing of Phil Vaudrin.

In those days at World a kind of kingmaker superiority pervaded its staff. The editorial powers there were insistent that I do a children's book about Ben Franklin. I researched the subject and believed that if I dropped out Ben's peccadilloes with the ladies, he was rather a stuffed shirt; I could not write the book with honest feeling and said so. The response was huffy: not "to hell with you" in so many words, but that was the effect. So we closed shop at World and I retained my integrity.

So, in those 1950's in New York, I learned that just as there are good-bad books, editors vary. And there were always golden moments to which I could cling. I remember one of those wonderful Friday evenings in summer when the city grows calm and lazy and filled with the magic of a deepening tranquillity. Allan Nevins was leaving Columbia to take a position at the Huntington Library in California and Carl Haverlin threw a little farewell party. We met at a private club somewhere in the Upper Fifties, perhaps two dozen of us, and the wine and dinner were excellent, the mood affectionate, the hours too short. Allan spoke with that straightforward, rather staccato voice that is surprisingly one of his most effective mannerisms. So few are the moments in a lifetime like this, I thought, when the day stands still to honor a man of Allan's simple humility, loyalty and superb accomplishments. Like wine, such a person ages memory with a peculiar richness. Alfred Knopf sat next to me that evening; I never have encountered a more charming dinner companion.

One other memory grows more precious with the years. The scene was the steps of the Senate wing on Capitol Hill. I sat between Lloyd Dunlap and Roy Basler, old friends I had known from the years in Springfield when both had toiled on the *Collected Works*. This day, when the nation's capital was celebrating the centennial anniversary of Lincoln's first inaugural, brought one of those shining mornings that Washington tosses so effortlessly into early March. Before the steps stood the podium and beyond was a mass of humanity. Across the way the sunlight bathed the Supreme Court building in brilliant whiteness as though emphasizing how clean in fact and spirit justice must be. Then down the aisle came two grand old men, Carl Sandburg and Sam Rayburn. They walked a bit unsteadily, linked arm in arm, and a great cheer went up. Like Henry Clay, both these white-haired old fellows had pressed their ears to the ground and listened to the sounds of approaching generations in America. And like the famous old Kentucky compromiser, each had tried to enrich the heritage that would await future Americans. The people knew. The cheers grew in volume. I glanced smilingly, briefly, at Lloyd and Roy. Emotion fringed all our eyes with moistness.

"You and Miers make a rare team," Carl Sandburg one day wrote to Paul Angle. We measured our friendship now not in years but in decades. For me to reach Chicago without seeing Paul amounted to the kind of heresy that I understood, and I had become an expert in directing baffled taxi drivers in how to find their way to 1902 Lincoln Park West where Paul lived in a house that had no business whatever being in Chicago for all that this neighborhood was called Old Town. "Paul," I said, "this farmhouse belongs on a Vermont roadside."

Paul nodded, immensely pleased with the treasure he had discovered within walking distance of his office at the Historical Society. A large, fenced-in back yard provided a spacious place for relaxing in warm weather. Across the street stood a Buddhist temple in what once had been a carriage house. Old Town, like most of Chicago, could run from near slums to luxury within a couple of blocks, and Paul hung a small baseball bat beside the back door in case a prowler awakened him at night. The trouble was the break-ins always came when the Angles were away. Walking home at night Paul invariably smoked a cigarette. "If an attacker seizes you and you give him a poke in the eye with a lighted butt, he'll damn soon let go," Paul said. Life in Chicago can be exciting.

In this Vermont farmhouse a thousand miles away from where it belonged, I watched the Angle children, John and Paula, grow up and go to college, marry and embark on their private lives. Vesta Angle was a splendidly vibrant personality, filled with an Irish love for fun and completely feminine in outlook. She and Paul had been sweethearts since their college days in Ohio and she was keeper of the scrapbook detailing Paul's rising career. And she was the family do-gooder, the volunteer hospital worker, the goer to charitable luncheons.

Moreover, Vesta possessed rare intelligence for an author's wife: she minded her own business unless asked for an opinion. Paul's bandbox study, where we frequently worked, was expertly arranged for the purpose. The right basic sources were here. A couch did fine for spreading out drafts of manuscript. A nude on the wall cleared minds that grew fuzzy and the room was removed from ordinary household noises and the sounds of traffic on Lincoln Park West. Occasionally, a child's shrill voice penetrated our privacy, but children are a pleasant reminder that life throbs on.

I do not remember that Paul and I ever once quarreled over any of our almost endless collaborations. We worked with complete respect for our individual abilities: in no small degree, each taught the other. Paul had the gift of a skilled editor, recognizing that excision was the key to fashioning a crisp, readable manuscript. He was, like myself, an intense stylist in writing, enjoying the hours that could go into the search for the right word, a lively turn of phrase. His literary idiosyncrasies were slight, whimsical, easy to live with. He did not, for example, like to use the verb "feel" as a synonym for "believe." "The only thing you should feel," he said, "is a lady's bottom," and insofar as no fannies were squeezed in the manuscripts we produced, we may never have used that verb. Paul also was obsessed with a conviction that no publisher ever should be allowed to remainder (that is, to sell at a cheap price) any book until five years after it had been published, a provision that drove some publishers crazy, but then publishers could drive us crazy, too.

Paul was an extremely successful author who never employed a literary agent, nor did he need one. I had worked through an agent early in my career and then had abandoned the practice. It was adding to an already complex creative situation a third party who was becoming a nuisance by resorting to the same tiresome cliché: "Perhaps this episode falls between two stools." The only image raised in my mind was of a baby in a loose diaper leaving his droppings all over the floor.

After the *Collected Works* appeared in 1953, Paul and I devoted ourselves to the somewhat Herculean task of reducing this massive bulk of Lincoln's writings to a single volume. We envisioned no scissors-and-paste job of excision that might take a month or two; we wanted with proper editorial interpolations to reconstruct Lincoln's mind, his personality, his times and the war he fought through his own words. After awhile we had read and reread so much of Lincoln's prose that we began to talk and to think like old Abe, but there are few better orientations for understanding the modern America in which his unfinished war endures. The wholeness of the man became astonishing: he was much more than the uncommon common man, as a shrewd observer once described General Grant; Lincoln had risen from the people so steeped in a moral force that he became the uncommon modern man whose meaning would be understood in an emerging Africa and breach the Iron Curtain. *The Living Lincoln* was published in 1955 and perhaps one of the best rewards Paul and I reaped from the toil that went into its creation was its selection among the three hundred and fifty books chosen by the Carnegie Corporation of New York as most descriptive of life in the U.S.A.

و‌ۀ

With the publication of *The Living Lincoln* I believed that I had discharged my last debt to the memory of my beloved grandmother, Nana, but I was wrong. Republican-dominated Washington was determined to squeeze every ounce of reflected glory from the sesquicentennial of their idol's birth. When I went to Washington to become editor-in-chief of the special commission Congress had appointed for this observance, I was asked, "How do you vote?" and gave what I considered the only appropriate response: "In a booth behind a curtain."

The man most responsible for bringing me to Washington was David C. Mearns, whom I had known since those days when we had both sat on the committee of *The United States Quarterly Book List.* "I know," I wrote in an introduction to one of Dave's books, "that it was a happy occasion, filled with laughter and warm-hearted conversation, and that I came away a wiser man; but in this sense I am always meeting David Mearns for the first time, for he possesses that rare gift of ageless companionship which, though the years may stiffen muscles, leaves the spirit nimble and the heart unburdened."*

Dave's acquaintance with Washington had begun as a blue-eyed toddler some sixty years before when McKinley occupied the White House, and for more than forty of those years he had been a devoted servant of the Library of Congress. He was a protegé of Herbert Putnam, that unforgettable Librarian of Congress whose "fortunate impress was upon everything he touched," including David Mearns. As Chief of the Manuscript Division, Dave had charge of some 16 million items ranging across every facet of American life; and he held as well the chair of history attached to the division through an endowment of William

---

*David C. Mearns, *Largely Lincoln*, vii–ix.

Evarts Benjamin of Vermont. Upon another occasion I said of Dave: "Whether a scholar's labors carry him into the still little used papers of the American Colonization Society or into the mass of documents of the League of Women Voters so popular with students of the current political scene, each is serving the national culture with equal passion. Each needs help, sympathy, appreciation, and a loyal friend, the qualities that make Dave Mearns a national institution among historians."

But it was as an off-hours companion that Dave really blossomed. His clear eyes twinkled with a kind wit he could not repress, and whenever we gathered at the Congressional Hotel or the Cosmos Club I was reminded of Tennyson's buoyant lines about The Cock, that excellent tavern on the north of Temple Bar:

> O plump head-waiter at the Cock,
> To which I most resort,
> How goes the time? 'Tis five o'clock—
> Go fetch a pint of port.

In the same way that Alfred Knopf was the nation's master instructor in publishing, so was Dave the man of magic in charging historical research with enormous vitality. He never demanded anything; his method of teaching was by artful suggestion of where to look or whom to see to turn up the missing part of a historical riddle. Invariably he was right: the range of his mind was a source of constant astonishment to me, and the devotion which he gave to an aging mother reflected the gentleness with which he plied his unofficial trade as a tutor in the art of historical fidelity. Not that he was without irritations: laziness, slovenliness, and stupidity ruffled his characteristic calm in no uncertain terms—a Mearns frown equaled a Knopf roar.

As for my duties as editor-in-chief of the Lincoln Sesquicentennial Commission, which consisted in producing for scholars the three volumes of *Lincoln Day by Day*, a sentence can describe the chore: I supervised a research staff in Washington and Springfield and applied the devotion to detail that must govern such professional editorial occupations. I could not have asked for a more congenial advisory committee: L. Quincy Mumford, the Librarian of Congress; Dave and Paul; Roy Basler, who now ran the Library's Reference Department; and Clyde Walton, Illinois State Historian and a friend of long standing.

The joy in the labor was the excuse for being in Washington twice a month over a period of two years. Even the rather pinched austerity of the Eisenhower Administration could not rob Lafayette Square of its gentleness in spring, or Pennsylvania Avenue of its exciting bustle, or The Hill of its magnetism as the seat of the mightiest government on earth. I was free to come and go as I pleased: it was a perfect life for a man who had submerged his physical disability in a love and trust in people.

To joke about Washington and its bureaucrats is part of our national tradition and, God knows, there are dunderheads who toil here at the public's expense, but the joke makers really do not know their capital city. From Monday through Saturday no other place in America works harder. Washington is a city of experts, a city of dedication. The hours are long, especially if one associated with a human fireball like the Honorable Fred Schwengel of Iowa, who began his day with breakfast meetings in the House dining room. Invariably Fred arrived ruddy-faced and scornful of those poor beggars like myself who had not jumped out of bed at dawn and unlimbered for the day with fifty pushups. Washington is the nation's crossroads where someone you have not seen for years happens to be "in town for the day." It is Looneyville and Dreamville and Get-Things-Doneville all rolled in one. The press emphasizes its disputes and mistakes; the vast amount of remarkable achievement that flows from Washington has become too commonplace for comment.

Part of my delight in Washington was resuming the friendship of Lloyd Dunlap, whom I had known in Springfield as a member of the editorial staff of the *Collected Works*. We assumed the names of the Lincoln boys—Lloyd was Willie and I was Tad—and between us in gratuities we practically supported Fats, the Negro piano player at the Market Inn. In and out of Washington we knew hundreds of friends in common—their wives, their kids, their present work, their good and bad points—for Washington is also Gossipville. If Fred Schwengel and Allan Nevins fell into an argument in the lobby of Boston's Palmer House over the proper way of doing pushups and ended the dispute by peeling off their coats and demonstrating individual techniques while other astonished hotel guests looked on, Washington knew about that performance next morning. It knew about who was sleeping with whom (and where and sometimes why), and which college president had been drunk as a hoot owl two weeks before, and what Carl Sandburg had said about the type of mind that produced a novel like *Tropic of Cancer* in a heavily censored press conference, and which collectors had been robbed of their eyeteeth by what dealers, and how Dave Mearns once had almost kicked Calvin Coolidge in the behind.

Friendships in Washington tended to rest on a different level than in New York or Chicago. Washington basically was also Help-Yourselfville, but whether you did well depended on the kind of mark you had made in life and the type of person you were. Convince your Washington friends that you were fighting for a right principle and an enormous amount of power could be generated. There were channels for making your voice heard on The Hill. And in the White House too, if that became important.

❧

What being in Washington demonstrated was the fact that when a writer leaves his well, life can acquire a sudden zest. Nor were Lincoln and the Civil War the sum of my intellectual interests. During these years I produced three books for the corporation that had achieved near perfection in the reconstruction of Colonial Williamsburg. A short plane flight connected these two interests; in fact, such was the difference in time between the District of Columbia and Virginia that I could fly from National Airport to Patrick Henry Airport and arrive four minutes before I started.

The change merited this Lewis Carroll touch of fantasy; Washington and Colonial Williamsburg were worlds apart. The charm of another century pervaded Williamsburg; here time had stopped when George Washington marched down to Yorktown and brought Cornwallis to his knee-buckles. Ed Alexander, a rangy, gentle scholar out of Wisconsin, who was in charge of publications at Williamsburg, was as stern a research disciplinarian as Dave, and I felt a deep gratitude to him for that fact. My more intimate associate was Jack Walklet, who produced another youngster each year so that when we all assembled in one room we took turns breathing. Jack loved fine printing, good writing, jazz records and bonded bourbon; he was a companion rather than a boss, and a cross word never passed between us.

Blood of Freedom (1958), a volume in the Williamsburg in America Series, was the book I did for Ed and Jack that brought me the greatest satisfaction; this book reconstructed the stories of colonial Jamestown, Williamsburg and Yorktown and steeped me in the traditions of an American nation struggling to be born. My congenial guide on these explorations was a lovable Tarheel, Hugh Rankin, who later joined the history department at Tulane University. Hugh was a big fellow who laughed most merrily at a good story on himself. He was, after all, unique in Rose Bowl history—alone, with the goal line unprotected, he had looked back, tripped over his own feet and missed a certain touchdown. Colonial history dripped from him like aphids from a tree in summer: it was he rather than I who brought those years of long ago to life. To settle Hugh at Nick's, below the bridge at Yorktown, with a bottle of beer and one of Nick's famous salads, was to guarantee an afternoon speeding by. He could tell a story with such hearty warmth that no one wanted to break the spell.

Now when I spoke to the handicapped about how crutches or a wheelchair could sprout wings, I was thinking of myself at home in New York, Washington, Williamsburg, Chicago, Springfield . . . whenever I returned, someone remembered that I needed a straw in my glass, my meat cut for me. I all but forgot that I had cerebral palsy for long periods of time.

܀

If Paul and I were to have peace of mind, there was still another task we must complete and in 1960 Simon & Schuster published *Tragic Years,* a two-volume documentary history of the Civil War. Between us we had invested a generation of research into this work, yet it was another little book, thrown together over a single weekend, that gave us almost equal excitement. *A Ballad of the North and South,* which recaptured the emotion of the war through the songs the people sang, had been intended solely for distribution by the Kingsport Press as a gift to its friends at Christmas. But this slim volume had an irresistible appeal, and soon Golden Records, a subsidiary of Simon & Schuster, inquired if we would like the work offered as a special record album.

People in "show biz," especially the entrepreneurs, are a queer lot. They run their businesses much as the Kremlin runs the Communist world: the intelligence of the public is not to be trusted. After a series of meetings with the staff at Golden Records, I never did fully comprehend what they had in mind. Somehow *A Ballad* was to be transformed into a mixture of Tennessee hoedown and North Carolina coon hunt; in any event, whatever historical fidelity the work contained was obviously expendable. "What do you think?" came the inevitable query. What we really

295

thought was neither quotable nor printable; we closed the door quietly, not wishing to disturb these obviously excitable people.

Again, we clung to an unwavering principle: integrity was a salable commodity. Within weeks the Chicago radio station of the Columbia Broadcasting System, working with the North-western University Glee Club, produced *A Ballad* without change as a one-hour special. The volume of the fan mail surprised every-one and the program was repeated by the CBS station in New York. Now Carl Haverlin of BMI caught up with the project; a new orchestration was composed by Normand Lockwood, a distin-guished musical scholar, and our "little orphan of the storm" at Golden Records was released by Associated Music Publishers. Many performances throughout the nation followed and the notices were excellent. Doubtless Paul was less astonished than I: he at least could strum a banjo and play a piano whereas my musical talent paralleled that of General Grant, whose tin ear could recognize only two tunes—the one that was "Yankee Doodle" and the one that was not.

Increasingly, as the centennial years of the Civil War ap-proached, I was discouraged by the flood of books it produced. In 1959 I had reviewed at least fifty Civil War titles for *The New York Times* and *The Saturday Review,* and I must have handled that many more volumes the following year. It was obvious also that Bruce Catton had the field monopolized; he had converted it into a big business. I knew Pete and Barbara Long, who were Bruce's research team. I had seen the book-lined room where red-bearded Pete combed every word on the subject ever written. Moreover, Pete and Barbara periodically were covering inch by inch the ground where the war had occurred. From somewhere had come a barrel of money to underwrite this talented pair in their researches; no one else could compete with them. Whether literary history or reportage (or, more likely, a combination of both) would emerge from this collaboration was an editorial question, and really quite beside the point: Bruce was equally gifted at either. Alone of all the other persons working in this period of American history, Bruce was Carl Sandburg's equal in capturing the public's imagination. His platform appearance—balding head, rimless glasses, a trace of a moustache—was that of a professor; his diffident manner, his almost monotone voice, his intensity of interest all added to this image; and he was of course an unusual spinner of tales, a man of superb talent. If anyone in the field was envious of Bruce's success, he was a fool. Bruce's books were lyrical in their composition.

Through my work with crippled children, I began to appreciate how much books could mean to youngsters. Perhaps no other branch of literature than writing for children has changed so radically during the past quarter of a century. The quality of craftsmanship easily is the equal of the adult field, and the art work is far superior. Yet the average person still remembers the books of his own youth—those pot boilers that Reed Silvers once ground out a chapter a night for $200 outright—and rather looks down his nose at those who devote their full energies to this labor.

"What is your work?" the staff physician once asked me when I was hospitalized in Chicago.

"I write books for children," I said.

"I know," the doctor said vaguely. He was willing to humor me up to a point. "But what do you do for a living?"

I resisted the temptation to reply that, if the truth were known, I actually operated a chain of bordellos. The poor man departed, shaking his head. No one had explained to him that the population explosion, the growth of schools and the increasing professional training of librarians not only had transformed books for children into an art form but also into a major industry.

If the author for youngsters is rarely advertised and is reviewed only in driblets, other compensations bolster his ego. One is the hundreds of charming letters that children write, for they still can afford to yield their affection with a wild abandon. The whole day is suddenly brighter when a ten-year-old begins his letter: "Mr. Miers, you write good." Or: "My sister let me read one of your books. It was too good to waste on a girl." Or: "My teacher may think she knows everything, but I surprised her plenty from what you taught me." Another compensation is the sales figures: a ten-volume history of the United States sold in the millions; a short biography of President Kennedy sold well over one million copies the first month; and my average sale per title far exceeds the average sale per title in the adult field.

It is an exacting task, this writing for youngsters. If your research is not honestly exhaustive, they will find you out. They insist on clarity, crispness, a sense of reality. A classic of literary criticism was achieved by an eight-year-old who once wrote a friend of mine: "Your book about penguins tells me more than I really want to know." If you write down to children these days, no matter what the old-fashioned librarians and educators say, you are in the same trouble as if you talk down to children. Their manner may remain polite but inwardly they are thinking: "Gee, glimpse this square—he'll wind up in Looneyville!"

It is often a lonely life when I am down in that well, a man fighting a typewriter, and without rigid self-discipline, I know most certainly, no free-lance writer can long endure. But in those weeks of isolation I remember the rewards. Among my books are titles that have been translated into French, Spanish, Arabic, Persian, Urdu, Bengali and Indonesian.

I think of a far-off Hindu, reading one of my books in Urdu, and wish I could meet him personally. Always I am reaching out to be with people. It is as though some mystical inner voice keeps telling me: "People don't care about your handicap. So what else is new, Buster?"

CHAPTER EIGHTEEN

Madaline
Williams

O*ne day in*
a tavern somewhere in the Midwest an old fellow in a black leather jacket stumbled across the room and placed an arm around
my shoulder. His breath was beery, his voice solicitous.

"Buddy, old buddy," he said, "what kind of sick are you?"

I explained as patiently and simply as I could the nature of
athetosis. The old fellow's head nodded. "A damn shame, buddy,
a damn shame," he mumbled. As abruptly as he had approached,
he stumbled away.

But there is another kind of sickness gnawing inside me that I find more difficult to explain, for its name is shame. It is caused by my race, my religion and the indifference of my friends. It is a sickness that first overwhelmed me when I realized how mutely my religion, my government and my friends had stood aside while Hitler murdered six million Jews. It is a sickness that leaves me writhing in frustration when I see the face of Governor George Wallace of Alabama or watch half-wrecks of white women with hair disheveled stomping the streets of New Orleans and screaming, "Kill 'em, kill 'em" at a Negro mother and her child committing no sin other than seeking to enter a school.

I know the cure for this sickness. A Russian named Pasternak gave it to me in a novel entitled *Dr. Zhivago:* "You in others —this is what you are, this is what your consciousness has breathed and lived on and enjoyed throughout your life, your soul, your immortality—your life in others."

About the dead Jews I can do nothing; about the living Negroes in America I have still time to try.

❧

Like tapestries, lifetimes acquire patterns: some bright and dominant, some shadowy and elusive. Sadness overwhelms me when I recall the child I once was, hawking newspapers in the Negro ghetto of Hackensack. Today, ridiculed and hated as "Whitey," that child would not fare so well. My effort to comprehend the tragedy that befell Paul Robeson was only a surface accomplishment: I shared his grief but not his torment.

I have been called a fool, a Commie, an egghead for my lifetime conviction that, by God's command, I am also my black brother's keeper, and often I have stood alone because of this belief. I remember well that meeting of the National Society when the discussion involved the selection of Houston, Texas as a convention site. Mine was the only negative vote. But the Houston hotel where the convention would convene could not guarantee to open its facilities to Negroes, and I cannot distinguish the person who hisses the word "nigger" in hatred and contempt from the person who speaks the word "cripple" in derision and derogation. Southern members then dominated the committee and they were never quite so friendly toward me after I made my lonely stand and insisted that my dissent be included in the record.

Upon occasion at the New York University Club I have suggested that we break the color line and admit a Negro to membership. My warmest friends turn chilly at the proposal. Like peevish children, they say, "I do not wish to discuss the subject," in much the same tone that parents once explained why they chained crippled youngsters to bedposts. The lawyers state in raised voices that a private club cannot be forced by law to admit a "nigger"; and, twinkling with triumph, they go off to gamble at dice and cards, which the law does forbid.

Weeks after I have dropped the subject, an opponent will seek me out, still full of fight. "I hope you've thought better of that crazy idea of filling the club with niggers," he begins. I smile. His conscience is troubled. "I can wait," I reply. "The force of history is on my side."

New Yorkers—and especially New Yorkers who join the University Club—have to be treated differently from other Americans. After Irving Berlin won the First World War for them by writing a song called "Over There," they lapsed into a world of unending amusements. Blondes, bootleggers, gangsters and very bad mayors became part of the big, happy, sophisticated existence that life was to them. They loved Texas Guinan when she called them suckers, and Mayor Jimmy Walker in his tipped derby, and the secret cellar stocked with booze at 21 during the bawdy prohibition years; they entertained Frank Costello at the Democratic Club ("You'll find him an *amusing* fellow," Meyer Berger promised when we lunched with this gang lord); and New Yorkers would not be found dead with a do-gooder who, by their definition, belongs somewhere west of the Hudson with cowpunchers and old ladies. As the Great Depression, the Second World War, the United Nations, the Cold War and the crazy Civil Righters invaded their city, New Yorkers became aware of enormous changes in the most personal of ways: these events dulled the edge of their fun. A Mike Quill with a transit strike was, in a sense, an amusement whereas Martin Luther King at a Harlem rally was not, so they would rather walk for Quill than listen to King. Aging children cannot stand to have their insularity destroyed; it spoils their relaxation.

If I resign from the Club because its membership does not yet realize the Negro is marching down Freedom Road and will never turn back, I gain nothing. When the admission of Negroes divided the Cosmos Club in Washington, to which I also belong, those who resigned or withdrew their applications aided neither humanity nor the Club. As wise old David Mearns knew from the outset, the victory of tolerance could only be won by the quiet pressure of those who remained. And so it was. The Negroes whom I now greet at Cosmos are charming and educated and an asset to one of the most distinguished clubs in America. Moreover there is not the least statistical evidence that, as a result of their membership, the number of mixed marriages has increased in the District of Columbia.

Because of my growing interest in the Negro problem Paul Angle once arranged for a guide—a Negro army officer in uniform—to take us through the Chicago South Side. We saw three distinct levels of Negro culture: we began in the quiet workingman's neighborhood where an evening was passed over a glass of beer in the same fellowship that we would have encountered among the Germans on the North Side; we moved into lusher surroundings where pimps and bookies mixed with those success-ful in business and the arts and the atmosphere became typically nightclubbish and brassy; and ended in the black-and-tan district where an occasional white was seen.

We rode in taxis that cruised along the streets, picking up or dropping off passengers wherever they pleased and never seeming to carry less than five riders. In one black-and-tan café where a rather racy dance was in progress an obviously drunken girl grabbed my leg. Her fingers were clamped with a kind of rigid spasticity. She hurt. I refused to look at the girl, who began to shout. The dance ended and the fingers loosened.

"Let's go," Paul and the guide said in unison. The air had turned electric.

We had learned very little from our evening in the South Side except to see part of a ghetto filled with a teeming popula-tion to whom we were suspicious intruders. The experience was depressing, not alone for the shabbiness of the place but also for the shabbiness of our comprehension. Never again would I think of the colored people from the background of a single white child wandering happily among the friends of Mattie and Emory in Hackensack. In Chicago I had experienced a fear that might easily have turned to terror; here my handicap was not cerebral palsy but a white skin.

My mother, who moved to the Washington Heights section of New York City soon after Father's death, never could sympa-thize with my interest in the Negro problem.

"You meet them on the subway," she said, "spitting on the floor and sticking knives into the seats and brushing up against white women in a crowd and see how much you like them then!"

I replied that I would not like any human being who acted in this manner. And I admitted that just as I would not tolerate a neighborhood that included slovenly, vulgar, intemperate whites, neither would I welcome a slovenly, vulgar, intemperate black as a next door neighbor.

My mother now was too old to change her prejudices; she judged by what she saw and never probed for causes. She was a devoted grandmother and not a social reformer. Let the politicians build more houses and better schools and find other jobs, if that was what was needed; she was approaching her three score years and ten and deserved to bask in the pleasure of her grandchildren. And I agreed.

Still, within my own heart, I was committed. I believed in fighting for the human dignity of all who were handicapped and, God knows, the Negro masses lived twisted, tormented, disfigured lives unequalled by any group in America. I felt helpless in this second sickness, for I wanted so desperately to do some small thing that might help.

And then Madaline Williams gave me a chance.

≈§

We were six gathered in a cubbyhole-office directly across the hall from where the New Jersey General Assembly convened. To the usual State House noises was added the sound of the press corps milling outside the door. Now and then a knock would sound and a head, peering at us, would inquire, "Anything yet?" We were meeting as members of the New Jersey Civil War Centennial Commission, appointed in part by the governor and in part by the upper and lower houses of the state legislature. We were not intended to make news of national interest, but today we might.

Donald Flamm was chairman of the Commission, a New York theatrical producer who invariably arrived with the haunted look of one who was giving up the most important opening night of his career. I recognized in Donald what I saw in Pat Knopf— a man who enjoyed living on the edge of a perforating ulcer— and I admired the belligerent steadfastness with which he could cling to his convictions. As attorney general, David D. Furman ranked next to the governor in executive power; he was warm-hearted and scholarly and would soon become a superior court judge. Joe Dempsey was a lawyer, a dedicated and stubborn advocate, and when crossed in what he considered an unfair manner his cheeks could light up like a bulb on a Christmas tree. Everett J. Landers was the Commission's salaried executive secretary; he was a former newspaperman who had overcome alcoholism, which made him an admirable fellow in my eyes; and to his efficiency and intelligence he added the valuable asset of being the friend of everyone in the State House.

But the shining personality in the room was Madaline Williams. She was a woman in her middle sixties, gracious in manner, mild in speech, alert of mind. Originally she had represented the General Assembly on the Commission, but after her election as Register of Essex County had been reappointed a citizen member. Throughout the state Madaline was admired as a Negro whose presence gave a warmth to any occasion. Her husband, Sam, had opposed her acceptance of membership on the Commission, for his long years of experience in working with the National Association for the Advancement of Colored People gave him an almost mystical perception of impending conflict.

"Sammy," I once teased him, "when you fellows take over the world will you remember I was your friend?"

The broad smile that lighted Sam's anthracite black face was wonderful to behold. "We'll remember you," he promised.

Just once did I ever notice Sam wince and that was one day when a later employee of the Commission boasted: "I was bawn in Lynchburg, Virginiah, and I'm a proud unreconstructed rebel." Sam also had been born in Lynchburg where his father, a schoolteacher, had argued that educators should be paid without regard to color. For this independent opinion the Williams family had been invited to leave Lynchburg quietly and quickly. The family had migrated to Newark, New Jersey, and Sam's mother had died as a result of the rigors of this enforced uprooting. So Sam, a child of Lynchburg, had become a Reconstructed Negro who could look back upon the place of his birth as a burg where Negroes could be lynched.

The crisis that Sam had feared for Madaline was little more than a month away when we six assembled at the State House on an afternoon early in March of 1961. The National Civil War Centennial Commission under the direction of General U. S. Grant III, had selected Charleston, South Carolina as the site of that year's National Assembly. Southerners were delighted with the choice, since it gave them the chance of reenacting the firing on Fort Sumter and glorying anew in humbling the Yanks (in fact, the chief emphasis of the national program appeared to be playing these games of cops and robbers, possibly in the hope that a century later the South could win all the battles).

But the times were tense with racial conflicts. Only seven years had passed since the United States Supreme Court had outlawed segregation in public schools. John F. Kennedy now occupied the White House, promising to be far more forceful than his predecessor in exerting moral leadership behind the Civil Rights movement. And as the spring of '61 approached, Negroes were mobilizing for a succession of "sit-ins" to dramatize the injustice of continued discrimination.

For weeks, at the direction of the New Jersey Commission, Ev Landers had been demanding guarantees from Washington that Mrs. Williams would be courteously received in Charleston. I, for one, had no illusions about the Francis Marion Hotel, which had been selected for the headquarters of the National Assembly; I had stayed in this hostelry which faces across the square from The Citadel. It was as segregated as a klan meeting. All of Ev's inquiries went unanswered by Karl S. Betts, the executive secretary of the National Commission. The circumstances reeked with suspicion. "To hell with Betts," Joe, Donald or I said; the attorney general never swore. Ev called J. Palmer Gillard, Jr., the mayor of Charleston, and he was no beater of the bushes. Mrs. Williams' appearance in his city, he said, would be "very embarrassing to all concerned" and under no circumstances would she be received as a guest in the Francis Marion Hotel.

Madaline was marvelous in her calm acceptance of these insults—the inexcusable silence of Betts, the blunt reply by Mayor Gillard, who could not recognize a child of God until he saw the color of the skin.

"I expected it," Madaline said with a quiet dignity that she wore like a coronet around her head.

The rest of us were nowhere near so composed. The subsequent resolution, which I introduced, was drafted by all of us. The chief function of the National Commission, that resolution insisted, was not only to commemorate the stresses the war had imposed upon the nation, but also to emphasize how later American action had contributed to "human freedom, justice, and the dignity of the individual." The National Commission, we contended, was the creature of Congress, supported by federal funds, and in sponsoring a segregated meeting in Charleston, where "custom and/or law" clearly denied "equal hospitality to members of the Negro race," the National Commission had abrogated "the fundamental concepts of human decency and the fundamental guarantees of civil liberties under the New Jersey Constitution." Therefore, we concluded, New Jersey declined to participate in the Charleston meeting and urged other state commissions to support cancellation of the National Assembly until it could be rescheduled in quarters accessible to all Americans.

I was in New York when the story broke in the press. An old Southern-born friend at the University Club burst into hysterical laughter. "Where the hell do you think this will get you?" he spluttered amid guffaws. "If Charleston doesn't want the nigger, let her stay home." And my friend delivered a lengthy harangue on states' rights—his state's rights, not mine.

More depressing was the reaction of a contact with the New York State Commission. The resolution, he clearly thought,

THE TROUBLE BUSH

was some kind of monstrous spoof and his reaction was the more surprising insofar as New York had a Negro commissioner in the distinguished historian, John Hope Franklin. "Jolly for you," I thought. "I am glad you can be so amused at a fine woman's embarrassment." I slammed down the phone.

My cynicism toward New Yorkers somewhat dulled the edge of this disappointment. What hurt more was the opinion of a Lincoln expert in Old Abe's home town that the action was "ridiculous." This was not the way to go about such things, I was told. Then, I inquired, what was the way? "Forget it," came the lame response. I called Starling, hoping her voice would cheer me up.

"Honey," she said, "you better get home. The phone hasn't stopped ringing. That resolution has stirred things up."

For the next several days the telephone kept ringing. From the State House in Trenton came Ev's voice in a steady stream of bulletins: get this editorial, read that column. From Washington came Lloyd Dunlap's drawling voice: "Hey, Tad, this is Willie. Uncle Dave wants you." Then would follow Dave Mearns' almost daily pep talk: "Keep up the good work, lad—I think you've got 'em on the run."

Both houses of the New Jersey Legislature adopted unanimous resolutions upholding the Commission's stand. Governor Robert E. Meyner, who had let the Kennedy bandwagon roll over his toes at the Democratic Convention the year before, offered no support, and the Republican gubernatorial candidate, former Secretary of Labor James P. Mitchell, spanked him soundly for his muteness when "a great principle has been attacked and must be unequivocally defended." My old friend, United States Senator Bud Case, reacted as I expected, whipping off a telegram to General Grant III, urging the removal of the National Assembly to a site where Mrs. Williams would not be subjected to "the indignity of segregation." Case had enlisted in this war for the duration; and another consistent battler was Hugh

J. Addonizio, then a representative in Congress and now mayor of the city of Newark. Addonizio read New Jersey's entire position into the *Congressional Record* and added his own tart comments anent "the shocking situation resulting from the segregation policies of Charleston, S.C." A mountain of newspaper clippings poured in, filled with editorial comment pro and con.

The South raged. Governor Ernest F. Hollings of South Carolina charged Bud Case and other New Jersey officials with playing politics, although Hollings' motives for this verbal blast-off scarcely seemed altruistic.

State Representative John May promised fellow Carolinians that he would "uphold the customs and laws of the state"; Mr. May spoke also as chairman for the South Carolina Confederate Centennial Commission, one of those organizations in the South that failed so conspicuously during the next four years to keep the once noble Confederate flag from degenerating into a mud-stained rag in the hands of the white supremacists and klansmen.

Southern editorial comment was far more emotional than factual: Mrs. Williams, insisted one school of opinion, had been deliberately placed on the New Jersey Commission to stir up trouble; another school of opinion emphasized the argument that New Jersey was not altogether above reproach in its treatment of Negroes and so rested its case upon the rather novel logic (so popular with Governor Wallace) that one evil justified another; and occasionally there were dark mutterings that the White House was being maliciously manipulated by "the integrating Yank."

In White House memoirs of those days Arthur Schlesinger, Jr., is content with the comment that the controversy made the President "very angry," but Theodore C. Sorensen adds: "In a note of high irony, the Civil War Centennial Commission under U. S. Grant III had to be told to use only nonsegregated facilities."* The poor old General was indisposed at his home in Clin-

---

*Theodore C. Sorensen, *Kennedy*, 477.

ton, New York and the executive committee of the National Commission convened in Washington under the chairmanship of William M. Tuck. A former governor of Virginia and then a member of Congress, Tuck was a tough old segregationist. Kennedy's "note of irony," if known to Tuck's committee, was brushed aside with a somewhat truculent announcement on March 21 that no change in the time or place of the National Assembly was contemplated.

Next day in the pose of a patriarch looking down his nose and scolding a child, Tuck told the President through a press interview that the National Commission possessed "no authority by which it can dictate to the hotel keepers as to the management of their property." To Tuck the issue was settled.

ୡଌ

But Tuck was basking in a Pyrrhic victory. Behind the scenes other strategists in the struggle for civil rights were marshalling their forces, and even an unsanctified military historian like myself could have told the Virginian that campaigns are not decided by any one battle. From his Senate office Bud Case found the action of Tuck's committee "incredible." Gentlemen whom Tuck perhaps never suspected—Carl Haverlin in New York, Dave Mearns in Washington, Ralph Newman in Chicago—were fashioning darts to tickle the hide of segregation. Other state commissions began tumbling in behind New Jersey's boycott of the Charleston meeting: first New York, then Illinois, then Michigan, Wisconsin and California in a rush.

Nor had Tuck reckoned with the Baptist conscience of that Iowa fireball, the Honorable Fred Schwengel. Fred sniffed smoke and looked for the blaze: how truly "unanimous" was the decision of Tuck's committee? Fred questioned two of the five members—Senator Ralph W. Yarborough of Texas and Bell I. Wiley of Georgia—and found them less than overjoyed with Tuck's pronouncements. Everyone in Washington, from the President to the doorman of the House restaurant, realized that Fred could not tell a lie even if he tried. And I knew Ralph Yarborough from my days with the Lincoln Sesquicentennial Commission; he was no pussyfooter on civil rights and once when he characterized Lincoln as "a man of conscience and not of consensus" he might have been describing himself. And I knew Bell Wiley, again no wheeler-dealer with human dignity. "Don't waste your time," Bell once told me, "trying to change the South with moral arguments. Hit 'em in the pocketbook—*that* they understand." Where Meyner still stood aloof from the struggle, the Democratic aspirant for the governorship, Richard J. Hughes, blasted the conduct of Tuck's committee as "incredible effrontery" to the President; moreover, added New Jersey's future chief executive, the action "gives ammunition to our enemies throughout the world." Madaline Williams had enlarged on this theme in an interview a day or so previously.

Tuck's major tactical error was in misjudging the Irish cussedness of John F. Kennedy. A press conference on March 23 gave the President his target range. What, he was asked, did he intend to do about the Charleston situation? Kennedy answered quietly. It was his strong belief, the President said, "that any program in which the United States is engaged should provide facilities and meeting places which . . . do not discriminate on the ground of race or color." The President admitted that he had exchanged letters with General Grant. "We cannot," Kennedy said, "leave the situation as it is."

Shortly thereafter the announcement was made that the National Assembly had been shifted from the segregated Francis Marion Hotel to the desegregated Charleston Naval Base. For two days the New Jersey Commission haggled before it consented to this compromise, and then agreed reluctantly under strong pressure from a White House source to "for God's sake, take the President off the hook."

My Southern-born friend sought me out at the University Club. He was baffled and upset.

"Think of it!" he expostulated. "One nigger beating the whole South!"

"One human being," I corrected. "And one very basic principle of human justice."

"Oh, the hell with that!" he shouted angrily. "With you and your kind helping, the niggers will soon take over the country!"

❧

My Southern friend was not alone in his bitterness. With a kind of heroic inflexibility, Tuck announced: "I do not acquiesce in this action." In South Carolina, State Representative Nat W. Cabell hoped that none who agreed with Kennedy's executive order "will impose their presence upon us." The cry was raised anew that Madaline Williams had been planted on the New Jersey Commission simply to bedevil the South, and in Louisiana the *Shreveport Times* sneered: "We are memorializing a bloody war that settled nothing except the question of who was the strongest." But *The New York Times,* reflecting upon the meaning of the war a century later, saw it as a conflict which had "destroyed a civilization, in blood and tears, in order to build a better one." Abraham Lincoln would have shared that judgment.

I write only of a pebble thrown into the great oceans of history. And yet it was important. Other executive orders from the White House followed the Charleston precedent until more productive civil rights legislation could be passed by Congress. More important to poor little frustrated people like myself, the apparent White House indifference toward the torment of the Negro at last had ended. U. S. Grant III resigned as chairman of the National Commission and Allan Nevins replaced him. A new spirit permeated the air. A handful of New Jerseymen, said John

Hope Franklin, not only had "chastised the nation" but also had "restored a measure of sanity and probity in national as well as local attitudes toward what the centennial should be."

Later efforts toward breaking the color line at the University Club have met with the same old hardened resistance. As a do-gooder from across the Hudson, I still wait patiently. As long as I can cling to my faith in the ultimate triumph of human decency, I can answer those who ask: "What kind of sick are you?"

The pressure of other commitments prevented me from attending the Charleston meetings. The treatment that the New Jersey delegation received, by every report, was unfortunate if it stood for a Southern chivalry that has been so long hallowed. But Madaline returned from Charleston as she departed: a quiet woman, composed, compassionate, modest, unbreakable, serene in human dignity. New Jersey well esteems her and the lovable Sam as symbols of the triumph Lincoln promised. Someday this land shall be blessed with a new birth of freedom.

Perhaps Madaline possesses a black skin as Starling possesses a white skin, but this fact never impresses me. Both are monumental women. Both enrich the lives of those around them. Both would have satisfied Pasternak, when he gave me the cure for my secret sickness: "Your life in others."

CHAPTER NINETEEN

The Arch

*A*ncient architects

lived by a proverb: "The arch never sleeps." The poet in Carl Sandburg could not resist this image, and his Civil War Centennial Address at the Library of Congress closed with stirring beauty: "When the arch holds all else holds. Love stands and hangs by an arch. The rainbow is an arch. Hate and pride breaks arches. Love and understanding build unbreakable arches."

In my life Starling and our children have been the arch.

In working with the parents of handicapped children one of the most frustrating experiences is trying to break through the conspiracy of silence that surrounds the subject of sex. Yet sex, like the instinct of self-preservation, is one of the locked-in powers that nature gives human beings. Both are enormous forces. Persons confined to wheelchairs have been known to walk away from the scene of an automobile accident. Meyer Perlstein tells the story of how in college a spastic's walking suddenly showed astonishing improvement. His therapist was in ecstasy over how well her treatments were working. And Meyer chuckles. "Treatments, my foot! That boy had met a girl and gone out on his first date and wanted to get to her house for more!"

To me the key to rehabilitation for any disabled person is a love that produces a good marriage and a happy family. "The one area in which the cerebral palsied can compete with anyone," Meyer Perlstein often has said, "is in having normal children." I approached fatherhood filled with ancient superstitions and fears, seeing myself as an inferior specimen to add his kind to the human melting pot; and I wish I could have heard Meyer then, counseling parents: "It is a waste of human material to discourage reproduction of many of our cerebral palsied, some of whom are really superior individuals and whose genetic traits would be valuable to our society."

If Starling shared my apprehensions, I never knew it. She carried her first child like a blimp moored to two masts; she was happy, hungry and anxious to discover what was keeping her awake with its infernal kicking at her belly; and in good time the youngster arrived. My Aunt Gert, who was my father's sister, was a great believer that men should watch their wives undergo the struggles of childbirth. "It's good for them," she said, still fussed by the memory of her own labor, and, clearly, Aunt Gert suspected that an occasional horsewhipping never spoiled any man.

Briefly I watched Starling in labor and terror filled my heart.

Resting between pains, she saw me. "You get out," she panted. "This is my job." She managed a smile, tired but tender. A nurse hustled me through the door. When our third child arrived I passed the time in the hospital kitchen, eating apples and playing bridge with two interns and an off-duty nurse. Aunt Gert would have been scandalized, but Starling thought I was making considerable headway as a partner in the kid business.

◆§

From the start I knew I was a limited father. I could not change diapers unless I wished to risk poking open safety pins into the poor infant's behind. I was no good at bottle feeding or, later, at training our children to eat with spoon or fork. My idea of burping amounted to exercising with a punching bag. In times of illness I could not administer doses of medicine unless the baby could hold his own spoon or sip through a straw. So I slept soundly while Starling did a great deal of dragging around the house at all hours of the night, which would have happened anyway for she was the kind of instinctive mother who awakened and sat up in bed if a baby sighed in his sleep.

For a goodly number of years raising a family became Starling's career, and she possessed very definite notions of where a husband belonged in this process. Foremost, his responsibility was to pay the bills, and in this task he deserved protection. Wives who sent their husbands off to work without their breakfasts, or who expected them to get their own breakfasts, were slackers in Starling's estimation. And she scorned also wives who demanded that husbands work all day and spend their evenings or weekends housecleaning, washing, shopping, punishing the youngsters for the day's naughtiness, and in similar ways bending to a reign of female tyranny. A man, by Starling's standards, needed rest, companionship, relaxation, a chance to build his own dreams for the morrow and freedom of movement. Starling's kind of marriage and parenthood was a love affair and not a trap, and I was very sorry that she could not patent the system and grow rich.

In many ways I was not a limited father. One of the principal requirements of living happily with a physical disability is taking the responsibility of putting others at ease with your handicap. It is not their duty to make the first move; they may not know how or they may be embarrassed or they may be afraid of doing the wrong thing. So a physically disabled person, if he has good sense, acquires many automatic reflexes. He smiles quickly. He offers a pleasant and neat appearance. He holds a door for a woman and steps aside to permit her to enter an elevator. He enjoys laughter and learns how to evoke it. He accepts personal inquiry without resentment. If a woman takes out a cigarette and he cannot light it, he frankly says so, avoiding strained moments (but he can offer her matches or a lighter). He admits his own limitations calmly so that others can take pleasure in helping him, but he does not intrude his personal problems into a conversation. What he does if he is an athetoid and someone suddenly places an ice cream cone in his hand I am not certain: the temptation as the cone crumbles is to dump the mushy lump into the biggest bosom within sight.

But aside from the ice cream cone, I was determined that my children through example and instruction should also acquire these reflexes, and I knew that as competitors in the race of human survival they would have a head start over a good three-quarters of the field. In the little helps that I required, I decided, I also could be a special father to them. They were being trained to be aware of the needs of another, to anticipate little ways in which to insure the old man's comfort and to live naturally and amiably with whatever handicaps others might have. Again, as human beings, they were ahead in the game of life.

I am not sure that I ever have looked upon David, Meredith, and William as children at all; to me they have been three distinct characters, quite dissimilar in nature, who have afforded me both joy and amusement. I have always agreed with Epictetus: "What constitutes a child?—Want of instruction; for they are our equals so far as their degree of knowledge permits." I know fathers who are great strap-wielders, whaling their kids mercilessly, who turn into the worst bullies in the neighborhood, but the old adage about sparing the rod is not for me: I have too much respect, both for myself and my youngsters, to slap them around. They know how I feel; they are not stupid; and they know it is to their advantage to get along with their dad. So that's how it is.

I think my children have enjoyed being treated as my equals. Since I enjoy privacy, I give them privacy. I have always been drawn to that school of psychology that believes it is good for youngsters to retire to the basement, hang up drawings representing their parents and sling mud balls at those images (it is nice if they clean up the mess afterward). But I like to get rid of my resentments. Why should not they? And I expected that somewhere along in adolescence the boys would subscribe to *Playboy* magazine, telling Starling: "If they ever begin collecting pictures of naked men we can start worrying."

⌘

For a decade after Starling's father retired our summers were spent at Martha's Vineyard, an island off Cape Cod where Mr. and Mrs. Wyckoff lived their last years. Both Starling and the children deserved these summers: a good part of their essential heritage existed here. A broken hip made Mother Wyckoff a semi-invalid in those final years, but her spirit and her love kept their buoyancy and the kids needed the quiet stability and serenity she gave them. Father Wyckoff, indulgent and loving, was an old sport, and the family champion at croquet. He adored Martha's Vineyard, with its personality and rolling contours so like

Monmouth County, New Jersey, where he had spent a country boyhood. Mother Wyckoff, who was city bred, was more inclined to share my cynical amusement at those weekly exhortations in the *Vineyard Gazette* over how we all had reached heaven seven miles at sea and should shout our hallelujahs each sunrise and sunset (except in August when invariably it rained for days and the fog horns drowned out such exultations).

"Sunnyside," where we spent two summers, was easily the most interesting residence we occupied on the island. This rambling old house, once the home of a sea captain, had been moved inland to stand in the middle of a farm. The dining-room floor, as a result, slanted upward so that we had the unique impression of eating on a hillside. Only part of the farm was planted in hay; there were miles of wooded land and fields abounding in the blueberries, grape vines and beach plums that grew wild on Martha's Vineyard. A half mile down a private road was a cove perfect for youngsters learning how to swim.

The place was as isolated as though we were living in another century, and we quickly acquired country habits. Invariably Starling and I were up by sunrise and enjoying our breakfast coffee on the lawn. We would watch the deer moving noiselessly toward the woods after some night's deviltry that we never discovered. A peacefulness lay upon the land and our spirits. Rabbits bounded through the tall grass and birds splashed in the puddles left by the night's brief rain; and then came the intrusive throb of the morning plane bound for New York City some three hundred miles to the south.

David was a fleeting visitor; we saw him only before his camp in New Hampshire opened or after it closed. In the mornings Meredith had her dancing classes; and young William, if left to his own devices, delighted in driving a neighbor's tractor. I wrote in the mornings, napped and read in the afternoon, and explored the hills and unspoiled beaches of this hundred square miles of island. The private yachts that harbored in Edgartown,

Menemsha and Vineyard Haven were a constant attraction. So, too, were the clay cliffs at Gay Head, where the descendants of the original Indian settlers still lived; and everyone on the Island looked forward to Illumination Night at Oak Bluffs when the place was strung with thousands of paper lanterns that for more than a century had been brought back from the Orient by the Methodist missionaries who summered here. There were paddle boats, an antique merry-go-round called the "Flying Horses" and hordes of cyclists pushing their wheels up the hills and looking quite ridiculous in their puffing defiance of the motorists flashing by.

The charm of the island was in forcing upon the family a different way of life—leisurely, even a bit lazy and sloppy, yet wonderfully close-knit. Kite-flying, croquet, the same card games were daily occurrences, and to have varied these routines would have spoiled the whole experience. The faithful daily visit to Mother and Father Wyckoff was a highlight: this, we all knew, was why we were really here. We were living by our hearts, and the rewards were rich within ourselves.

Labor Day closed the adventure. We crowded on the deck of the Islander which would ferry us back to the mainland. Handkerchiefs waved wildly until we no longer could see Starling's parents. Tears flowed unashamedly. Then, storing away another summer's memories, we watched the shore of Cape Cod drawing closer and we began gabbling like chickens over the other world, the other way of life, in which we also dwelled.

≈§

My own mother was born to have grandchildren. They were her crowning glory. At any hour of the day or night, if an emergency arose, she came racing like a fire horse laced to the traces. The children idolized her. She was Muz to them, the bearer of endless gifts, usually broken within an hour, for where Muz believed they should be entranced watching monkeys spin around when wheeled across the floor, the youngsters were far more enchanted by pulling out the fur and throwing the household into a panic by stuffing the fuzz up their noses.

Muz played games with them. She read books by the hour. She drew pictures and walked obediently behind as their tricycles scattered stray dogs and deliverymen from the sidewalks. She hopscotched and danced and sang five million renditions of "Rudolf the Red-Nosed Reindeer." She took them to the zoos, amusement parks, museums, theaters, and braved the boat ride to the Statue of Liberty; she hiked them over Civil War battlefields and through thousands of miles of corridors in the Smithsonian Institution and to the top of the Washington Monument, and, I am sure, if she could have found a diving bell, they would have explored the floor of the ocean.

Any reservations Muz may have held toward Starling as a daughter-in-law were dispelled by one wonderful accomplishment: Starling produced babies—chubby, rosy-cheeked babies who could be cuddled and bathed and dressed and fed and wheeled and picked up and bounced on the knee and trussed up against pillows and defended from silly dogs that thought babies were to be sniffed at like rabbits and licked like lollipops. Meredith made her delirious—a little girl to dress! But she had sense about children and when one day our young lady flung off in a temper tantrum and planted her frilly bottom in the middle of the road amid blood-curdling howls, Muz could leave her there until nature restored sanity. A neighbor picking up the child and indulging its outburst put Muz in a murderous mood that reddened her face for years when she thought of "that old meddler."

She was a grand matriarch, I thought, watching her surrounded by doting grandchildren. She could still spark with sensitive indignation when one of the boys remarked that she was "rather fat," but they needed to learn to hold their tongues. She still loved fluffy dresses and fancy hats and gay parasols—

old age was no bedfellow she would tolerate. To the end, a writer studying a book was not working. "Earl's only reading," she would say, justifying any interruption. But the children knew better: Starling had drilled the fear of God in them—when Dad was in the study they kept out. About Muz nothing could be done: she moved like a planet in her own orbit.

An infatuation of Muz's last years—this woman who had scrimped and saved and endured hard sacrifices to raise her own family—was horse races. She devoured scratch sheets, and worked out systems and, hanging over the rail, carried on animated conversations with fellow devotees of the sport of kings. When she lost, Edith and I were the fools who had forced her to go. Occasionally, she harangued us angrily for frittering away money, but at the next suggestion of going to the races she flew to fetch her hat, pocketbook and scratch sheets. "I go for the sport of it," she declared, which is what all horse players say; but they go to win. Deep down, they know that they can't and won't. As Eddie Arcaro once said, "If I could win betting 'em, I wouldn't ride 'em." Even when they hit a winner and the cashier hands over the pay-off, they understand the track is only lending them the money. Sooner or later they will bet it back. And Muz, like Edith, always could say with a thrilling self-righteousness: "I've never been such a sap that I've lost the rent money!"

What a tender memory it is to recall Muz in her seventieth year wedged tight against the rail, hat waving at the ponies pounding down the stretch, the crowd roaring. Muz could out-shout all the railbirds. She may have prayed for a winner when the horses broke from the gate, but she was too shrewd to rely on divine intervention now. There was only one way a horse could win—he had to run faster than the other nags—and to do that he had to be rooted home by the sheer indomitable spirit of the two-dollar bettor! Muz rooted 'em with a fishmonger's bawl: "Come on, damn you, you lop-eared glue factory!" And she often won! To hell with the jockey and the horse—Muz brought them home. It was against her nature to back too many losers.

When I researched the Grant book, I took Muz with me. She was an inexhaustible traveler, ready to start at four in the morning, reluctant to retire at midnight—it was no wonder she wore out a car and a son. It was a memorable journey: Muz ecstatic when she found a horse parlor just outside Biloxi, Mississippi; Muz tramping the French Quarter in New Orleans; Muz enraged to find the grass mowed on the Confederate side but unattended on the Union side of the battlefield at Vicksburg; Muz sizzling the hide off the traffic cop who dared to give her a summons for passing a stop street in some now forgotten Illinois hamlet; Muz the guest of honor at dinner with Ben and Sally Thomas and Roy and Virginia Basler in Springfield, with Larry and Barbara Linck in Hinsdale, with Paul and Vesta Angle in Chicago. She was living high and was equal to the occasion.

Muz died sensibly within seconds of a heart attack. I insisted that the hymn, "Onward, Christian Soldiers," be sung at her funeral, for as such she had lived for seventy-two years. Driving down from New York to Colt's Neck, I was filled with awe for all this woman had accomplished, for her family and for her handicapped child, by clinging to her simple country faith that if all of life's troubles were hung on a bush, you would still pick your own. Now she rests beside Father close to their beloved baby, LeRoy.

And if I only knew what a Trouble Bush looked like, I would plant it there.

⋘

I have only feared death once, and then not for myself alone. In 1953 Starling and I were flying home from a meeting of National Society and fortunately had crossed the mountains before the plane encountered a storm with thunderheads rising more than twenty thousand feet above the earth. About an hour out of New York we had climbed as high as the DC-6 could go and still could not escape the storm. Suddenly the plane went out of control and in four or five minutes (but perhaps less) we fell to 3,000 feet in a series of three dives, seconds apart. In one dive the plane seemed to turn over so that we believed we were falling upside down. In each dive the plane plummeted faster than the pull of gravity; we were like travelers in outer space, bodies without weight, and any loose object—suitcases, pocketbooks, the leaves of the book I was reading, rugs, coats, money—drifted by us and could be deflected by a touch of the hand.

On the first dive a woman who had gone into the lounge was caught with her seat strap unfastened; her screams were pitiful. A stewardess, who had gone to the woman's assistance, was picked up like a feather and flung against the ceiling; then, when the plane pulled out of the dive, she crashed to the floor. People sobbed. On the second dive, Starling's seat belt began to slip after the arm rest between us had floated away; we both clung to the end of the strap for if it had let go, I could not have helped her.

I wrote Larry Linck afterward: "When our plane landed at LaGuardia on Sunday the doctors and ambulances were waiting. We were, I guess, a miracle plane, for none of us expected to get out alive; there were three stretcher cases that we know of —the woman behind us had her ribs cracked—and the cabin of the plane was a shambles." For days we both lived in a state of shock: within minutes, our children could have been deprived of both parents!

Some years later when I rode in an ambulance through the congested streets of Chicago to Augustana Hospital my mood was quite different. No one had told me yet that I could not bleed to death with a lung hemorrhage, and looking through the big glass window at the harried work-bound drivers bucking traffic on the Outer Drive, I felt only a dull resignation toward whatever the mystery of life must unfold. I knew that Starling would join me as soon as she could make the necessary arrangements at home, for she is tenaciously a wife in such emergencies; and meanwhile I conserved my strength to do battle with nurses insisting I hold still while they took my pulse, for nowhere across all of God's green earth has anyone taught a nurse that if an athetoid could control these random tensions he would not be cerebral palsied. The prospect of death brought only sadness: there was still so much ahead for the children that I would like to witness.

David as the first child, and for four years as an only child, must have weathered the hardest stresses: he was a Holy Experiment entrusted to parents who, like everyone else, were completely unequipped for the God-role into which they were thrust. Everything was not only a first for him but for us. He was the world's first baby to have colic, a fever, diarrhea, a cold, to develop a screaming imagination and to roll from the sofa onto the floor. Gradually he proved not quite so fragile as sugar candy. It was truly a relief. In fact, he rested while we fretted over washing diapers and boiling bottles and mixing formulas and stopping the furnace from pouring noxious smoke through the registers. From the start nature left him thoroughly endowed to grow huskier while we grew wearier. He was lucky, too, when Meredith came along and was a girl so that we had an only son and an only daughter; and when Bill arrived we kept their identities by having an oldest child, an only daughter, and a youngest child. This is a very nice way to raise three children, if you are clever enough to arrange it.

I had more leisure and strength to give to David—raising one child is cheaper than three—and so I taught him how to break windows with a baseball and skin his knees at touch football and fall off a two-wheeler until my back started going out and I retired to the bench and Muz took over. He would sit for hours, happily pulling the stuffing out of the furniture, while I told him stories about "the magic table leg" that somehow managed to overcome all of his enemies, foreign and domestic. In almost all the books I wrote for children as the family increased and there was more necessity to keep at the typewriter, our own youngsters crept in as characters, and I hope that fact gave them pleasure.

By nature I could not be a professional pal to my kids, reminding them of what a fine old man they had because he took them on hikes or boat rides or fishing trips; I did what I could and wished to do, and we were all square when the deal was ended, for I had enjoyed their company as much as they possibly could enjoy mine. One of the boys was denied membership in the local scout troop because his dad flatly refused to go on overnight hikes (indeed, could not go, with his bad back). I had no sympathy for Little League enterprises after hearing parents scold their youngsters for not hitting the ball in the clutch. Bossy parents who mix their egos into childhood games by stressing winning over having a good time are an obnoxious breed to me. And I could write a most macabre tale about a father who, brooding over how his son had disgraced him by striking out with the Little League bases loaded, drank himself into a royal rage and went home and murdered his wife.

I could only give my children what I was, naturally and honestly. I shared with them my own happy cynicism toward the human race: most of all, I wanted them to know that all people blunder and their own childhood failures should not be overemphasized. I wanted them to be at ease with the great and the near-great, and they can greet any living being with a smile and a firm handshake. From the time they could toddle I took them out to dine so that they would know that good manners were not an abstraction—maybe they forget their manners at home, but they had better learn how to shine in meeting the outside world. And whenever I could I took them with me on my travels for I wanted them to live naturally on trains and in hotels and to fix in their minds an image of what a sweeping, majestic country was this land of their birth. And they do know America: not as words in a textbook but as a spirit that pulsates in their memories.

I suspect that I am an odd character to them. When Meredith was eleven and in the sixth grade, our local Parent-Teachers Association instituted Friday evening dances. The hostess was a reddish-haired woman, round as a pork barrel, whose notion of a dance must have been gleaned at some hot spot along U.S. 1. When the music started she ordered all the lights turned off. The poor kids stumbled around, bumping fannies and stepping on one another's feet, when an astonished voice demanded through the darkness: "What the hell is going on here?" Meredith did not need the lights turned on to know her father had arrived. The lights stayed on, too.

Periodically the kids' relationships with schools have moved me to blind fury, whether the institutions were public or private. Sight reading was the great educational fad when David was in grade school. The teachers had invested their money in learning what it was all about and, by God, the kids were going to cram it into their heads or bust (and some of the kids did bust, for, as state specialists in juvenile delinquency ultimately discovered, the frustrations engendered by this fad did considerable damage). David was one of those whose temperament and eyes were not geared to sight reading, but his teacher insisted that the fault was ours. "You don't buy the boy no books," she said. As it happened, David lived in a house where there were books in the living room, dining room, study, and bedrooms; there were books in the attic and books in the cellar; and David's personal library exceeded one hundred volumes. So we ignored the teacher and sent this boy to a good reading clinic where he was taught to read phonetically and the love for books that had been bred into him on Starling's knees was revived.

It was not my fault that David ever graduated from high school. Repeatedly I had been needled by his English teacher to help the boy with his themes. So I did. I taught David what writing was: meticulous research, rewriting, a tightening of phrase and thought, a groping for images to convey emotion, an experience in personal growth. The boy toiled for hours, enjoying the venture for he could see a creative work growing in his hands. The school exploded. The work was too professional; no student could write this well; I must have ghost-written the theme. I marched into the principal's office, tasting blood. The reason why kids did not write well, I raged, was because composition was taught by nitwits who had not the least comprehension of how to inspire joy and freedom in the exercise. I recalled an old rule of the book trade: never publish a brilliant textbook for it exposes the trite mentality of the teacher expected to use it. The principal apologized. He pleaded for my help in writing his doctoral dissertation. I'd be damned if I would—my days of meddling with the educational system had ended.

But I had gained. I had seen David awakened, fired, responding to a challenge. Some day, in school or out, he would find the right level of men who could rouse him to genuine mental growth; he would meet, as I had, a Carl Rollins or an Alfred Knopf or a Paul Angle. Few of the great teachers of a lifetime are found in classrooms.

Each child has suddenly delighted me with an unexpected insight into the future adult. I remember one of those summer days when Meredith served as a counselor in a crippled children's camp in Pennsylvania.

"Miss Merry," a child wheedled, "I've got my undies on backward and can't find the pee-pee hole."

"Then change them, silly," Meredith said calmly.

A child in braces implored: "Miss Merry, I fall down."

"Then pick yourself up."

The children loved her. She gave them their self-respect, treating them as equals. Outside the home, they turned around their undies and struggled back on their feet, proud of the self-reliance they achieved. They held my daughter's hands and walked down the camp path, happy and singing. And I glimpsed Starling the woman in Meredith my child and experienced a contentment that a thousand straight A's in school could not have afforded.

And that satisfaction, too, I have gained from Bill. A small printing press given him one Christmas has grown into a bigger press and a well-equipped small print shop in the cellar. Through the graphic arts Bill has found an outlet for a real creative impulse. He is a studied craftsman who enjoys careful work. He has discovered within himself a capacity for mental excitement and growth and pride. No one can do this for him beyond affording an opportunity and quiet encouragement. To make education a drudgery—or to make it a fear as it must be for those contemplating getting into college today—is to sell out to mediocrity and the computerized mind. The world must have more than machines; machines fly over cities and drop machine-made bombs in machine-like patterns; but no machine can help the little child left weeping amid the debris. Another human being must do that—a David, a Meredith, a Bill.

If children are to grow into Pasternak's immortality—"Your life in others"—then the essence of their maturity cannot substitute mathematics for tenderness or physics for compassion or mechanical drawing for beauty or success for God or the computer for the unfolding mystery of life. Perhaps the boys believed Muz was "rather fat," but she was deliciously soft when they needed comfort; pressed against her bosom, suddenly aware that the sunlight lay upon the rug like a golden sword, they were taught a wisdom for which all philosophers grope. Teaching involves all the senses.

᷎

One day a pretty girl appears. "Dad," your eldest says, "this is Karen." And you know your children will marry and have their children. And when your first grandchild is born you say to your wife: "Linda Kim? What kind of name is that? It sounds like a Chinese laundry." And you are scolded and told: "It's their life and their child," which of course it is. You feel as though the story of your life is a little like the motto carved on the entrance to the National Archives Building in Washington: "What is past is prologue."

And so another Trouble Bush is planted. And will grow up just fine.

INDEX

Index

American Mercury, The, 221
American Story, The, 284
Amherst College, 151
Angle, John, 288
Angle, Paul M., 194–202, 205, 232, 233, 234–35, 287–89, 292, 295, 301–302, 323, 328
Angle, Paula, 288
Angle, Vesta (Mrs. Paul M.), 288, 323
Antioch College, 244
Appel, David, 181, 183
Appleton, D., Century & Co., 138
April, Margaret, 182
Arcaro, Eddie, 322
Armed Forces Institute of Pathology, 262
Arnold, Sir Edwin, 135
Ashland, Ky., 267
Associated Music Publishers, 296
Associated Press, 97–98, 185
Atlanta, Ga., 229–30
Atlantic City, N.J., 217–18
Austen, Jane, 88
Austin, Louis L., 259

B

Backfield Feud, 138–39
Baker, Louise (Mrs. Howard Wilson), 244–45, 267
Ball, Lucille, 268
Ballad of the North and South, 295
Baltimore, Md., 177, 253
Bara, Theda, 65
Barbour, Ralph Henry, 87
Barnard College, 74
Barrie, Sir James M., 88
Barton, Betsy, 244–45
Baruch, Bernard, 164
Basler, Roy P., 210–12, 286–87, 292, 323
Basler, Virginia (Mrs. Roy P.), 211, 323
Battle Creek, Mich., 248–49
Bender, Dr., 23–24

Bennett, Agnes, 75
Bergen Democrat, The, 100–101
Bergen Evening Record, The, 90–97, 98, 100, 160
Berger, Meyer, 236, 301–302
Berlin, Irving, 301
Betts, Karl S., 306, 307
Bevan, Aneurin, 259
Bierce, Ambrose, 143
Biloxi, Miss., 323
Bleak House, 88
Blickensderfer, Joseph P., 213
Block, Herb (Herblock), 235
Bloomington, Ill., 193
Boise, Idaho, 267
Bookmaking and Kindred Amenities, 159
Book-of-the-Month Club, 165, 195–96, 198, 284
Boston, Mass., 261–62
Bound Brook, N.J., 144–45
Bowman, Chancellor John, 209–10
Boys Life, 87, 144–45
Brandt, Joseph P., Director of Princeton Univ. Press and President, University of Oklahoma, 166, 204, 213
Brett, Philip Milledoler, Acting President of Rutgers University, 129–30, 155, 206
Brill, E. Hopkins (Hop), 119–22, 127, 154–55, 161, 163, 166, 242
Bristol, Va., 238
Broadcast Music, Inc.; see Haverlin, Carl
Brockway, George, 279
Bronk, Detlev, 213
Brontë Sisters, 88
Brooklyn Dodgers, 36, 37
Brooklyn, N.Y., 16, 17, 23–24, 26–39, 44, 104, 107, 140, 173, 228, 260, 269–70, 277
Brooks, Elwood M., 267
Brown, Richard, 204–205
Browning, Elizabeth Barrett (Mrs. Robert), 257–58
Browning, Robert, 156, 257–58
Buenos Aires, Argentina, 212
Bunn, George W. (Gib), 193–94, 200, 232

332

Index

Miers, Emma Swannell (Mrs. William Schenck), mother, 16, 18–25, 26–28, 30, 33–34, 38–43, 44–47, 48, 49–50, 52–54, 56–59, 61–62, 66, 77, 79-80, 82–85, 89–92, 99, 100, 104–107, 112, 123–124, 125–127, 131, 136, 141–142, 303–304, 320–23, 329

Miers, Karen (Mrs. David W.), daughter-in-law, 330

Miers, LeRoy, brother, 22–23, 323

Miers, Linda Kim, granddaughter, 330

Miers, Meredith, daughter, 187, 216, 317–18, 319–20, 321, 325, 327, 328–29

Miers, Sarah Conover (Mrs. William), grandmother, 19, 31–33, 33–34, 48, 74, 124, 193

Miers, Starling Wyckoff (Mrs. Earl Schenck), wife, meeting, 127–28; courtship, 128–30; parents, 129, 130–31; threatened college expulsion, 131–32; crisis with Will, 133–35; employed at Rutgers, 137–39; marriage, 141–42; reaction to handicapped man, 143–44; to Albert S. Johnson, 145; help in book design, 159, 161; going ahead, 164; mother, 168; brother's death, 170; 175, 208; third pregnancy, 216, 218; agrees I quit Rutgers, 218–19; letters from the South, 229; the *Christmas Card Murders*, 231; in Miami Beach, 243–44; in San Francisco, 275; 308; home life and children, 315–30

Miers, William Holmes, son, 218, 317–18, 319–20, 321, 325, 329

Miers, William Schenck, father, 18–25, 30, 35, 38–43, 44–47, 48, 49–51, 54–55, 59, 61–62, 66, 70–71, 72–73, 76–77, 78–81, 85, 96–97, 106, 112, 123–24, 125, 130–31, 141–42, 170–71, 281–82, 313, 314, 323

Milligan, Archer G., 119

Milltown, N.J., 188

Mitchell, Harry A., 267

Mitchell, James P., U.S. Secretary of Labor, 308

Mitchell, Margaret, 230

Mohawk Stamp Company, 78–82

Morison, Elting, 284

Morris, John, 160–61

Morrow, Anne (Mrs. Charles A. Lindbergh), 97

Morrow, Ambassador Dwight, 97

Mount Holyoke College, 74

Mumford, L. Quincy, Librarian of Congress, 292

Murrow, Edward R., 281

N

Nation, The, 151

National Association for the Advancement of Colored People, 305

National Boy, The, 89

National Health Institute, 262

National Park Service, 271

National Research Council, 213

National Society for Crippled Children & Adults, Inc., 40–41, 245, 262, 265, 273–74, 277, 300, 323

Netherlands Club, New York City, 284

Nevins, Allan, 182, 200–201, 283, 284, 286, 312

Newark, N.J., 81, 93, 305

Newark Evening News, 120

New Brunswick, N.J., 104, 105, 103, 111, 121, 142, 166, 173, 183, 207

New Jersey Civil War Centennial Commission, 304–11

New Jersey College for Women (Douglass College), 120–21

Newman, Ralph G., 182–83, 204, 232, 283, 310

New Orleans, La., 229, 265–66, 267, 323

New Salem, Ill., 183, 193

New York, New York, 138, 207, 227–28, 231, 239, 240, 261, 293, 295, 323

New York Civil War Centennial Commission, 307–308, 310

New York Democratic Club, 236

New Yorker, The, 221

Index

Wegener, Theodore H., 267
Werner, Heinz, 180
Westminster Press, 172–77
West Point, N.Y., 191
Wheat, Zach, 58
Wichita Falls, Tex., 81, 267
Wilcox, Ella Wheeler, 60–62
Wiley, Bell I., 310–11
Wilhelm, C. H. (Curley), 162–63, 165, 178, 208, 222
Will, Allen Sinclair, dean, School of Journalism, Rutgers University, 114, 133–36, 145, 169, 215
Williams, John L. B., 138
Williams, Madaline (Mrs. Samuel), 305–13
Williams, Samuel, 305–306
Williamsburg, Va., 294–95
Willkie, Rev. Harold, 242–43, 245
Wilmington, Del., 173
Wilson, Howard, 245, 267
Wilson, President Woodrow, 32

Wisconsin Civil War Centennial Commission, 310
Wisconsin, University of, 154
World Publishing Co., 285, 286
Wyckoff, Florence W. (Mrs. Holmes S.), 129, 138, 318–20
Wyckoff, Holmes S., 129, 138, 318–20
Wyckoff, John, 170
Wyckoff, Starling; see Mrs. Earl Schenck Miers
Wynkoop, Ross H., 91–100

Y

Yale University, 151, 157, 159
Yarborough, Senator Ralph, 310–11
Yellow Springs, Ohio, 244
Yorktown, Va., 294
Youth's Companion, 87

PRINTED IN U.S.A.